"Marty O'Connell is a man of great wisdom and experience in options trading and shares with the reader a wealth of insight into the minds of options traders, especially those who are trading with other people's money."

> Didier Varlet
> Chairman and CEO of Carr Futures
> Senior Regional Officer
> North America of Crédit Agricole Indosuez

"Marty O'Connell's practical approach to managing risk has influenced scores of derivatives professionals trading in the industry today. His new book is a welcome disciplinary guide to risk taking."

> Christiane Mandell
> Managing Director
> Bank of America

"Here is a sophisticated book that's fun to read, packed with insight, and laced with common sense. Not only that, Marty O'Connell writes in plain, declarative English without a trace of dull-witted financial, academic, or traders' jargon. Clearly, with these kinds of subversive credentials I predict the book has no future in the modern financial library."

> Jim Piper
> Managing Director
> North American Capital Markets Practice
> Stanton Chase International

The Business of
options

The Business of
options

Time-Tested Principles and Practices

MARTIN P. O'CONNELL

John Wiley & Sons, Inc.

New York • Chichester • Weinheim • Brisbane • Singapore • Toronto

Published by John Wiley & Sons, Inc.

Published simultaneously in Canada.

This publication is designed to provide accurate and authoritative information in regard to the subject matter covered. It is sold with the understanding that the publisher is not engaged in rendering professional services. If professional advice or other expert assistance is required, the services of a competent professional person should be sought.

Library of Congress Cataloging-in-Publication Data:

O'Connell, Martin P.
   The business of options : time-tested principles and practices / Martin P. O'Connell.
     p. cm.
   Includes index.
   ISBN 0-471-40557-4
   1. Options (Finance)   I. Title.
HG6024.A3 O246 2001
332.64′5—dc21

                                                                                    2001017813

Printed in the United States of America.

10 9 8 7 6 5 4 3 2 1

preface

My entry into the options business in June 1977 was typical for the time. I was a native Chicagoan who had a nonfinancial job in Southern California when I experienced the lure of the Chicago Board Options Exchange (CBOE) floor. I quit my job, emptied my Newport Beach apartment, moved back to Chicago, and rented a CBOE seat that was half owned by a saloon keeper. I had saved some money (I was single) and I decided that it would be better to lose it all than to spend the rest of my life wondering what I had missed.

One of the first things I was told in Chicago was that I had already missed it. The CBOE had been open for just over four years, and the real money had already been made. If only I had been there in 1974, I might have made a ton.

Like many options beginners, most of what I had heard about options involved mathematical tricks—make a trade, then do this, then do that, and at the end you make money. After a little experience, I noticed that there was much more to options trading than a few tricks. It was complicated and uncertain. I was a little dismayed that I hadn't found a fountain of easy money, but, in one way, I was pleased. This was starting to look like a real business. It could grow and evolve. There might be long, rewarding careers for people who had some breadth and depth to their skills, could build expertise over time, and would adapt to changing opportunities. I hoped that I would be one of those people—especially since it seemed like a lot of fun.

The options business has evolved further than I ever imagined. Now, at the beginning of the twenty-first century, it is more dynamic than ever. As its activities reach far and deep into the worlds of commerce and investment, it continues to tempt otherwise responsible people to try to get by on a few tricks—to take the easy way out.

This is a book for people who want to approach options in a business-like way. It is not designed for a complete beginner, but it does not require an extensive background. No single part of it is difficult, but many parts have broad implications and interrelate with other parts. It is not easy and it doesn't offer a formula for success. This is a business.

There is plenty of mathematics in this book, but I have worked hard to make it as simple and intuitive as I can. In a few cases, I "cheated" on the math when it seemed that utility was more important than perfection. I had hoped to write the entire book without a graph or an equation, but I didn't quite succeed. I encourage the reader to become immersed in the *practical* math of options, but to remember that option mathematics are only the beginning. This is a business.

Observations and generalizations about human behavior abound in this book. Many of them are oversimplified. They are offered, not as sociological truths, but rather as food for thought. I'm not offended if you think some of them are not worthwhile.

NOTES ON THE TEXT

This book is written for market participants and their managers. It is partly for option *dealers* and other profit center traders. That is, it is for people whose jobs are to trade options to make money. It is also for option *users,* such as corporate hedgers and institutional investors. There are some concepts and tools that both dealers and users need to master, and Part One of the book addresses many of them. Everyone should read Part One. Part Two addresses the application of these concepts and tools to the business of dealers. Users can skip this section. Finally, Part Three addresses user applications.

Many of the chapters conclude with a section titled *Loose Ends.* This material is offered for readers who would like to pursue a chapter's subject matter a little deeper. The *Loose Ends* tend to be more mathematically taxing, but they don't begin to approach "rocket scientist" complexity. There is no discussion of the modern exotic options, which are an important and interesting part of some options businesses, but which require a level of mathematics that seems inappropriate for this book.

This book is designed to be read from the beginning. Each chapter is written with the assumption that the reader understands the previous chapters (except that understanding Part Three does *not* require an understanding of Part Two). However, it is never assumed that the reader has looked at the *Loose Ends.*

In this book, there is quite a bit of slang and words with vague meanings. For most of them, I have used quotation marks. There are also a lot of option terms of art; that is, normal words that have a special meaning in the options business. These are set in italic when they first appear, and, in some instances, when they appear again. I have taken the easy way out of the problem of pronouns and gender. Throughout the text, unless reference is made to a specific woman, the male forms (he, him, etc.) are used exclusively and are intended to be gender neutral.

The approach taken in this book is applicable to options on a wide variety of financial instruments. For simplicity, I have tried to minimize the number of different examples and to use underlying instruments that would be familiar to many readers. Equity and foreign exchange (FX) examples are prevalent, primarily because equity and FX people sometimes don't adapt well to bond or money market examples. My apologies to the interest rate option traders.

Many examples assume 0% interest rates. This assumption often facilitates the development of a better intuitive feel for option dynamics and decisions. In some cases, however, the examples simply worked better with positive interest rates. It is not important for the reader to figure out why particular interest rate assumptions were made.

Finally, the text assumes that readers have at least a surface familiarity with market structure and option terminology. If you are in the options business, you've probably had plenty of opportunity to learn the difference between a put and a call, which options are in-the-money, what a strike price is, and so on. If you haven't, you won't have trouble finding a broker, dealer, futures exchange, securities exchange, or Web site to help you out.

MARTIN P. O'CONNELL

Chicago, Illinois
May 2001

acknowledgments

I am most grateful to the many people who have given me the industry exposure and the ideas that have made it possible for me to offer advice in the options business. Among them are Dick Belden, Ed O'Connor, Mike Greenbaum, Warren Shore, Jim Piper, Maureen Murphy, Peter Kellogg, Jim Porter, Jim McNulty, Nassim Taleb, Ted Craver, John Kruse, and Chris Mandell.

This book's content especially bears the imprints of Mike Greenbaum and Jim Piper. My career of offering options advice began in the late 1970s when Mike turned the First Options seminar program over to me. Along with an audience and a fee, Mike gave me some excellent concepts and frameworks for thinking about options and for talking about them. I'm sure that many of the ideas that I still use today—and think of as my own—were put into my mind by Mike.

Jim Piper was my partner for 17 years in the options advisory business. We worked together to produce seminars, consulting projects, and trading advice over a time when the industry, and our views of it, experienced mind-blowing evolution. Over the years, our thought processes became more and more compatible. Eventually, we didn't know or care about what our roles had been in developing most of our ideas.

contents

Option Concepts
and Tools

CHAPTER 1

Are You Too Anxious to Win?

Before about 1979, computers were not in widespread use among professional options traders. In part, this was because of the limited availability of useful hardware and software, but the more important reasons were personal and cultural. Members of the Chicago Board Options Exchange (CBOE) and its competitors usually were not the products of graduate schools or of corporate management development programs. They were more like Wild West characters who wandered into town with no identity, no relevant history, not even much money. Many of them (myself included) had never made a trade on a stock or options exchange. Most had a lot of confidence and tolerance for financial risk. Many had good mathematical instincts, but few had classical mathematical expertise or an aptitude for computer work. Almost all were sole proprietors, trying to learn the business and to find a way to make a few hundred dollars a day. Social graces weren't required.

In this environment, the potential applications of computers weren't just ignored, they were scorned. Real men didn't use mathematical models and they didn't hedge their positions. A "stand up" market maker was supposed to make a living by making markets for the public in individual options or by taking shots on stock price direction.

Eventually, of course, the power of computerized analysis could not be kept out, and many traders—some looking for magic—gave it a try. They soon learned that their new tools couldn't protect them from their human weakness and inexperience.

In 1979, it became trendy to have a secret computer program that would calculate the probability of winning on a particular position. These *theoretical probabilities* were discussed as *facts* by some of their users. Since many of us thought of ourselves as "born winners," it made sense to us that we should have large positions that would almost surely be profitable. It was common in 1979 to hear a trader say something like "I did a 99.1 today." That meant he had put on a position for which his (questionable?) program calculated a 99.1% probability of success.

It doesn't take much imagination to think up a position (or a bet) that has a very high probability of winning, but, on average, will be a loser. No doubt, many of these 1979 positions fall into that category. In most of them, though, the long-term average result was not the big problem. The big problem was *remote risk*. It is common sense that, if your sole criterion for a position is that it has a 99.1% chance of winning, then maybe somewhere buried in that other 0.9% is a nuclear bomb. Among the remote nuclear bombs waiting for the 1979 crowd were:

- *The Saturday Night Massacre:* In October 1979, the Federal Reserve raised the discount rate by 200 basis points on a Saturday night. Markets went crazy during the following week. In some cases, call prices rose as stocks collapsed.
- *The Hunt Brothers' silver disaster:* The Hunt Brothers were billionaires who bought a lot of silver in the late 1970s. In late January 1980, silver prices finally peaked at about $50/ounce, and then got ugly. The real panic came two months later when the price collapsed from $22 on March 24 to $12 on March 27. Apparently, silver was big enough to take the stock market with it. The Dow Jones Industrial Average (DJIA) decline was only about 20%, but it seemed like a nuclear bomb to some options traders. Other traders survived the decline, but got caught by the whip at the bottom.

In the options business, there can be a powerful temptation to seek out positions that have high probabilities of success, but that also come with excessive remote risk and/or negative expected returns. Good dealers, speculators, and hedgers can overcome this temptation, both at the individual level and at the institutional level.

In practice, we often find that option traders think differently from other traders regarding expectations about the probability (or frequency) of winning. For example, if you talk to a foreign exchange spot trader who has just put on a position, you might notice that he really believes he's going to make some money. He might even have reasons. Then, later, when he talks about the trade, he's likely to use language that reflects that belief. He might say, "I was right on that position." This means that the subsequent market action proved that his trade was brilliant. Alternatively, he might say, "I was wrong." That means that the subsequent market action demonstrated that his trade was stupid.

In contrast, a good option trader can be expected to think quite differently. A good option trader will frequently make a trade even though he thinks it will probably lose money. Sometimes, this is hard to explain to the boss.

"You mean, we make trades, even though we think we'll lose money on them?"

"Yeah, that's a basic part of our strategy!"

In the options business, simple statistical concerns are often well clarified through the use of gambling examples. In this case, a dice example helps. Suppose I would like to bet that I can roll a 4 in a single roll of one die. Of course, if you insist on even odds, I'm not going to bet because I know I only have one chance in six of winning. On the other hand, if I can get 10 to 1 odds, I am going to make that bet. I am going to make it fully expecting to lose, and I am still going to think about it as a business.

Notice that the word "expect" might be used here with two different meanings. I expect to lose (meaning I'll probably lose) but I have a positive expected return in the statistical sense. If I am in the *business* of trading options to make a *profit,* it is the *statistical* expectation that matters most. Usually, the appropriate attitude is to be *statistically passive.* That is, I don't care how likely I am to win *this time.* I want to win *on average.* This is the attitude of an insurance company or a casino.

Suppose I make the 10-to-1 bet and roll the die and get a 2 instead of a 4. Was I wrong? Of course not. I'm no dumber than before the roll, and also no dumber than if I had rolled a 4. If I had rolled a 4, the result might make me feel brilliant. That feeling would be simple emotional weakness. To be statistically passive is not just to make a trade without thinking I know the result. It also requires ignoring the temptation to think that the result indicates the quality of the trade.

Our business is full of snappy inane slogans. Often these slogans sound clever and insightful. Many of them are stupid—or even dangerous. My candidate for the worst of them is "You're only as good as your last trade." Sometimes, traders say it and sometimes the boss says it. Weak bosses often say it indirectly. They can be too quick to praise or reward short-term successes and too punitive about short-term losses. Such bosses eventually get exactly what they deserve—their employees find ways to give 10-to-1 odds that I can't roll a 4.

I don't want to be in the kind of business where you're only as good as your last trade. I can't "know" what's going to happen all the time. In the options business, the pros are statistically passive.

CHAPTER 2

What's Different about Options?

Options are multidimensional and nonlinear. That's it! That's what makes options what they are, and that's what makes the options business different from other businesses.

A popular 1970s slogan among CBOE members was "The whole purpose of being a market maker is to have time working for you." Unfortunately, these traders often learned the hard way that their "free" time decay came with some very undesirable nonlinearity in their exposure to underlying stock price movement. This kind of inclination to believe that we don't have to take the bad with the good is a common human weakness that seems to appear everywhere in the options business.

NONLINEARITY

Most people who are new to options come from a one-dimensional, linear world. For example, if I buy 1000 shares of IBM at $100 per share, I have one significant dimension of exposure: stock price. If the stock price rises, I make money; if it declines, I lose. There's not much more to worry about. Furthermore, I'm likely to think of my position as linear. If IBM goes to $90 or $120, I'm still 1000 shares long. If my boss wants to impose risk limits on my trading, the rules are likely to be simple: How many shares (or dollars worth of stock) am I allowed to be long or short?

In the options business, it's easy enough to design a position that "feels" about 1000 shares long in IBM. Such a position, however, is not likely to be linear. If IBM were to go to $90 or $120, the option position would probably feel like it's long more than 1000 shares, or less than 1000 shares. Maybe at $90 or $120, the position would even feel short.

Nonlinearity is pervasive in the options business, and it causes much discomfort, confusion, and wishful thinking, especially for people who are accustomed to linearity. Many of the tools and terms that we use and misuse are driven by the unspoken fantasy that we can make the nonlinearity go away—or that we can keep only its benefits.

ADDITIONAL DIMENSIONS

When we think about option positions, there is a lot more to worry about than the movement in the *underlying price*—that is, we usually have more dimensions of exposure.

Time is one of these dimensions. Usually, even with no change in the underlying price, an option position will make or lose money because of time passing. Furthermore, even if the underlying price does change, we would expect our profit and loss (P&L) to be different because of the passage of time. We usually expect the effect of time on our P&L to be nonlinear.

The third major dimension of option exposure is *volatility*. It is obvious to most participants in the options business that volatility is an important and complex subject. It is discussed in considerable detail throughout this book, especially in Chapter 6. For now, we can simply say that option P&L's are affected nonlinearly by apparent changes in market perceptions about volatility. This is likely to be important with or without a change in underlying price and with or without the passage of a significant amount of time.

When we analyze option opportunities, P&L dynamics, or risk, it is useful to think in terms of a multidimensional nonlinear puzzle in which most of the action is driven by changes in these three major dimensions of exposure: *underlying price, time,* and *volatility*. These dimensions sometimes "act" individually, sometimes in combination. Certainly we should expect that a business that operates in this kind of puzzle is likely to be more complex and confusing than one that is one dimensional and linear.

In practice, option analysis can be even more complicated. Chapter 6 describes several aspects of volatility that make it inappropriate to think of it as a simple dimension (like underlying price or time). In addition, option positions are often influenced by other variables such as interest rates, dividends, and bond coupons. Usually, these variables are not as important as underlying price, time, or volatility, but in some circumstances, they can be very important.

WHY DOES IT MATTER?

It is the *multidimensional, nonlinear* character of options that provides flexibility and variety to hedgers and speculators. It often permits hedgers to focus on specific fears, and to hedge against them while retaining some desirable aspects of their exposures. Similarly, it gives speculators the flexibility to zero in on narrowly defined views, and to bet on them quite specifically. It provides a seemingly endless list of potential market inefficiencies (both real and imagined) that can look like profit opportunities to traders.

The same multidimensional, nonlinear character produces the risk complexity that we must deal with in the options business. Compared to the risk in most other financial vehicles, option risk seems more complicated, more time consuming, more expensive to manage, and often scarier. This doesn't make options riskier than other financial vehicles, nor does it make the options business a bad business, but it certainly makes it different.

It is very important for the options business participant to face up to the fact that options are different from other instruments and that their multidimensional nonlinear character is not going to go away. In the 1970s (when *options* meant *stock options*), the CBOE and other exchanges were heavily populated by *stock pickers*. These were traders who thought of themselves as skilled at guessing stock price direction. Many had good track records in the securities business and were attracted by the leverage, low margins, and low transaction costs of the options business. To them, options were "little stocks."

Most of these traders "busted out" because options are not little stocks (or little foreign exchange contracts or little swaps or little futures). It is true that the action in an option position can sometimes be dominated by the direction of the change in the underlying price. It is also true that it sometimes makes sense to use options to assume or adjust a directional exposure. But, there is a lot of multidimensional nonlinear exposure in the options business, and to ignore some of it is to invite disaster.

Twenty-five years later, we don't have many professional options traders who try to imagine a one-dimensional linear world (although temporary lapses are common). Today this problem is bigger among bosses (e.g., senior managers at trading banks or corporate treasuries) who would like options to be different from what they are. My advice to these people is to accept reality. Your old skills, instincts, and rules of thumb are likely to bring trouble in the options business. If you want to be competent in this business, get ready for a whole new way of thinking.

Strategic Concepts and Principles

Many of the concepts and principles that we use in the options business are statistical. Some are simple. Some are not. Some have powerful implications for decision making. None are so universally applicable that they make our decisions easy.

To clarify statistical issues, options instructors and authors frequently rely on gambling examples, such as the dice example in Chapter 1. Over the past 30 years, the game of roulette has been used, in various ways, as a vehicle to shed light on the options business. Here is my version.

ROULETTE RULES

In the United States, roulette wheels usually have 38 slots, numbered 1 through 36, 0, and 00. A player bets that the ball will come to rest in a particular slot. For simplicity, we'll assume that the price of the bet is $1. An employee of *the house* spins the wheel and drops a ball onto the wheel. Eventually, the ball comes to rest in one of the slots. If the ball comes to rest in one of the 37 slots that the player didn't select, *the house* wins the $1. If the ball comes to rest in the slot selected by the player, the player wins the *prize,* which is $36.

It is easy to see that, on average, *the house* should win money. It's also easy to see that, with a slight change in the rules, the player would win on average. For example:

- If there were only 35 slots, the player would win, on average, even though he would lose almost every time.
- With 38 slots, the player would win, on average, if the prize were $40.
- With 38 slots and a prize of $36, the player would win, on average, if the price of the bet were only 90 cents.

This is a game with three variables: price, prize, and number of slots. The expected average outcome is a function of all three.

MARKET PRICE/THEORETICAL VALUE/EDGE

Imagine a 38-slot roulette game in which the prize is $36, but the price can vary. You might want to be *the house* when the price is $1, but the player when the price is 90 cents. In either case, you would expect good results on average, but you might have bad results for a little while.

There is, of course, a price between 90 cents and $1 at which the player and *the house* would expect to break even on average. That price is $36 ÷ 38 = 94.74 cents. For simplicity, we'll say that the break even price is 95 cents. At that price, neither the house nor the player would have a long-term advantage, but we'd expect some money to change hands in the short run. We call this 95 cents the *theoretical value* (TV) of a roulette bet.

What is this theoretical value? It is the statistical value of the bet. It is *not* necessarily a good guess of what the price of the bet would be in the real world (in fact, we expect the price to be some other number, namely $1). Also, it is not necessarily a good indicator of the result of a single bet.

Relating this theoretical calculation to the real world, we could say that the reason roulette is usually a profitable business for *the house* is because it charges $1 for a bet that's worth only 95 cents. That is, *the house* has an *edge* of 5 cents.

Market price (MP)	=	$1.00
Theoretical value (TV)	=	0.95
Edge	=	$0.05

And, of course, in the real world, *the house* in a roulette game wins about 5% of the gross.

SHORT-TERM INVISIBILITY OF THE EDGE

Think for a minute about what your experience would be if you were *the house* in a roulette game in which one player bet $1 on each spin of the wheel. You would have a long series of $1 wins, occasionally interrupted by a $35 loss. On average, you would make about 5% of the amount bet.

You might like this experience for two reasons. First, you might like having the edge. You might even imagine that you are making 5 cents on each bet and that the short-term profits and losses are just *noise* that you live through on your way to your expected long-term profit. Second, you might like the experience because you like winning almost every time (remember Chapter 1?). You might even get addicted to collecting that $1 each time, and you might forget that, in the long run, only 5 cents of it will be yours. Likewise, that 5 cents would be little consolation when you had your inevitable $35 losses. In other words, the short-term ups (+$1) and downs (−$35) are so large that, for a while, the edge might be *invisible*. Your attention could be so fixed on the short-term cash flows that you might forget what matters in the long run.

This short-term focus can be a problem if it affects your behavior. For example, you might be so happy about winning $^{37}/_{38}$ of the time that you might start selling some bets for 90 cents. Even at 90 cents, you would win almost every time, and it might take quite a while for you to notice that, on average, you're losing.

Similarly, if you were to find a game in which you could buy roulette bets for 90 cents, you would have about a 5 cent edge and you might like the short-term action. This situation might be especially attractive to someone who likes to sleep at night. He might be willing to live through a lot of little losses in order to be sure that all of the big surprises would be in his favor. In the world of financial markets, "trend followers" often prefer this kind of exposure.

Of course, the buyer of 90 cent roulette bets also must be careful that his preference for the short-term exposure doesn't tempt him to get more action by paying $1. At $1, he can still sleep at night until it occurs to him that he doesn't have a business. He has a negative edge that can be invisible for a while, but will eventually be overwhelming.

In the options business, it's very common for traders, hedgers, bosses, and organizations to have preferences for exposures that resemble one side of the roulette game. That is, they might like:

- To win almost every time, or
- To have small losses and big gains.

It is important to distinguish between such preferences and the expectations for long-term performance.

MAKE MONEY/MANAGE RISK

After reading the previous discussion of the short-term invisibility of the edge, you might be tempted to conclude that, in the options business, we should not worry about short-term ups and downs; rather, we should focus on the long term expected result—the edge. That approach is too simplistic.

Suppose you are offered the following career opportunity: As your sole source of income, you can be *the house* in a roulette game. Normal odds would apply, but the wheel would be spun just once a day. Each time the game is played, one player would bet $10,000 on one of the 38 slots. If he loses, you win $10,000. If he wins, you lose $350,000.

Does this career opportunity look like a good business to you? Think about the following:

- For a while, you'll probably make $10,000 a day, and you might get used to it.
- Occasionally you'll lose $350,000 in a day—this might even happen for two or three consecutive days.
- On average, if you survive, you expect to make the 5% edge (i.e., $500/day).

What's good about this opportunity? You expect to make $500/day and you don't have to work hard.

What's bad? You have to live through some big losses. Are the anticipated $350,000 setbacks too big to make this a sensible business? That is debatable, but think about some possibilities:

1. Would you like it better if the bet were $20,000/day? You'd expect to make an average of $1,000/day, but on your bad days, you'd lose $700,000.
2. With $4,000 bets, your exposure would be only $140,000/day, but you'd have to live on $200/day.
3. Most people would take this kind of opportunity if they could expect to average a profit of $500/day with small ups and downs. In this example, however, the $350,000 daily exposure would discourage most people— even if they had $350,000 to lose.

In roulette, as in any business, we have two basic concerns: *profitability* and *risk*. Profitability is the expected result (in the statistical sense)—in this case, the $500 edge. Risk is our expectation for short-term ups and downs. In most businesses, there are many risks of various magnitudes. In this example, we worry only about the $350,000 losses.

It should be apparent that, in a sound business, there should be reasonable profitability and reasonable risk. If either is missing, we don't have a business. In this example, the $500 profitability might be adequate, but, if the risk is excessive, it is not a business.

Some readers might think: "This isn't too much risk. I'd do it." Maybe I would also, but at some risk, I'd say no! If I had to take a 1 in 38 chance of losing $10,000,000 to make an expected $500/day, that would be too much risk. The general principle here is: Even with a real expected profitability, there can be so much risk (compared to the expected profitability) that the opportunity is not a business.

Notice that, in this example, the player's risk seems much more acceptable than *the house's*. Does this mean the player has an acceptable business? No. He has negative profitability. For a sound business, both profitability and risk must be reasonable. Maybe neither side has a business. The player's problem is profitability; the house's problem is risk.

How many times have you heard someone say: "Just manage the risk. The profitability will take care of itself"? *It won't.* You can manage risk with random bets at the race track, but, in the long run, you won't come out ahead unless you find an edge.

Throughout this book, when profitability and risk are discussed, we will talk about basic activities: *make money* and *manage risk*. In this context, make money will not refer to the P&L of a particular transaction. It will refer to improving our expected profitability. Manage risk will mean improving our exposure to the wide variety of ups and downs we might expect. Whenever I'm considering an option trade, I ask:

- Would I do it to make money?
- Would I do it to manage risk?
- Am I trading off one against the other?

SPREADS

In a real roulette game, *the house* is quite satisfied with a 5% edge, but it would like to be exposed to less severe ups and downs than we would have in the simple example just described. That is, *the house* would like to manage the risk. One approach is to do what traders might call a *spread*. For example, instead of having one player bet $10,000 on one number, *the house* might be able to get two players to bet $5,000 each on *different* numbers. This arrangement would seem like a spread because the results of the two bets would be negatively correlated.

Table 3.1 compares our expectations for this spread approach (Strategy 2) to those of the one-bet approach (Strategy 1) that was previously discussed. Notice that the two strategies have identical expected profits: $500/day. If you were to choose between these strategies, you couldn't do it on the basis of profitability; you'd have to focus on risk. In Strategy 2, you'd expect to suffer more frequent losses, but the losses would be smaller.

A similar comparison could be made for option trading. Suppose you and I are both foreign exchange option dealers, and we each sell an at-the-money call on £10,000,000 for a nice fat price. Then, suppose you spread

TABLE 3.1   Two Strategies

	Strategy 1: 1 Player $10,000 Bet 1 Number	Strategy 2: 2 Players $5,000 Bets Different Numbers
Gross Action	$ 10,000	$ 10,000
Edge	$ 500	$ 500
Best Result	+$ 10,000	+$ 10,000
Worst Result	−$350,000	−$170,000
Probability of Worst	$\frac{1}{38}$	$\frac{2}{38}$

off your exposure with a £5,000,000 spot trade, while I put my position in my book and forget about it. After a few years of this kind of behavior, we'd probably make about the same amount of profit. You would probably be about even on all of your *spot* trades. Our cumulative profits would probably be close to the edge in our *option* trades. What was the purpose of your spread? You did it to manage risk, not to make money. The spread gave you more acceptable short-term expectations while you waited to make your edge on average in the long term.

Getting back to the roulette example, consider this: If you could afford an occasional $350,000 hit, would there be any reason to manage the risk by changing to Strategy 2? Usually, the answer would be *yes,* especially if you had the opportunity to do bigger size at the same price. Then, the risk management features of the spread would enable you to assume a bigger position with more than a total edge of $500/day.

The same considerations apply to the £10,000,000 option example. Your spread position enables you to responsibly sell more overpriced calls and to have a bigger total edge. A naked call seller can afford to sell only a few.

DIVERSIFICATION

Another approach to risk management is *diversification.* In Table 3.2, we see the comparative effects of having two players making $5,000 bets on separate roulette tables.

In Strategy 3, our expected daily profit is still $500, and our worst case is a loss of $350,000 (both players might win). However, an effect of diversification is to make the worst case much less likely. Player A should win $\frac{1}{38}$ of the time, but Player B should also win only $\frac{1}{38}$ of *those* times. Hence the big ($350,000) loss should only occur $\frac{1}{38}$ of $\frac{1}{38}$ of the time.

TABLE 3.2 Three Strategies

	Strategy 1: 1 Player $10,000 Bet 1 Number	Strategy 2: 2 Players $5,000 Bets Different Numbers	Strategy 3: 2 Players $5,000 Bets Separate Tables
Gross Action	$ 10,000	$ 10,000	$ 10,000
Edge	$ 500	$ 500	$ 500
Best Result	+$ 10,000	+$ 10,000	+$ 10,000
Worst Result	−$350,000	−$170,000	−$350,000
Probability of Worst	$\frac{1}{38}$	$\frac{2}{38}$	$\frac{1}{1444}$

Clearly, diversification, like spreading, is a risk management technique. It enhances our profitability only to the extent that it enables us to do bigger size. While the general concept of diversification is useful in the options business, its application is somewhat less simple. In roulette, we assume that the results on different tables are uncorrelated. In the financial markets, correlations are usually difficult to predict.

PRICE ORIENTATION/TRADE ORIENTATION

In 1981, my partner Jim Piper and I decided that we might make some money by selling option advisory services to institutional investors. At the time, the options business was dominated by equity options. A few institutions were using them in connection with their stock portfolios, but at most institutions, people were afraid of options and/or hoping they would go away. Jim and I figured they just needed some good advice.

We didn't have much trouble getting appointments to meet with senior investment people—they were interested. Most of the conversations didn't go far, though. It was a couple of years too early. They were just starting to think about options, and they were going to do it their way. The classic response came from the senior investment officer of a large insurance company. He said they hadn't made any trades yet, but they recently hired two MBAs who were doing a study to find out "what kind of option trades work." At that point, I figured the conversation was over. This guy was looking for the magic trade. It reminded me of the late 1960s when people would say, "Nobody's ever been fired for holding IBM."

It is very common in the options business for a person to have a strong preference for a particular kind of trade or position. Sometimes, such a person thinks he has found something special. Many dealers and exchange market makers prefer *short premium* positions. Sometimes, their bosses require them to have *long premium* positions. Many corporate foreign exchange managers prefer *zero premium* trades. In each of these cases, the person has a *trade orientation,* meaning, there is a certain kind of trade or position that he favors.

Price orientation is the opposite of trade orientation. A trader with a strong price orientation is one who might say, "Show me any position. At some price, I'll do it. At some other price, I'll do the opposite. If I can't get a good price, I'll do nothing."

Generally, if you trade options to *make money,* a trade orientation is a weakness. There simply aren't any positions that can be relied on to offer an adequate edge. A "profit center" trader needs a price orientation. He needs to shop around for market inefficiencies. In contrast, if the primary purpose of your trade is to *manage risk,* a trade orientation might be appropriate. You'd like to manage your risk with trades that provide an edge, but, if the market won't cooperate, you need to be realistic about your priorities. Many risk management decisions require profitability-versus-risk trade-offs—will you accept a less-than-perfect hedge if it allows you to avoid some negative edge?

Most participants in the options business have trade orientations. Some people are overwhelmed by them; others can feel them come and go. Often, trade orientations are influenced by the unfounded fantasy that positions that "worked" in the past will "work" again in the future. Trade orientations can give us false security or can relieve us of the burden of making difficult decisions.

My advice: Know yourself!

CHAPTER 4

Getting a Feel for Option Dynamics

Chapter 2 introduced the *multidimensional nonlinear* character of options and identified underlying price, time, and *volatility* as the three dimensions that usually dominate the action. Beginning in Chapter 5, we discuss the mathematical models that are used in the options business to help us make money and manage risk in this multidimensional nonlinear world. We will look at the models' inputs and outputs, their strengths and weaknesses, and their uses and misuses.

Before exploring the models, however, it is useful to develop a rough feel for option price dynamics and risk. Consider Example 1.

EXAMPLE 1

You are a dollar-based option trader, looking at 90-day European style (i.e., no early exercise) options on the British pound sterling (£). The spot price of £ is $1.6500. The 90-day forward price is also $1.6500. All $ and £ interest rates are 0.00%. All option positions will be held, unhedged, until the expiration date.

What is a fair price (in the sense of the 95 cent theoretical value of a roulette bet) of a sterling call with a strike price of $1.7000? Buying this out-of-the-money (OTM) call is a little like buying a roulette bet (see Chapter 3) or like betting that you will roll a 4 in one roll of a die (see Chapter 1). That is, the call buyer will have a chance for a big profit, but he will probably lose the entire price of the call. In 90 days, the price of a pound will probably be less than $1.7000 and the call will probably be worthless. However, you should still be willing to pay something for the call just as you should be willing to pay something for a roulette bet. The arithmetic is simple:

£ Price in 90 Days ($)	Call Payoff ($ per £)
Below 1.7000	0
1.7200	0.0200
1.7400	0.0400
1.7600	0.0600
1.7800	0.0800
and so on	and so on

If we knew the probability of *each* sterling price above $1.7000, we could probably calculate a satisfactory value for the call. Unfortunately, unlike in the betting examples, in this case we aren't very confident that we know what the probabilities are. We have to guess.

Our fair value for this call might be uncomfortably sensitive to our probability guesses. For example, if we thought there was a good chance of a big pound price move (say a 35% chance of finishing above $1.7000 and a 10% chance of finishing above $1.8000), we might think this call is "worth" $0.0250 or $0.0300. On the other hand, if we thought a big rally in sterling was less likely (say a 20% chance of $1.7000+ and only a 1% chance of $1.8000+), we might value the call at only $0.0050 or $0.0075.

For simplicity, let's assume that we made careful guesses for the probabilities of every sterling price above $1.7000 and that we used these guesses to calculate a fair value of $0.0100. Now, let's think about where we are in our three-dimensional, nonlinear puzzle:

■ Underlying price: $1.6500
■ Time: 90 days
■ Volatility: moderate

What does moderate volatility mean? Not much at this point. So far, we haven't defined *volatility,* nor have we suggested a way to describe or measure it. We'll save most of that for Chapter 6. For now, we'll say that volatility is a characteristic of the price of the pound. It describes the extent to which the price of the pound tends to make big moves in short periods of time. Moderate volatility means we don't have reason to believe that the pound has an unusually high or low probability of experiencing big price moves in the next 90 days.

Taking this analysis a little further, we can see that our $0.0100 call value is a function of underlying price, time, and volatility. We can also see that a change in any of these dimensions would be likely to change our idea of the value of the call. Consider three hypothetical situations:

1. What if the underlying price were $1.6600 instead of $1.6500?

   The higher underlying price would probably make us increase our guess of the probability of each expiration price above $1.7000. That is, we would think there would be more chance for each of the results that would produce a positive payoff. This would make the call worth more than $0.0100—perhaps $0.0125.

2. With the pound at $1.6500, what if this were a 60-day call instead of a 90-day call?

   The shorter time period would probably make us decrease our guess of the probability of each expiration price above $1.7000. There simply wouldn't be enough time for the pound to have a good chance to make a move to a price that would give us a big call payoff. Hence, we would probably think the 60-day call would be worth less than $0.0100—perhaps $0.0060.

   Notice that this is not a volatility consideration, since volatility is the extent to which the price of sterling tends to make big moves in *short* periods of time. Our call payoff is dependent on net sterling price movement. With moderate volatility, we might think there is a decent chance for a big net movement in 90 days, but not much chance in 60 days.

3. What if this were a 90-day call with the pound trading at $1.6500, and we expected unusually high volatility instead of moderate volatility?

   Of course, the unusually high volatility expectation might make it quite likely that the pound price will go down to $1.5500 or even $1.4500. We don't care about that, however, because the payoff at $1.4500 is no worse than the payoff at $1.6000. In this example, the only volatility that matters is the kind that can send the pound price above the $1.7000 strike price. If we expect unusually high volatility, we probably think there is a higher than normal chance for each of the high-payoff expiration prices. This view might lead us to raise our call value from $0.0100 to $0.0150 or $0.0200. It might even produce a value of $0.0400 or $0.0500. These values can be *very* sensitive to the volatility assumption.

What is a fair price of a sterling* put *with a strike price of $1.6000? In many ways, we should think of this OTM put as similar to the call with the $1.7000 strike price. Table 4.1 shows the expiration payoffs.

In the call example, it was suggested that the call might be valued at $0.0100. In light of the similarity of these payoffs, we might conclude that the put values should also be $0.0100. This conclusion would be sensible if we thought that the probability of any net decrease in the price of the pound

TABLE 4.1 Expiration Payoffs

Call ($1.7000)		Put ($1.6000)	
Net £ Change	Call Payoff	Net £ Change	Put Payoff
Down	0	Up	0
Up < $0.0500	0	Down < $0.0500	0
Up 0.0700	$0.0200	Down 0.0700	$0.0200
Up 0.0900	0.0400	Down 0.0900	0.0400
Up 0.1100	0.0600	Down 0.1100	0.0600
Up 0.1300	0.0800	Down 0.1300	0.0800

was equal to the probability of a net increase of the same amount (i.e., our expectations were symmetrical). Of course, our assessment of the probabilities might be very different for big down moves than for big up moves. In that case we might value the put at more or less than $0.0100 (see box on page 23).

Now, as in the call example, let's look at some changes that might affect the put value.

1. What if the underlying price were $1.6600 instead of $1.6500?

   Because at $1.6600, the put would be $0.0600 out of the money, we would probably conclude that we would have a lower probability of any payoff and the value of the put would be less than $0.0100—perhaps $0.0080.

2. With the pound at $1.6500, what if this were a 60-day put instead of a 90-day put?

   As in the call example, the shorter dated put would be worth less than $0.0100.

3. What if this were a 90-day put with the pound trading at $1.6500, and we expected unusually high volatility?

   As in the call example, the increased likelihood of big moves in the underlying price would make the put worth more. Also, as in the call example, the only volatility that matters is the kind that can send the pound price through the strike price—in this case, $1.6000. To the extent that pound price *increases* are possible, we don't care whether they are likely to be big or small.

ASYMMETRIC EXPECTATIONS FOR THE POUND

On Wednesday, June 10, 1987, only two trading days remained until the expiration of the June foreign exchange options traded at the Philadelphia Stock Exchange. At the close of business, the spot price of the pound was $1.6580. The June 162.50 puts were 3.30 out-of-the-money, while the June 167.50 calls were only 1.80 out-of-the-money. Nevertheless, the closing price of the 162.50 puts was 0.40, while the price of the 167.50 calls was only 0.30.

Was this an inefficiency? Not necessarily! There was to be a British General Election on June 11. Most people thought that the Conservative Party would do well enough for Prime Minister Margaret Thatcher to continue in office, but it was certainly not a sure thing. No doubt many people thought that, if she retained her position the pound would have a minor "relief rally" but probably not enough to send it through $1.6750 by the end of the week. On the other hand, in the unlikely but possible event that the Conservatives were beaten, the June 162.50 puts could be worth plenty.

This asymmetrical set of expectations was reflected in the short dated options. No similarly extreme asymmetry was noticeable in longer dated options since the election effect was merely one of a large set of potential events that gave them value.

As it turned out, the Conservatives won, but the rally fizzled. The pound ended the week at $1.6525.

What is a fair price of a sterling call with a strike price of $1.6000? Buying this in-the-money (ITM) call is not very similar to buying a roulette bet. It is more like buying a sterling forward contract. If you could buy the call for $0.0500 instead of buying the forward contract, your expiration P&L comparison would be as shown in Table 4.2.

On a comparative basis, the call is clearly a bargain at $0.0500. For any final pound price above $1.6000, the call and the forward perform equally. Below $1.6000, the call out performs—maybe by a lot. This price relationship would not endure in either the real world or the theoretical world. With the pound at $1.6000 there would be plenty of bids for the call at $0.0500 because owning the call at that price would be obviously preferable.

How would we decide how much more than $0.0500 would be a fair price for this call? As in our previous examples, we would have to guess some probabilities. If we were sure that the pound price would not be below $1.6000 in 90 days, there would be no reason to pay more than $0.0500; but

TABLE 4.2 Expiration P&L Comparison

£ at Expiry	Call P&L	Forward P&L
$1.5250	−$0.0500	−$0.1250
1.5500	−0.0500	−0.1000
1.5750	−0.0500	−0.0750
1.6000	−0.0500	−0.0500
1.6250	−0.0250	−0.0250
1.6500	—	—
1.6750	+0.0250	+0.0250
1.7000	+0.0500	+0.0500
1.7250	+0.0750	+0.0750
1.7500	+0.1000	+0.1000
1.7750	+0.1250	+0.1250

if we think there is a good chance that it will be well below $1.6000, a higher call price is justified. In other words, buying this call is a lot like buying the forward and getting an insurance policy that covers our exposure below $1.6000. We should have to pay something for that insurance, and the amount we should pay should be related to its possible values under different expiration scenarios as well as to the likelihood of these scenarios occurring.

Of course, we have already considered the possibilities of various pound price moves to below $1.6000. Our guesses for these probabilities formed the basis for our "fair value" calculation for the $1.6000 put discussed previously. If $0.0100 is the value of that put, we would expect the value of the $1.6000 call to be

$$\$0.0500 + \$0.0100 = \$0.0600$$

That is,

$$\text{ITM call value} = P + V$$

where P = *Parity*, that is, the amount by which the call is in the money
   V = A *volatility ingredient* which is the amount we should pay for the feature of limited downside exposure

Now, consider the same dimension changes that we considered in valuing the OTM call and put:

1. With the underlying price at $1.6600, both P and V would be different. P would be $0.0600 while V might be only $0.0080 for the same reasons that the $1.6000 put might be worth only $0.0080. Hence, at $1.6600,

$$P + V = \$0.0600 + \$0.0080$$
$$= \$0.0680$$

That is, a $0.0100 increase in underlying price would increase the value of the ITM call, but only by $0.0080 because of the decrease in the volatility (i.e., insurance) ingredient.

2. With the pound at $1.6500, a 60-day ITM call would be worth less than the 90-day ITM call. P would still be $0.0500, but V would be lower because all of the expiration prices below $1.6000 would be less likely. Perhaps,

$$P + V = \$0.0500 + \$0.0060$$
$$= \$0.0560$$

3. With the pound trading at $1.6500, the 90-day ITM call would be worth more than $0.0600 if we expect the pound price to be unusually volatile. In that case, P would still be $0.0500, but V would be greater than $0.0100 because the "insurance" would be so valuable. Once again, the value of the $1.6000 call would change by the same amount as the value of the $1.6000 put. Consequently, the only kind of volatility that matters is the kind that would make this call finish *out-of-the-money*. As in the previous examples, it is the likelihood of a movement *through the strike price* that adds value to the option. We don't care about the likelihood of big moves *away from* the strike price, even when the option is in-the-money.

Sometimes, the volatility dynamics of an option can be the opposite of what your instincts might tell you. If you were considering buying the $1.6000 call with the pound at $1.6500, you might ask yourself what the chances are of a big collapse in the pound price. If you thought there was a pretty good chance of a collapse, your instincts might tell you not to pay much for the call. In fact, the likelihood of a pound price collapse makes the call worth *more* because its limited downside exposure makes it attractive compared to the forward. Likewise, if you thought there was *very little* chance of a significant pound price decline, you might think of this call as an attractive "buy" and you might be inclined to "pay up" for it. In this case, however, the call would be worth *less* because the feature of limited downside exposure wouldn't be worth much. You should ask yourself how much you should pay for insurance against events that seem very unlikely. If the call price is much more than $0.0500, maybe you should buy the forward instead.

What is a fair price of a sterling put with a strike price of $1.7000? In the ITM call case (above), we compared a *long* forward position to a *long* call position and concluded that the ITM call was worth $P + V$; that is, it was worth a premium over parity to account for the attractive feature of limited downside exposure. A similar thought process can be useful for the ITM $1.7000 put if we compare a *long* forward position to a *short* put. Table 4.3 displays the data for this comparison with a put price of parity ($P = \$0.0500$).

As in the case of the ITM call, the forward and the ITM put perform equally if the option finishes in-the-money. However, the short put *under performs* the forward if the pound finishes above $1.7000. By selling the put instead of buying the forward, we are giving up some of our upside potential. We need to charge a *volatility premium* for the put if the put sale is to be "fair" compared to the long forward. Hence,

$$\text{ITM put} = P + V$$

where P is parity ($0.0500) and V is a volatility premium which compensates the put seller for giving up some of the upside potential of a long forward position. As in the case of the ITM call, the ITM put is worth more than parity only to the extent that it is likely that the pound price might move through the strike price (i.e., above $1.7000). We don't care about the likelihood that the pound will finish much *lower* than $1.6500, because such a result is equally undesirable for the short put and the long forward.

Given this analysis, what probabilities should we guess to come up with a value for the $1.7000 put? We need the same guesses that were necessary

TABLE 4.3   Put Performance

£ at Expiry	Put P&L	Forward P&L
$1.5250	−$0.1250	−$0.1250
1.5500	−0.1000	−0.1000
1.5750	−0.0750	−0.0750
1.6000	−0.0500	−0.0500
1.6250	−0.0250	−0.0250
1.6500	—	—
1.6750	+0.0250	+0.0250
1.7000	+0.0500	+0.0500
1.7250	+0.0500	+0.0750
1.7500	+0.0500	+0.1000
1.7750	+0.0500	+0.1250

for the $1.7000 call discussed earlier. If our fair value for the $1.7000 call is $0.0100, then for the $1.7000 put we would have

$$\text{ITM put} = P + V$$
$$= \$0.0500 + \$0.0100$$
$$= \$0.0600$$

What would happen to this value as a result of a change in underlying price, time, or volatility expectations? Let's consider three scenarios:

1. With the underlying price at $1.6600, P would be only $0.0400, but V would be *higher* because the put seller would be giving up more opportunity above $1.7000. As in the $1.7000 call, V might be $0.0125 and

$$P + V = \$0.0400 + \$0.0125$$
$$= \$0.0525$$

As in the ITM call case, a $0.0100 change in underlying price produces a change in put value, but the change is less than $0.0100 (in this case $0.0075) because of the effect of the changing volatility ingredient.

2. With the pound at $1.6500, a 60-day ITM put would be worth less than a 90-day put because the volatility ingredient would be lower, as in the ITM call case. Perhaps,

$$P + V = \$0.0500 + \$0.0060$$
$$= \$0.0560$$

3. Also, as in the ITM call case, our expectation of high volatility would make the ITM put worth more. That is, with the pound trading at $1.6500, a put seller would have to charge more to be appropriately compensated for giving up the potential profits above $1.7000.

CONVERSION RELATIONSHIPS

It should be obvious from the analysis in this chapter that there can be a close relationship between the value of a call and the value of a put that has the same strike price and expiration date. In this chapter's simple example, the relationship is easy to understand.

Suppose, with the pound at $1.6500, we were to buy the $1.6000 call for $0.0600 and sell the $1.6000 put for $0.0100. The net price of the combination would be

$$\$0.0600 - \$0.0100 = \$0.0500 = P \text{ (parity)}$$

TABLE 4.4   Expiration P&L Comparison

£	L Call/S Put Price	L Call/S Put P&L	L Forward P&L
$1.5250	−$0.0750	−$0.1250	−$0.1250
1.5500	−0.0500	−0.1000	−0.1000
1.5750	−0.0250	−0.0750	−0.0750
1.6000	—	−0.0500	−0.0500
1.6250	+0.0250	−0.0250	−0.0250
1.6500	+0.0500	—	—
1.6750	+0.0750	+0.0250	+0.0250
1.7000	+0.1000	+0.0500	+0.0500
1.7250	+0.1250	+0.0750	+0.0750
1.7500	+0.1500	+0.1000	+0.1000
1.7750	+0.1750	+0.1250	+0.1250

Comparing the expiration P&L of this combination to the expiration P&L of the forward, we have the results shown in Table 4.4.

At expiration, this long (L) call/short (S) put combination performs exactly as the long (L) forward position. Hence, with the call in-the-money:

$$\text{Call value} - \text{Put value} = P \text{ (parity)}$$

That is, at any given underlying price, a higher put value requires a higher call value and a higher call value requires a higher put value.

Notice that, in this example, the value of the call/put combination is not affected by time to expiration or by volatility expectations. The combination is worth parity.

In a more complicated example, this combination might not be worth parity, and might not perform exactly as the underlying contract, but usually the relationships are close. Hence, we often refer to a long call/short put combination (with identical strikes and expirations) as a *synthetic*. In this example, it is a *synthetic forward*.

The expected similarity in behavior of forwards and synthetic forwards provides a number of synthetic relationships that option market participants find useful. For example,

L Forward
S Call
L Put

can be thought of as a long forward and a short synthetic forward. It is often called a *conversion* or a *forward conversion*. Similarly,

S Forward
L Call
S Put

is often called a *reverse conversion* or a *reversal*.

In our example, these relationships are riskless because the synthetic will perform exactly as the forward. In many other examples, a conversion or reversal might have some small risk. In some examples, the risk might be substantial.

The thought process that makes a conversion or reversal a low risk position can lead us to other useful synthetic relationships. For example, we might think of

L Forward
L Put

as a synthetic L call.

Or,

S Forward
L Call

as a synthetic L put.

These synthetic relationships are usually so simple that they rarely provide easy profit opportunities. They do, however, serve as analytical tools that often help us understand our position or consider trading alternatives.

LOOSE ENDS

Example 1 is quite simple and it produced simple relationships. In the real world, at least three additional levels of complexity require attention:

What if the options have a cost of carry? That is, what if interest rates are positive and we have to pay for options with cash?

For a European style option on a forward or a futures contract, the effect of interest rates is straightforward—the value of the option should be discounted by its carrying cost over its life.

For example, in the case of the ITM £ call, with a 6% U.S. dollar interest rate, we would discount the 90-day option value by about 1.5%, Table 4.5

TABLE 4.5 ITM Call Values

£	$i = 0\%$	$i = 6\%$
$1.6500	$0.0600	$0.0591
1.6600	0.0680	0.0670
Change	$0.0080	$0.0079

shows the effect of this discounting for two different underlying prices, and also the effect on the option's sensitivity to underlying price change. You can see that, while the option's value and dynamics are influenced by the level of interest rates, the impact is relatively small compared to the effects of changes in underlying price, time, or volatility expectations. You can easily imagine, however, that in a case involving longer dated options and higher interest rates, cost of carry considerations could be more significant.

What if both the options and the underlying instrument have a cost of carry? This is typically the case for options on common stocks, bonds, and spot foreign exchange, as well as for cash settlement stock index options.

EXAMPLE 2

Today is March 20. You are a dollar-based stock option trader looking at 3-month (June) European style options. The underlying stock, XYZ, is trading at $100 per share. The current 3-month interest rate is 4%. XYZ is expected to pay a $0.50 quarterly dividend. The next expected ex-dividend date is May 20.

---

1. *What is a fair price for a June 90 call?* As in Example 1, we can compare owning a June 90 call at parity (i.e., 10) to owning the common stock of XYZ. What's different?

   a. The shareholder must pay $100 per share while the option holder must pay only $10. The option holder is thus better off by interest (i) on $90 for 3 months:

$$i = \$90 \times 4\% \times \tfrac{1}{4} \text{ year}$$
$$= \$0.90$$

This amount should be added to the value of the option because it is a benefit to the option buyer.

b. The shareholder receives the $0.50 dividend ($D$). The option holder does not. This amount should be subtracted from the value of the option because the dividend makes the option less attractive compared to owning XYZ stock.

c. The call owner has the benefit of limited downside exposure. Thus, as in Example 1, the call value should include a volatility (or insurance) premium. This premium should equal the value of the June 90 put. To calculate it, we have to guess the probability of XYZ trading (at expiration) at each price below $90. If we assume that our value for this put is $1.00,

$$\text{ITM Call value} = P + i - D + V$$
$$= \$10 + \$0.90 - \$0.50 + \$1$$
$$= \$11.40$$

A few comments might be helpful:

- i = Interest on the *strike price,* not on the price of XYZ.
- D is frequently unknown. We often have to guess.
- As in Example 1, V could be much higher or lower than $1.00, depending on our volatility expectation.
- For simplicity, we have ignored the second-order effects of interest on the interest and dividend flows.
- We could have arrived at the same option value by assuming that a 3-month forward contract on XYZ traded at $100 + i$ (on 100) $- D$ = 100.50. If we think of our option as a call on this forward contract, we would have $P = 10.50$. After adjusting for interest on 10.50 and adding a $1.00 volatility ingredient, we would once again arrive at a call value of about $11.40.
- What if XYZ traded at $101? Then,

$P = \$11$
$i = \$0.90$
$D = \$0.50$
$V = \text{perhaps } \$0.85$

$$\text{Call value} = P + i - D + V$$
$$= \$11 + \$0.90 - \$0.50 + \$0.85$$
$$= \$12.25$$

■ As in Example 1, a $1 increase in XYZ produces less than a $1 increase in the call value because of the change in the volatility ingredient.

■ With XYZ at $100, the synthetic stock (L June 90 call / S June 90 put) should trade for $10.40 ($P + i - D$). It should trade for more than parity because the benefit of saving interest on $90 (the strike price) exceeds the disadvantage of missing the $0.50 dividend.

2. *What is a fair price for a June 110 put?*

As in Example 1, we can compare a long XYZ position to a position of short June 110 put at $10.

a. As in the case of the June 90 call, the S June 110 put position has a substantial interest advantage. In the put case, it amounts to interest on $110 ($100 saved by not buying XYZ stock *plus* $10 generated by the put sale). Thus

$$i = \$110 \times 4\% \times \tfrac{1}{4} \text{ year} = \$1.10$$

should be *subtracted* from the value of the put because this interest advantage makes us more anxious to *sell* the put.

b. Since the put seller doesn't collect the dividend, we should *add* $0.50 to the price of the put. That is, a put seller should charge more for passing up the dividend.

c. As in Example 1, the put seller should charge a volatility premium because, by selling the put rather than buying XYZ stock, he is giving up his potential profits above $110.

Should this volatility premium be $1.00 as it was for the June 90 call? Should our expectations be symmetrical with a midpoint of $100? Remember, a 3-month forward contract would probably trade at $100.50.

If $V = \$1.00$, our put value would be

$$P - i + D + V = \$10 - \$1.10 + \$0.50 + \$1$$
$$= \$10.40$$

Notice that, in this example, the June 110 put would be worth much less than the June 90 call. In both cases, $P = 10$ and $V = 1$, but, because XYZ has a cost of carry, i and D are significant and have different effects on the values of the options.

What if there is a cost of carry for both the options and the underlying instrument, and the options are American style (i.e., they can be exercised on any day)?

Generally, the right to exercise an option before its expiration date can only make the option worth more. In many cases, it is unlikely that it will ever be worthwhile to exercise early. In those cases, the American-style option isn't worth much more than the comparable European-style option. In some cases, however, the option is "worth more dead than alive" and the right to exercise early can be worth a lot.

Usually, options are exercised before expiration when cost-of-carry considerations overwhelm the value of the option's limited loss feature. For example, in our June 90 call example, suppose on May 19 (1 day before XYZ goes ex-dividend) XYZ traded for $120 and $i = 2\%$. With the option $30 in-the-money and with only 1 month until expiration, the likelihood of XYZ falling below $90 might seem insignificant.

Then, using our prior calculation

$$\text{Call value} = P + i - D + V$$
$$= \$30 + \$0.15 - \$0.50 + 0$$
$$= \$29.65$$

As a European-style option, this call is worth only $29.65, but it is worth $30 if it can be exercised today. We would probably choose to exercise now—before the dividend gets away.

Similarly, what if on May 20, after the stock is ex-dividend, XYZ trades for $80 with $i = 6\%$. The European-style, June 110 put would be worth

$$P - i + D + V = \$30 - \$0.55 + 0 + 0$$
$$= \$29.45$$

Here again, the option would seem to be worth more dead than alive. With little or no dividend or volatility value, an American-style put holder would be likely to opt for the cost of carry advantage of exercising and generating $110 in cash.

It is useful to think of the right to exercise early as an option on an option. How should we value that right? How much extra value should we assign to an American-style option? This decision can be complicated, but it boils down to:

- What scenarios could take place that would make the option worth "more dead than alive"?
- How likely are these scenarios?
- If these scenarios take place, what financial benefits would early exercise bring?

A good mathematical model can help us deal with these issues.

CHAPTER 5

Option Valuation Models

Mathematical option valuation models play an important, but often misunderstood, role in the options business. They are powerful tools that help us make money, manage risk, and measure our profits and losses. For most professional market participants, they are essential. In recent years, however, they have taken on a mystique that isn't justified by their quality. They were never intended to be perfect or to be the magic answer to any business problem.

Throughout the twentieth century, there were a variety of attempts to develop frameworks or models for the pricing of options and similar financial instruments. This activity accelerated in the early 1970s, culminating with the publication of "The Pricing of Options and Corporate Liabilities" by Fischer Black and Myron Scholes in the May/June 1973 issue of the *Journal of Political Economy*. Although the model described in that article applied only to European-style options on common stocks that do not pay dividends, the Black-Scholes approach was broadly applicable to different kinds of options and different kinds of underlying instruments. Since 1973, many theoreticians and practitioners have attempted to modify this model for specific applications or for ease of calculation. Occasionally, the Black-Scholes framework has been somewhat changed, but, for the most part, these modeling efforts have been incremental improvements, not breakthroughs of the magnitude conceived by Black and Scholes.

The publication of the Black-Scholes model nearly coincided with the April 26, 1973, opening of the Chicago Board Options Exchange (CBOE)—an event that we Chicagoans identify as the beginning of the modern era of options. Apparently, these two events were largely unrelated. There is little evidence that the early Black and Scholes work was motivated by commercial concerns, and their model was rarely used by traders during the early years of exchange trading. As the industry matured, however, the options business gradually recognized the power of the models and the need for sophistication in position selection and risk management. By the 1980s, when bank dealing rooms discovered options, model usage was a routine part of the business.

This book does not include a specific formula or algorithm for any theoretical value or other output of an options valuation model. Such information is available in many publications. Even more important, there is plenty of commercially available software that adequately enables options professionals to make theoretical calculations. Our emphasis in this book is the *application* of this software to the business of options.

THE NOBEL PRIZE

In addition to Fischer Black and Myron Scholes, there were other significant contributors to the development of option thinking in the early 1970s. Most notable among then was Robert Merton, who, at the time, was a colleague of Scholes at MIT.

In 1997, Scholes and Merton were awarded the Nobel prize for their work. Unfortunately, Black died too soon to be so honored.

ELEMENTS OF AN OPTION'S VALUE

Generally, option models calculate theoretical values for option prices as a function of three or more variables. As you recall in Example 1 in Chapter 4, we looked at how the value of an option on the pound could be sensitive to the underlying forward price, time, and volatility expectations. That is,

$$TV = f(FP, t, V)$$

A mathematical model can, given values for *FP*, *t*, and *V*, calculate a theoretical value for an option. This theoretical value can be viewed as similar to the 95 cent value of a roulette bet (which was a function of two variables—the prize and the number of slots). The "logic" of the calculations used in our models might not exactly correspond with the thought process discussed in Chapter 4, but it can be useful to think of these models as precise calculations that semi-realistically address most of the issues raised in Chapter 4.

As described in Chapter 2, some options prices and values are influenced by additional variables such as interest rates, dividends, and bond coupons. For these options, we need a model with more than three independent variables. Rarely, however, do additional variables affect the general approach of the models we use. Occasionally, one of these additional variables plays a very important role in the pricing or risk of an option position, but usually the big three—underlying price, time, and volatility—are dominant.

MODEL ASSUMPTIONS

All option models are based on specific, simplistic assumptions. Among the most common and most important assumptions are:

1. Volatility is continuous, constant, and known. This means (a) the underlying price moves 24 hours a day, 7 days a week. It never stops; and (b) the volatility of the underlying price never changes during the life of the option—that is, there are no periods during which the underlying price movement is livelier or quieter than normal; and (c) everyone knows how volatile the underlying price is going to be.
2. Option markets are efficient. That means that all options trade at their theoretical values. The implication is that the model is "correct" and that the option price "knows" the values of the input variables, including the future volatility of the underlying price.

Of course, these assumptions are not exactly correct. Sometimes, they are not even close. This situation, which is to be expected in financial modeling, can be disturbing. Are our models wrong? Do they produce incorrect values? Are the calculations based on variables that don't exist in the real world?

WHAT IS A MODEL?

In March 1985, I was one of four speakers at a two-day Interest Rate Options Seminar presented in London by E.D. & F. Man Financial Markets, Ltd. The other three speakers, Myron Scholes, Mark Garman, and Eduardo Schwartz were well-known professors with years of modeling experience. Needless to say, their perspectives on the options business were much different from mine.

Because almost all of my presentation time was scheduled for the second day, I was able to spend most of the first day listening to the other speakers. I was quite anxious to do this not only because I knew they were professional teachers, were brilliant, and thought differently than the traders I knew, but also because I wanted to be able to help the audience reconcile their comments with the things that I would have to say.

In the course of one of Dr. Scholes' presentations, the seminar began to break down a little. One of the participants was quite persistent in hassling Dr. Scholes about perceived imperfections in his model. Finally, things came to a head when the guy said: "Your model is just wrong." Dr. Scholes, who so far had not said anything funny or ironic, came back with: "Of course, it's wrong. That's why we call it a model."

The answer to each of these questions is *yes*. As sophisticated as our option models are, they are just models. They are not reality. They are tools to be used by knowledgeable professionals. In using them, we need to continually ask ourselves whether imperfections in our model or its inputs are material to the decisions we are making. In most situations, our models work well enough for the options business to be a sensible one. Sometimes, however, model problems are severe. Occasionally, we find ourselves in situations where the models are useless. It is our job to be aware of model problems, to anticipate them, and to react to them appropriately.

MODEL USES

If our model calculations were perfect and if everyone knew correct values for the input variables, the options business would be pretty dull. Options would always trade at their theoretical values, expected profits would always be zero, and there would be no P&L surprises. Career opportunities would be less than promising.

In fact, model imperfections require us to think about our models in different ways. For example, we can use our model to produce a *statistical calculation of value,* much like the 95 cent value of a roulette bet. We would have to observe or guess values for each of the input variables, and then, let our model use these inputs to calculate option values. We might try to *make money* by trading options whose prices look a lot different from their theoretical values. Even if *risk management* were the purpose of our option trading, we might use these values to try to avoid giving up too much *edge*. Of course, none of this would be possible or necessary if the "perfect market" assumption were correct.

Alternatively, we could use our model for option *price prediction.* In the theoretical world, this would be no different from calculating an option's statistical value, but, in the real world, it's very different. Using a model for option price prediction requires us to make different kinds of guesses. Now, we are looking for the equivalent of the $1.00 price of a roulette bet. Among the questions to consider: Does the market "think" like our model? What values for the input variables are "they" using and who are "they" anyway?

In the real world, option prices are established by supply/demand forces and perceptions that don't have to be consistent with the assumptions of our models. Nevertheless, option professionals frequently use models for price prediction, especially for:

- ■ Looking ahead to the prospects for trading out of an option position before expiration,

- Mark-to-the-market accounting, and
- Risk analysis.

For all three of these activities, we need to continually be aware of the frailties of our models and of the consequent magnitude of the uncertainties of any calculation. There are many traps, and they are not easy to deal with.

A CLASSIC MODEL MISUSE: THE 2000 U.S. PRESIDENTIAL ELECTION

On election day, November 7, 2000, U.S. television networks continued their practice of competing to "declare" the winners of various contests, including the presidential race in each state. They claimed to have sophisticated models to project results, using a variety of input data including actual results and postpolling information. Apparently, five television networks and the Associated Press all relied on the same surveys conducted by Voter News Service. In the case of the 2000 Florida vote for president, some of the networks acted like an amateur options trader who was too anxious to have a position.

Some networks declared Vice President Al Gore to be the winner in Florida even before all of the polls were closed. They stuck with this projection for hours, even as Governor George W. Bush's people insisted that they liked their chances. At about 10:00 P.M., however, it became apparent that the models' imperfections were material, and the networks declared the Florida race "too close to call." Later, at about 2:15 A.M., the same models projected a Bush victory and the networks declared him the winner.

Of course, this wasn't the end. After Mr. Gore called Governor Bush to congratulate him, the Democrats received additional results that gave them hope. Mr. Gore retracted his phone conversation and, by morning, the networks changed their projections again, declaring the race "too close to call." Since the nationwide election was close enough for Florida's 25 electoral votes to determine the winner, the situation developed into a long administrative and legal battle. The result remained in doubt for more than a month before Governor Bush prevailed.

What's the moral for option traders? Mathematical models are imperfect. There are many temptations to rely on them for more than their quality can justify. The consequences of such aggressive trading can be severe.

CHAPTER 6

Volatility

At first glance, volatility appears to be just another input variable in the imperfect mathematical models we use to value options and to manage risk. It isn't. Volatility is a nasty, messy concept that is difficult to understand and even more difficult to discuss. In an industry that is full of verbal nonsense, volatility is most often the subject of ridiculous and frustrating conversations. In my career, I have given several hundred volatility seminars, and I haven't been satisfied with any of them.

On the other hand, volatility is probably the most important subject in the options business. It is almost always "where the action is." It is fascinating and challenging. Its complexity is good for us. If it were simple and predictable, the options business would probably be trivial and devoid of much opportunity.

THE PROBLEM OF LANGUAGE

One of the obvious problems with volatility is the confusion resulting from multiple uses of the word. While the term is used with many different meanings in the business, these meanings tend to fall into two distinct categories:

1. We frequently use the term, *volatility,* as a characteristic of a commodity price. This characteristic is often called *actual volatility.* Simply speaking, actual volatility is the extent to which a commodity price tends to make large moves in short periods of time. If a commodity's price has changed substantially and rapidly in the recent past, we might say it has been very volatile. If we expect it to be quiet for a while, we might say we predict low actual volatility.
2. We also use the term volatility to describe the level of option pricing. To most option market participants, it makes sense that option prices should be higher if we expect the underlying commodity price to be very volatile, and lower if we expect it to be quiet. Hence, it is natural, if

we see a relatively high option price, to imagine that the option price "implies" that the underlying commodity price will be very volatile. This *implied volatility* is a characteristic of an option price. It seems to be related to actual volatility (a characteristic of the underlying commodity price), but the two concepts are very different.

Too often in our business, the word volatility is used with no adjectives and it is difficult to know what kind of volatility is being discussed. Common sense tells us that we would be better off using two different words for these two kinds of volatility. To my knowledge, no one has really solved this problem in English or in any other language.

WHAT MAKES VOLATILITY DIFFERENT?

As discussed in previous chapters, it is useful to think of an option's theoretical value as a function of three major variables and, perhaps, some minor variables. That is,

$$TV = f(FP, t, V, ...)$$

where FP = Forward price (or futures price) of the underlying
                    instrument
            t = Time to expiration
            V = Actual volatility of the underlying instrument over the
                    remaining life of the option

In thinking about the meanings of these variables and their application to a valuation model, it seems that the volatility variable presents some special problems. It is helpful to think of these problems in two categories: *units* and *uses*.

Units

If you are a careful observer of American stock index prices, one feature that you have probably observed is their actual volatility. You can remember some periods of time during which the S&P 500 index has been quiet. Other times it has been wildly volatile. It might be a little harder to remember all of the many periods during which its actual volatility has been between these extremes.

What if someone asked you, "How volatile has the S&P 500 been over the past 12 months?" How would you answer? What units would you use?

Would you quantify volatility in miles? liters? ergs? Of course not. Such units are not helpful in describing volatility. In fact, in the real world, *there are no good units of volatility.* If you want to tell someone how volatile a commodity price has been, you probably need to itemize every change in price along with the time of each change. Anything short of this would be an incomplete description of its volatility.

Note that we don't struggle with this units problem in thinking about other major variables. Underlying prices usually have understandable units. We might quantify a gold price in dollars per ounce, or a foreign exchange rate in yen per dollar, or a common stock price in dollars per share. Even indexes usually have straightforward units expressed in "points." Similarly, we usually feel comfortable expressing time to expiration in days.

The absence of good, simple, descriptive units of volatility is a real problem in the options business. We can deal with this problem, however. Since there are no good units of volatility, we simply make up some bad units and incorporate these bad units into our thought processes and mathematical models. The following is a *rough* description of how we do it.

We begin by thinking about the likely movements of our commodity price (in this example, a stock index price) over short periods of time. We measure these moves in percentages (e.g., up 1.27%, or down 0.5%). The most common time horizon is one trading day, but, conceptually, a shorter or slightly longer time would be acceptable. Thus, we are thinking about the distribution of one-day changes in the index price expressed in percentage terms, or

$$\text{Daily change} = \frac{\text{Today's price} - \text{Previous day's price}}{\text{Previous day's price}}$$

or

$$\frac{P_n - P_{n-1}}{P_{n-1}}$$

For a given period of time, we would say that a very volatile index would be one whose price had frequent large daily percentage changes. The direction or sequence of these changes wouldn't be considered.

Our models assume that, over the life of an option, the probability of a 1% daily move in the index price is constant. Likewise, we assume that the probability of a move of any other magnitude (in %) is constant. In specifying volatility, then, the big question is: What are those probabilities?

Our model further assumes that a normal distribution (or bell curve) describes the distribution of daily index price moves. The peak (or midpoint) of this curve is where the index price is unchanged. Then, the probability of an index price move of any magnitude is determined by the standard deviation of the bell curve. For example, if 1% is a one standard deviation move, then on any given day there would (theoretically) be about a 38% chance of a move of less than 0.5%, about a 68% chance of a move of less than 1.0%, and about a 95.5% chance of a move of less than 2.0%. A daily move of greater than 3% would have only about a 0.3% chance of occurring.

Under these assumptions, the only unknown is the standard deviation (SD). Given a standard deviation, we would know the probability (looking forward) or the frequency (looking backward) of every possible daily percentage move. That is, we would be able to completely describe the actual volatility of the index price simply by specifying the standard deviation of the curve of daily price changes.

With this approach, it would make sense that our unit of volatility would be a one-day, one standard deviation move in percentage terms. For a variety of reasons, however, the convention in the industry has been to use an annualization of that standard deviation (calculated by multiplying the daily SD by the square root of the number of trading days in a year). So, for a commodity that moved with a one day, one SD move of 1%, we would say its actual volatility was

$$1\% \times \sqrt{250} = 15.8\%$$

As a general rule, then, a commodity price's actual volatility is about 16 times its one-day, one SD move in percentage terms. This "magic number" of 16 is quite useful in getting a feel for price action. For example, for a $50 stock that moves with a 40 volatility, a one-day one-SD move would be about

$$\frac{40\%}{16} \times \$50 = \$1.25$$

What's Wrong with This Approach? This approach to volatility quantification is oversimplified in several ways that can be important to the management of an options business. Here are three examples:

1. We assume that actual volatility is constant over the life of the option. Common experience tells us to expect some actual volatility variations over time.
2. This approach calculates actual volatility using only one data point per day. In practice, the daily percentage change might understate or overstate the actual volatility experienced during the day. (Remember, to really communicate volatility, we'd have to itemize every index price

change along with the time of each change.) Over the years, there have been a lot of attempts to "estimate" volatility using different data inputs (such as daily range). None have produced satisfactory results. As of this writing, daily change is still the most popular, but we can expect more innovation.

3. We assume that a bell curve describes the distribution of index price moves. In practice, this assumption seldom matches our experience or our expectations. In some cases (e.g., Mexican peso), most traders see asymmetry in their expectations. In most cases, traders anticipate "fat tails" and a "tall middle." That is, given a standard deviation, we often expect more than 38% of the moves to be less than 0.5 SD. We also expect more 3+ SD moves than the theoretical 0.3%.

Uses

Even after deciding on some units for volatility, our problems are not over. The next set of problems arises from the question: What volatility numbers should we use? For the other major variables (underlying price, time) we usually don't have a big problem. We normally value options using the *current* underlying price. Granted, we could worry that the bid, offer, last trade, and next trade might be different prices or might be unknown, but in most cases this is a small problem. Likewise, the time to expiration is usually known, although you might argue that not all days or hours should count the same (since actual volatility is not expected to be constant).

Finding the "right" volatility numbers is more troublesome. In the theoretical world of our models, volatility is known, constant, and continuous and we value options by using the actual volatility that the underlying price will experience over the life of the option. Unfortunately, actual volatilities are not known nor constant nor continuous. Likewise, implied volatilities tend to be unstable and difficult to predict.

In reality, there is no one single volatility number which should be used for all applications of the models. Rather, there are many different kinds of volatility, each of which might have a role in our analysis and our decisions. Figure 6.1 contains a *volatility category matrix* that can be useful in thinking about some different kinds of volatility.

In Figure 6.1, we have identified two broad categories of volatility: *actual* and *implied*. For each of these categories, we have rectangles representing *historical, future, forecast,* and *current volatilities*. Each of these eight rectangles requires some comments.

1. *Historical actual volatility* is a description of the volatility of a commodity price during some period of time in the past. Of course, for every commodity, there are a very large number of historical actual

FIGURE 6.1 Volatility category matrix.

	Historical	Future	Forecast	Current
Actual				
Implied				

volatilities. For example, we could discuss the actual volatility of the S&P 500 index over the last week, over the last month, over the last year, or for the decade of the 1970s. It is unlikely that any two of these historical actual volatilities would be the same, since actual volatility is not constant. Sometimes analysts like to weight the data in calculating historical actual volatility. It is common to see exponentially weighted calculations in which the most recent data have the heaviest weightings.

It is important to remember that no historical actual volatility calculation is magically "correct" or directly applicable to a trading decision. Such calculations are simply descriptions of past activities.

2. *Future actual volatility* refers to the volatility that a commodity price will exhibit during some period of time in the future. Since actual volatility is not constant, future actual volatility will be different for different periods of time. Usually, the period of time we are concerned about is the remaining life of a particular option. In an ideal world, we would value an option by inputting this volatility into our model. Of course, we can't do this because we won't know the future actual volatility until it becomes historical.

3. Since we are usually concerned about a stock index's future actual volatility, but we don't know what it will be, we might make an *actual volatility forecast*. An actual volatility forecast is someone's *guess* of what the actual volatility will be during some period of time in the future. The term *forecast* is a euphemism for *guess*. We can make our guess seem more sophisticated by calling it an *estimate,* but it's still a guess.

Clearly, there is a big difference between a *forecast* and a *future actual volatility.* A forecast is our guess for what the future will be. We make the guess in advance. Future actual volatility is the volatility that the index price actually experiences over a particular period of time. We can measure it, but only after it has already taken place.

Likewise, *historical actual volatility* is very different. Often, traders want to imagine that they can "estimate" *future actual volatility* by applying statistical analysis to historical actual volatility. In fact, historical data might be useful in *forecasting* the future, but it is important to remember that, no matter how sophisticated the methodology, we are still *guessing*.

A few more comments on actual volatility forecasts:

■ There is no correct way to make a volatility forecast. It's forecasting. Good luck!

■ You can expect large discrepancies between your forecast and the future actual volatility. Also, methodologies that "work" pretty well for a while might not work as well later. Market dynamics can change.

■ In anticipation of these large expected errors, *the single most important step you can take in risk management in options is to make sure you have room to be very wrong in your volatility forecast (for actual or implied)*.

■ Despite the difficulty and frustration of making actual volatility forecasts and living with them, it is pretty hard to run a good options business without them. In theory, it is possible to run an options business without having your P&L exposed to the actual volatility of the underlying instrument. In practice, almost no one does it. Before you expose yourself, you probably should make some kind of a guess.

4. There is no such thing as *current actual volatility*. Actual volatility includes a change in price and a change in time. With no change in time it's a meaningless concept.

5. For any option, *current implied volatility* is the *future actual volatility* that we would have to assume in order to reconcile an option's current price with our option valuation model and with the current (presumably known) values of the other variables. For example, we might have a three-month call on an index futures contract:

Strike price	= 100.00
Underlying index futures price	= 100.00
Call price	= 3.00
Interest rate	= 0%

In our model, $TV = f(FP, t, V, i)$.

We know FP, t, and i. We don't know TV (the option's statistical value) or V (future actual volatility). However, if we assume that the option price and our model are compatible, we can solve for an implied V that will make

$$MP = f(FP, t, V, i)$$

In this case, $V = 15$ is the only volatility that "works." It is the *current implied volatility* since it is the only assumption for *future actual volatility* that is compatible with our model, with the option's price, and with the current values of the other variables.

Of course, a higher option price would produce a higher *implied volatility*. For example, with a call price of 4.00, the implied volatility would be about 20.

It is easy to imagine that an option's implied volatility represents the market's consensus forecast for the future actual volatility. Theoretically, this is the way the world should work. In reality, the relationship between market expectations and implied volatility is indirect at best. Certainly, if the whole world thinks markets will be quiet, it is difficult for option prices to stay high. On the other hand, the "market" doesn't have to think in the terms of our model (who believes the bell curve?) and market participants can be driven by forces that have little to do with perceived value.

One sign of this kind of market behavior is the common phenomenon of different options trading at different implied volatilities. In the above example, the 3-month call with a 105 strike might trade for 1.00. The implied volatility (IV) of this option would be about 13.8. Of course, the same option might trade for 1.50, in which case its IV would be about 16.8. Neither of these IVs would be incompatible with a 15.0 IV for the 3-month call with a 100 strike.

6. Just as we might be interested in the history of a commodity's actual volatility, we might also consider its *historical implied volatility*. As discussed in this chapter, we can measure a commodity's historical actual volatility over different *periods of time* and find different levels because actual volatility is not constant. In contrast, we do not measure implied volatility over a period of time. We measure it at a *point in time*. Still, for a given commodity, there are many historical implied volatilities, because implied volatilities vary over time. Furthermore, even for a single point in time in the past, we are likely to find different implied volatilities for the various options on a particular commodity.

7. *Future implied volatility* is the implied volatility of an option's price at a specific point in time in the future. We might be very concerned about this. For example, an option's implied volatility at the end of next

month could be very important to us if we plan to trade out of it then or if we would like to calculate our P&L by marking the option to the market.

8. An *implied volatility forecast* is someone's guess of the implied volatility at which an option will trade at some point in time in the future. While such a guess is difficult to make and is likely to have a large expected error, it can be an important element of a trading or hedging strategy. Many bank option dealers claim to be good forecasters of implied volatility. Some of them are.

CALCULATION OF HISTORICAL VOLATILITY

For a closer look at the rough mathematics of volatility, we refer to Table 6.1, which breaks down some historical volatility calculations based on the closing prices of the March S&P 500 futures (SPH) traded at the Chicago Mercantile Exchange. These calculations give us 5-day *historical actual volatilities* for various time periods during January 1998. The 5-day calculations are chosen for demonstration purposes only. They are no more or less useful than 6-day, 20-day, 60-day, 250-day, or any other calculation.

To calculate a 5-day historical volatility, we need 6 consecutive closing prices (i.e., 5 daily changes). The first 1 SD move (through Jan. 8) is

TABLE 6.1 Historical Volatility Calculations

Date	SPH Close	% Change	(% Change)^2	1 SD Move	5-Day Vol
Dec. 31, '97	979.10				
Jan. 2, '98	984.70	0.572	0.327		
Jan. 5, '98	986.90	0.223	0.050		
Jan. 6, '98	971.00	−1.611	2.596		
Jan. 7, '98	974.00	0.309	0.095		
Jan. 8, '98	961.20	−1.314	1.727	0.979%	15.48%
Jan. 9, '98	929.50	−3.298	10.877	1.752	27.70
Jan. 12, '98	945.50	1.721	2.963	1.911	30.21
Jan. 13, '98	959.50	1.481	2.192	1.890	29.88
Jan. 14, '98	963.30	0.396	0.157	1.893	29.93
Jan. 15, '98	955.10	−0.851	0.725	1.839	29.08
Jan. 16, '98	968.40	1.393	1.939	1.263	19.97
Jan. 20, '98	985.20	1.735	3.010	1.267	20.03
Jan. 21, '98	975.40	−0.995	0.989	1.168	18.47

calculated as the square root of the mean of the squares of the individual changes. That is,

$$\sqrt{\frac{0.327+0.050+2.596+0.095+1.727}{5}}=0.979$$

Then, the 5-day historical actual volatility is calculated by "annualizing" this number; that is, by multiplying by the square root of the number of trading days in a year (presumed to be 250):

$$0.979\times\sqrt{250}=15.48$$

To calculate the next 5-day historical actual volatility (through Jan. 9), we drop the Jan. 2 change from the calculation and we add the Jan. 9 change. This change (−3.298%) is only about twice as large as the next biggest change in the sample, but it is squared in the standard deviation calculation. As a result, not only does the 5-day vol jump to 27.70%, but we have a situation in which a single piece of data dominates the calculation. In fact, even if the other four daily changes were 0.00%, we would still have a 5-day vol of 23.32%, that is,

$$\sqrt{\frac{10.877}{5}}\times\sqrt{250}$$

This phenomenon of a volatility calculation being dominated by a single "outlier" is no small problem in the options business. It is a reminder that our models are imperfect and our concept of volatility is weak.

In Table 6.1, the Jan. 9 outlier disappears from the 5-day calculation on Jan. 16. As of this date, the 5-day historical actual volatility drops from 29.08% to 19.97%. This change illustrates the difficulty produced by using a particular time period to measure historical actual volatility. Clearly, if, on Jan. 16, you asked what the historical actual volatility was, you would get very different answers for different time horizons (e.g., the 6-day vol was 28.03% because it included the big drop on Jan. 9).

Which number is more meaningful? Really, neither. They are just different facts about the past. However, this "sudden change" problem makes it easy to understand why many people look at exponentially weighted volatilities. With such weighting, pieces of data lose importance gradually over time, rather than suddenly (as in Table 6.1).

OPTION PRICES AND IMPLIED VOLATILITIES

It is not easy to get a feel for the relationship between an option's *price* and its *implied volatility*. (Note that this is the same as the relationship between an option's *value* and our actual volatility forecast). Table 6.2 displays a variety of prices for a call on a stock index futures contract. In each case the call has a strike price of 100.00, but we show call prices under different combinations of assumption for underlying price, time to expiration, and implied volatility.

Let's begin by looking at the 60-day, at-the-money (ATM) situation with an implied volatility (IV) = 20. The call price is 3.23. Notice that, with IV = 16, the price is 2.59. Within rounding, the price is about proportional to the implied volatility. This is typical of at-the-money options where the underlying is a forward or futures contract. Similar proportionality exists in the 120-day example. Even for options on other kinds of underlying instruments (e.g., common stocks), it is usually a good rule of thumb to think of the relationship between price and IV for ATM options as linear. This relationship is approximate, however, and it breaks down noticeably at very high IVs and/or long times to expiration. (Clearly, in the absence of unusual circumstances, a call price should not exceed the underlying price, and a put price should not exceed the strike price.)

Returning to Table 6.2, as we reduce the underlying price to 98 or 96, the call price remains about proportional to the IV. As we move further out-of-the-money, however, the linearity breaks down. With the futures at 90.00, an IV increase from 16 to 18 for the 60-day call produces more than a 75% increase in option price (0.13 to 0.23). A further IV increase to 20 produces a smaller percent increase (0.23 to 0.35) but a bigger tick increase. In such an out-of-the-money example, it is useful to think of the value of the option as coming mostly from the tails of our model's bell curve. These tails can really "pop up" as we increase the curve's standard deviation.

Moving on to an in-the-money example (e.g., futures at 108.00) the 60-day call value is dominated by its parity ingredient (8.00). Note, however, that the premium over parity responds to IV changes in ways similar to the out-of-the-money (OTM) examples.

It is also worth noting (although it might be obvious to many) that the relationship between IV and call price becomes more financially dramatic as we increase the time to expiration. For example, with 2 days to expiration, the underlying at 100.00 and a call price of 0.58, the IV would be 16. In contrast, with a call price of 0.72 (only 0.14 higher) our IV would be 20. That is, with not much time to expiration, our model needs a much higher volatility assumption to justify a slightly higher option price. In contrast, in the 60-day example, the same IV increase produced a 0.64 change in call price. In the 120-day example, the price difference is 0.91. It is not hard to

TABLE 6.2   Option Prices and Implied Volatilities

Call on index futures contract
Strike price = 100.00
Interest rate = 0%

Futures Price	Prices for 60-Day Calls (IV =)			Prices for 120-Day Calls (IV =)		
	16	18	20	16	18	20
90.00	0.13	0.23	0.35	0.54	0.78	1.05
92.00	0.29	0.44	0.61	0.87	1.17	1.50
94.00	0.57	0.78	1.01	1.33	1.69	2.06
96.00	1.02	1.29	1.56	1.93	2.34	2.76
98.00	1.68	1.99	2.30	2.71	3.15	3.60
100.00	2.59	2.91	3.23	3.66	4.12	4.57
102.00	3.73	4.05	4.36	4.78	5.23	5.69
104.00	5.11	5.39	5.68	6.07	6.50	6.93
106.00	6.67	6.90	7.15	7.50	7.90	8.30
108.00	8.39	8.57	8.77	9.07	9.42	9.79
110.00	10.21	10.34	10.50	10.74	11.04	11.37

see that for long-dated options, a small change in IV can produce a big P&L swing. Looking at ITM and OTM examples, we see a different kind of price sensitivity. In each case, however, more time means that bigger option price changes result from IV changes.

THE RELATIONSHIP BETWEEN ACTUAL VOLATILITY AND IMPLIED VOLATILITY

Questions regarding the interactive dynamics between actual volatility and implied volatility can drive you to extreme frustration or worse. Do implied volatilities respond to historical actual volatilities? Do implied volatilities predict future actual volatility? Are they so closely related that I can just worry about one of them?

Conceptually, they are very different. For example, *current implied volatility* should be based on market expectations for the *future actual volatility* of the underlying instrument over the life of the option. In practice, such expectations often seem to be influenced by recent actual volatility (e.g., a quiet market in the recent past might lead us to expect a quiet near-term future). Sometimes, however, pending news or other considerations might make the world "think" that future actual volatility might be very different from the recent past.

In making an implied volatility forecast, we are guessing what "the market's" expectation will be at some point in the future. This expectation might be influenced by the actual volatility experienced between now and then, but it might not be.

If markets were efficient, today's implied volatility would be a good forecast for future actual volatility. In practice we usually see big divergences between implieds and future actuals. Actual volatility is hard to forecast, whether the forecaster is an individual or a very large group.

Working in a world of so many different kinds of volatility is both challenging and frustrating. It certainly isn't easy. My advice: Be conscious of the whole volatility category matrix. Keep looking for relationships, but don't expect them to be simple or reliable. Volatility is a mess that must be constantly sorted.

LOOSE ENDS

Lognormality

Our discussion of the units of volatility was based on the simplistic view that our models assume that the distribution of short-term index price moves is a bell curve with a midpoint (median) of 0.00. This view is a pretty good one, but it breaks down if we think about it a little more. Let's think about this in three steps:

1. We know that for *really* big moves, the index can go up farther than it can go down. Certainly, it can go from 100 to 250 easier than it can go from 100 to −50. It can probably go from 100 to 190 easier than from 100 to 10. Even for small moves, there seems to be more room to go up. If we look at 1% moves as "typical," then, with the index starting at 100.00, five consecutive up moves would give us

101.00
102.01
103.03
104.06
105.10

while five consecutive down moves would give us

99.00
98.01
97.03
96.06
95.10

This arithmetic might lead us to think that our theoretical distribution should not be perfectly symmetrical.

Here is a related thought: Shouldn't a move from 100 to 105 be about as likely as a move from 105 to 100? Now we are comparing a +5.00% move with a −4.76% move. I am suggesting that a price increase from P to $P(1+x)$ should be about as likely as a decrease from

$$P \text{ to } \frac{P}{(1+x)}$$

Notice that

$$\log(1+x) = -\log\left(\frac{1}{1+x}\right)$$

Then, instead of a normal distribution, we might assume a lognormal curve with more "room" for big up moves and less "room" for big down moves.

2. When we thought about the distribution of index price movements as a normal distribution, it made sense to assume that the median corresponded to a move of 0.00. How about a lognormal curve? If we assume a median of 0.00, it looks too good. That is, we'd have a *positive expected return*. For example, the +5.00% moves and the −4.76% moves would give us about a +0.12% expected return. To account for this apparent "unfairness," our lognormal distribution should have a median corresponding to a slight down move. That is, in our lognormal (theoretical) world there should be more down days than up days. For commodities that aren't exceptionally volatile, the daily impact of this effect should be small.

3. How does this affect our handling of volatility? In short, we don't measure our daily changes in percentage terms

$$\frac{P_n - P_{n-1}}{P_{n-1}}$$

Instead, we measure them in logarithmic terms. That is,

$$\log_e \frac{P_n}{P_{n-1}}$$

For most commodities on which options are traded this distinction is not very important. Except for very large moves,

$$\frac{P_n - P_{n-1}}{P_{n-1}}$$

is usually not very different from

$$\log_e \frac{P_n}{P_{n-1}}$$

For example:

A Daily Change	B $\log_e \frac{P_n}{P_{n-1}}$
+0.5%	0.00499
+1.0	0.00995
+2.0	0.01980
+3.0	0.02956
+5.0	0.04879
+10.0	0.09531
−0.5	−0.00501
−1.0	−0.01005
−2.0	−0.02020
−3.0	−0.03046
−5.0	−0.05129
−10.0	−0.10536

Certainly the numbers in Column B are different from those in Column A, and for 10% moves they seem substantially different. For most financial commodities, however, a 10% daily move is very unusual. When such a move occurs, our assumptions break down in many ways (e.g., constant volatility? fat tails? representative data?) and it might not help much to worry about the distinction between

$$\frac{P_n - P_{n-1}}{P_{n-1}} \text{ and } \log \frac{P_n}{P_{n-1}}$$

However, for some financial commodities (most notably, equities in 2000 and 2001), daily moves of 5% or 10% can be so commonplace that this distinction really matters.

Table 6.3 compares the 5-day historical volatilities from Table 6.1 with the calculations we would get based on log P_n/P_{n-1}. In this example, most of the logarithmic calculations produced slightly higher 5-day vols because the big moves on Jan. 6 and Jan. 9 were down moves, and, in a lognormal world, a big move of down $x\%$ is considered "bigger" than a move of up $x\%$.

Drift

For commodities that have a positive or negative cost of carry (unlike forwards or futures), our actual volatility calculations usually make adjustments for a risk-free rate of return. For example, for equities, we assume that stocks drift up at the risk-free rate except on ex-dividend dates. Likewise, we assume that foreign exchange rates drift according to the interest differentials.

In theory, each day's data for historical actual volatility should reflect price changes that are adjusted for theoretical drift. In practice, this is usually unimportant because daily drift is usually quite small compared to a typical one SD move. One exception would be a high dividend stock. Another would be a low volatility currency pair with a big interest rate differential.

While drift problems are usually not very important in measuring actual volatility, they can become significant in dealing with the early exercise feature of American-style options.

TABLE 6.3   5-Day Historical Actual Volatility for SPH

5 Days Ending	Based on % Change	Based on log $\dfrac{P_n}{P_{n-1}}$
Jan. 8	15.48%	15.59%
Jan. 9	27.70	28.08
Jan. 12	30.21	30.53
Jan. 13	29.88	30.14
Jan. 14	29.93	30.19
Jan. 15	29.08	29.33
Jan. 16	19.97	19.84
Jan. 20	20.03	19.90
Jan. 21	18.47	18.38

Intraday Volatility

Earlier in this chapter, actual volatility was described as the extent to which a commodity price tends to make large moves in short periods of time. To really describe historical actual volatility, we would have to report every change in price along with the time of each change. Since this is impractical, we usually focus on daily price changes, that is

$$\log \frac{P_n}{P_{n-1}}$$

and hope that these changes do a good job of reflecting the actual volatility experienced on each day.

What if, to get an indication of how volatile a commodity price had been on a given day, we looked at the daily range instead of the daily change? Of course, in most situations we would expect a daily range to be greater than the daily change. For example, for a commodity that experiences a 15.8% actual volatility, we would expect a "typical" (i.e., 1 SD) daily change to be about 1%. For such a commodity, we would probably expect a "typical" daily range to be 1.5% or 2%. Hence, if we want to use daily range as the basis for an actual volatility calculation, we might be able to adjust the observed range down to a sensible daily change that would be "comparable."

The mathematics of this adjustment are not complicated if we assume that our intraday volatility is constant and continuous and that all of the price action is between the daily recorded high (H_n) and low (L_n). That is, we'd have to assume that all of the action took place while our market was open. Under these assumptions, the magnitude (but maybe not the sign) of the daily change should be about 60% of the daily range. That is,

$$\log \frac{P_n}{P_{n-1}} = \pm.6 \ \log \frac{H_n}{L_n}$$

In the real world, this relationship would vary. Table 6.4 presents an example of how historical volatility calculations can differ if they are based on the daily range instead of the daily change.

In this example of 13 trading days, 6 had close-to-close changes that were small (less than 60%) compared to the daily range and 7 had relatively large close-to-close changes. The mean of the ratio was 0.635. On three of the days (Jan. 6, 15, 20) the range and the change were virtually identical. We might want to conclude that, on those days, the daily change overstated

TABLE 6.4   Differing Historical Volatility Calculations

Date	SPH Close	SPH High	SPH Low	$\log \dfrac{P_n}{P_{n-1}}$	$\log \dfrac{H_n}{L_n}$	Ratio	5-Day Vol Close to Close	Range
Dec. 31, '97	979.10							
Jan. 2, '98	984.70	985.50	973.80	0.00570	0.01194	0.477		
Jan. 5, '98	986.90	992.50	976.50	0.00223	0.01625	0.137		
Jan. 6, '98	971.00	987.30	970.50	−0.01624	0.01716	0.946		
Jan. 7, '98	974.00	974.80	960.50	0.00308	0.01478	0.208		
Jan. 8, '98	961.20	977.40	960.60	−0.01323	0.01734	0.763	15.59%	14.83%
Jan. 9, '98	929.50	963.30	926.00	−0.03354	0.03949	0.849	28.08	21.81
Jan. 12, '98	945.50	948.50	915.00	0.01707	0.03596	0.475	30.53	25.71
Jan. 13, '98	959.50	959.80	944.50	0.01470	0.01607	0.915	30.14	25.58
Jan. 14, '98	963.30	966.20	954.10	0.00395	0.01260	0.313	30.19	25.37
Jan. 15, '98	955.10	963.20	954.80	−0.00855	0.00876	0.976	29.33	24.57
Jan. 16, '98	968.40	972.50	952.50	0.01383	0.02078	0.666	19.84	20.00
Jan. 20, '98	985.20	985.80	968.60	0.01720	0.01760	0.977	19.90	14.93
Jan. 21, '98	975.40	985.50	967.70	−0.01000	0.01823	0.549	18.38	15.37

the actual volatility, but we can't be sure. We could have had several large "whips" between the high and the low. On one day (Jan. 5) the close-to-close change was very small, but the daily range was not. For that day, it is safe to assume that the daily change understated the actual volatility.

On two days, the daily range did not include the previous day's close. This should make us a little uncomfortable with our calculations—what else is the daily range missing? In this example, however, the resulting errors might be minimal.

Generally, the calculated 5-day vols were quite different for the different methods. This is a hint that we should be hesitant to conclude too much from any actual volatility calculation. By coincidence, almost all of the range-based 5-day vols were lower. This is because the dominant big days (Jan. 6, 9, 20) had ranges that were surprisingly close to their daily changes. Another example might be quite different.

You can go crazy trying to decide what data to use to "estimate" historical actual volatility or what to expect regarding intraday volatility or what historical data to use in forecasting. There is also a lot of opportunity for statistical nonsense and "folk wisdom" in this area. Be suspicious! Remember, since our assumptions are always false, our conclusions are usually questionable and limited.

CHAPTER 7

Greek Letters

So far, in this book, there has been much attention given to the *multidimensional, nonlinear dynamics of options*. While this broad view should always be kept in mind, it is often useful to zero in on narrow pieces of our exposure. We often look at our exposure to one variable at a time, and we might look only at our incremental exposure to a variable, temporarily ignoring the potential effects of nonlinearity.

It is a custom in the options business to use Greek letters to quantify incremental, one-dimensional aspects of our exposure. While these Greek letters tell us very little about the expected *profitability* of our option position, they are powerful, *but imperfect, risk management* tools. They usually cannot completely (or even adequately) describe our risk, but they describe some important aspects of our risk, and they can help us make *some* simple, but important risk management decisions.

Throughout the options business, we find many variations in the definitions and applications of Greek letters. In this book, there is no attempt to comprehensively list and describe all of the terms that are in use. Rather, we concentrate on four common useful calculations: *delta, gamma, theta,* and *vega*.

DELTA

Suppose we would like to consider an option position's exposure to a potential change in the underlying price, assuming no change in other model variables (such as time and implied volatility). Table 7.1 gives us some useful data for a simple call position. For a call with a 100.00 strike price, Table 7.1 assumes that time to expiration, implied volatility (IV), and interest rates are fixed at 120 days, 16, and 0%, respectively. Under these assumptions, Table 7.1 shows what the call price would be for 11 different possible underlying futures prices.

TABLE 7.1   Effect of Futures Price on Options Price for a European-Style Call on an Index Futures Contract

120 days to expiry
Strike price = 100.00
Implied volatility = 16
Interest rate = 0%

A Futures Price	B Call Price
90.00	0.54
92.00	0.87
94.00	1.33
96.00	1.93
98.00	2.71
100.00	3.66
102.00	4.78
104.00	6.07
106.00	7.50
108.00	9.07
110.00	10.74

It is clear from the data that the exposure of the call price to a change in futures price is not a stable one. For example, if the futures price were to move from 92.00 to 94.00, the option price would increase from 0.87 to 1.33. That is, given these assumptions, the option price would change by

$$\frac{1.33 - 0.87}{94.00 - 92.00} = 23\% \text{ as much as the futures price}$$

For a futures price move from 100.00 to 102.00, the option price would change by

$$\frac{4.78 - 3.66}{102.00 - 100.00} = 56\% \text{ as much}$$

For a move from 106.00 to 110.00, the comparable calculation would be

$$\frac{10.74 - 7.50}{110.00 - 106.00} = 81\%$$

This kind of variability in the exposure of our option position to a change in the price of the underlying instrument is a significant concern in the management of option position risk. It might seem obvious that, under any set of circumstances, we should similarly quantify our exposure to a variety of hypothetical underlying price moves. Then, we should ask ourselves if any of those exposures are excessive. In practice, most people in the options business prefer to simplify this analysis by focusing on the option position's exposure to an *incremental* change in the underlying price. This exposure is commonly referred to as the *delta* (Δ).

Numerical Definition

We can define the delta of an option as

$$\frac{\text{Change in option price}}{\text{Change in underlying price}}$$

for an incremental change in underlying price, with all other model variables held constant. In other words, in Table 7.1, delta is change in Column B divided by change in Column A for a *very small* change in Column A.

It is worth noting that deltas for individual options are frequently expressed as *whole numbers* even though they describe exposure as a *percent* of underlying price movement. Hence, an option with a delta of 25 would be one whose incremental exposure would be 25% of that of the underlying price (assuming other variables are fixed). Also, for individual options, we frequently identify deltas without reference to their sign. Although puts have negative deltas, we might say a put has a 30 delta when its incremental exposure is calculated as −0.30.

Table 7.2 includes a delta for each of the option prices in Table 7.1. For example, with the futures at 92.00, the option's delta is 19. This means that, if no other variable changes, as the futures price moves incrementally through 92.00, the option price moves about 19% as "fast" as the futures price. Scanning down Table 7.2, as the futures pass through 94.00, the option price moves about 26% as "fast" as the futures price. Given these deltas of 19 and 26, it is probably no surprise that, on average, between 92.00 and 94.00, the option price change is 23% as large as the futures price change.

With the futures price at 100.00, the delta is 52 and the at-the-money (ATM) option price moves by about half the amount of the futures price change. Finally, as the option becomes in-the-money (ITM), its relative price movement continues to increase. At 110.00, why is the delta 86? Think back to Chapter 4. In this ITM option price of 10.74, we have 10.00 parity and a

TABLE 7.2   Effect of Futures Price on Delta for a
European-Style Call on an Index Futures Contract

120 days to expiry
Strike price = 100.00
Implied volatility = 16
Interest rate = 0%

A Futures Price	B Call Price	C Δ
90.00	0.54	14
92.00	0.87	19
94.00	1.33	26
96.00	1.93	34
98.00	2.71	43
100.00	3.66	52
102.00	4.78	60
104.00	6.07	68
106.00	7.50	75
108.00	9.07	81
110.00	10.74	86

0.74 *volatility* ingredient; that is, 0.74 is the market price of 120-day insurance against the futures finishing below 100.00. If we increase the futures price by 0.01, the parity ingredient also increases by 0.01 (it has a 100 delta), but the insurance ingredient declines slightly, so the option price increases by only about 86% of the futures price increase. Clearly, as we continue to increase the futures price, the volatility ingredient approaches 0.00 and the delta approaches 100.

Graphical Definition

For readers who think more easily using graphs instead of numbers, we can similarly define delta in graphical terms. Figure 7.1 is a graph of the data in Table 7.1.

Point A represents a futures price of 100.00 and an option price of 3.66. Point B represents a futures price of 102.00 and an option price of 4.78. Dotted line AC represents a futures price change of 2.00. Dotted line CB represents an option price change of 1.12. Dotted line AB has a slope of 1.12 ÷ 2.00 = 56%, indicating that, over the 2.00 futures price change, the option price moves by 56% of the move in the futures price.

FIGURE 7.1 Effect of futures price on options price for a European-style call on an index futures contract.

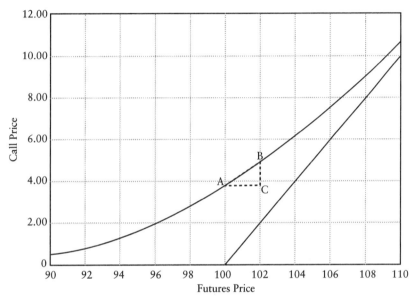

120 days to expiry
Strike price = 100.00
Implied volatility = 16
Interest rate = 0%

To calculate a delta for the option with the futures at 100.00, we need to keep Point A fixed, but reduce the size of triangle ABC until it approaches infinitesimal size. As the triangle becomes very small, Line AB looks like the tangent to the curve and its slope approaches the slope of the curve with the futures at 100.00. In this example, that slope is about 0.52.

Hence, an alternative definition of delta: Delta is the slope of the curve of option price versus underlying price with fixed values for time, implied volatility, and any other model variables. That is, delta is the first derivative of the option price with respect to underlying price.

Problems in Using Delta

Since a delta calculation can give us important information about our exposure to underlying price movement, it can be a powerful and important tool for risk analysis and management. At the same time, it can be a limited and sloppy tool for a variety of reasons:

1. A delta is an output of the same mathematical model that we use to calculate *theoretical values*. Hence, it is subject to problems related to several of the issues discussed in Chapter 5, including:

   ■ The model assumptions are false. They don't exactly reflect the real world.

   ■ Like the theoretical value, the delta is variable-dependent. In Table 7.2, it is clear that an option delta can be different for different underlying prices. Likewise, at a single underlying price, we can find significantly different deltas if we change time, implied volatility, or even interest rates.

   ■ In Chapter 5, we distinguished between the use of models for price prediction and their use for statistical calculation of value. In Chapter 7, we have discussed delta as a tool for "predicting" a change in option price. We can't really count on the accuracy of such "predictions" since the market doesn't have to "think" like our model and especially since implied volatilities might change. In contrast, we could calculate a delta as an incremental change in *theoretical value*. In that case, we would run our model using an *actual volatility forecast* instead of the option's *current implied volatility*.

2. The delta merely describes *incremental* exposure. It ignores *nonlinearity*. Hence, it doesn't necessarily tell us anything about exposure to discrete changes in underlying price. For example, in Table 7.2, with the futures price at 90.00, the option has a 14 delta. With a futures move to 96.00, the option price changes by more than 23% of the 6.00 futures price change. In another example, this discrepancy could be much more extreme.

3. Delta is a risk management tool that addresses only one variable: underlying price movement. In many option positions, exposure to underlying price movement is a minor (or even insignificant) part of the position risk. The more important exposure might be to the passage of time or to implied volatility change. A delta doesn't begin to address these exposures.

Nondefinitions of Delta

In the options business, it is common to hear two other "definitions" of delta. They are worth discussing, but I suggest that you reject them.

1. *Equivalent underlying position.* If you were the owner of the call in Table 7.2 with the futures at 94.00, and a delta of 26, it would probably occur to you that, if the futures price increased by 0.04, you would be about 0.01 better off. Likewise, if the futures declined by 0.04, you would probably lose about 0.01. After a while, you might think of your option position as "equivalent" to 26% of a futures position. That's dangerous.

   I admit that in my early years of giving stock option seminars to market makers, I was known to define delta as the "stock equivalent position." I stopped using that definition in the early 1980s when I saw bank foreign exchange managers go too far with the concept of "equivalence." They wanted to regard an option position's delta as *the same exposure* as an "equivalent" foreign exchange spot position. Of course, this led to disasters. A spot FX position is one-dimensional and linear. An option position is *multidimensional* and *nonlinear*. An option position's risk is unlikely to be exactly the same as the risk of *any* size spot position. Hence, I don't like to use the word "equivalent" in a definition of delta. The phrase "somewhat similar for limited purposes" might be more appropriate.

2. *Probability of the option finishing in-the-money.* If you think of an option's delta as its probability of finishing in-the-money, you might have a pretty good "rule of thumb." In Table 7.2, with the futures at 92.00, the option probably would have about a 19% chance of finishing in-the-money. Likewise, it might have about a 60% chance with the futures at 102.00, and an 86% chance with the futures at 110.00.

   However, in the mathematics of our models, it just isn't true. The delta is not equal to the theoretical probability of the option finishing in-the-money. Often the delta and the theoretical probability are pretty close. Sometimes, they are not close at all.

How to Think about Delta

In the options business, we often find situations in which the most important exposure of a position is its sensitivity to underlying price movement, and in which the biggest part of this exposure is stable (i.e., it is "fairly linear" and not too sensitive to changes in other variables). In such a situation, a delta can be a very important risk indicator. However, delta management is *not* a risk management program. A delta addresses only limited aspects of an option position's risk. Furthermore, a delta calculation does not produce a firm number in the way that a foreign exchange spot position has a size. A delta is a "soft" number that is model-dependent and variable-dependent.

It is seldom a good idea to ignore a large delta, but it is dangerous to assume that an acceptable delta can assure us that our risk is acceptable.

GAMMA

In reviewing Table 7.2, we might ask: Why do we care about delta? The simple answer is: Because we are concerned about *risk*. More specifically, we would like to quantify our exposure to underlying price change.

It should be clear that a delta does not fully describe the risk of our option position—not even the exposure to underlying price movement. Another part of that exposure is the instability of the delta as the underlying price changes. It is a practice in the options business to use the Greek letter, *gamma*, to describe the rate at which a delta changes as the underlying price changes. Like delta, gamma is an incremental calculation. It is defined as

$$\frac{\text{Change in delta}}{\text{Change in underlying price}}$$

for an incremental change in underlying price, with all other model variables held constant. In Table 7.2, gamma is change in Column C divided by change in Column A for a very small change in Column A. Often, gamma is referred to as the "delta of delta." The most common unit of gamma is "deltas per big figure change in underlying price," but sometimes other units are used.

Table 7.3 expands Table 7.2 to include gammas and also extends the deltas to three significant figures. With the futures at 90.00, the 2.63 gamma indicates that, as the futures price moves up through 90.00, the delta is increasing at an *incremental* rate of about 2.63 deltas per 1.00 move in the futures. As in the case of the delta, the gamma changes as the futures price changes. At 92.00, the delta changes at a rate of about 3.26 deltas per 1.00 move in the futures. Given these gammas, you might guess that, over the 90.00 to 92.00 range, the option's delta would increase at an average rate of about 3.00 deltas per 1.00 move in the futures.

With this guess, it is not a surprise that, over the 2.00 range, the option's delta increases from about 13.5 to about 19.4.

Table 7.3 demonstrates a typical pattern of gamma dynamics in that gamma tends to be high when the underlying price is close to the strike price (in this case, gamma peaks with the futures near 98.75). In contrast, gamma declines as the delta approaches 0 or 100. All of the gammas in Table 7.3 are positive because, for a European-style call, higher underlying

TABLE 7.3 Effect of Futures Price on Gamma for a European-Style Call on an Index Futures Contract

120 days to expiry
Strike price = 100.00
Implied volatility = 16
Interest rate = 0%

Futures Price	Call Price	Delta	Gamma
90.00	0.54	13.5	2.63
92.00	0.87	19.4	3.26
94.00	1.33	26.5	3.80
96.00	1.93	34.5	4.18
98.00	2.71	43.1	4.37
100.00	3.66	51.8	4.34
102.00	4.78	60.3	4.12
104.00	6.07	68.2	3.74
106.00	7.50	75.2	3.25
108.00	9.07	81.2	2.72
110.00	10.74	86.1	2.19

prices always produce higher deltas (assuming, of course, no change in other variables).

Graphical Considerations

The graph in Figure 7.1 is almost horizontal for very low futures prices. It approaches a slope of 1.00 for high futures prices. Near the strike price, it has a more prominent curve. Of course, if the graph were a straight line, its slope would be constant. In that case, the delta would be the same for all underlying prices. For the delta to change, the graph must curve. A gentle curve indicates a "slowly" changing delta. A curve that is very convex or concave would indicate a big positive or negative gamma. Gamma, then, is the rate of change of the slope. It is the second derivative of the option price with respect to the underlying price.

Because of these graphical dynamics, the term *curvature* is often used to describe the effect on a delta of a change in underlying price. Usually, the term, curvature refers to gamma (sometimes called *unit curvature*). Sometimes, however, we look at a different option characteristic known as *percent curvature*. By percent curvature we mean gamma divided by delta. This is the rate at which an option's delta changes as a percentage of the option's delta (per unit change in underlying price, with other variables constant). Again, the data in Table 7.3 is typical of that for European-style options in that percent curvature is highest for low delta (OTM) options, and lowest for high delta (ITM) options.

Gamma and percent curvature are different, but related, measures of the dynamics of option price and value. For some analytical purposes, it makes sense to think first about gamma; for others percent curvature is more useful.

Uses and Limitations of Gamma

Like delta, gamma gives us some specific information about a position's exposure. In some situations it describes the most important aspect of our risk; in others, it is insignificant.

Also like delta, gamma is model-dependent, variable-dependent, incremental, and one-dimensional. It is simply another limited risk management tool.

THETA

In defining delta, we considered an option's incremental exposure to changes in one variable (underlying price) with other variables (principally, time and implied volatility) held constant. In risk management, we might also be concerned with the option's incremental exposure to time changes. *Theta* can be thought of as the "delta of time." It is

$$\frac{\text{Change in option price}}{\text{Change in time}}$$

for an incremental change in time with all other variables held constant.

Theta's units are usually points per day, ticks per day, or dollars per day. The theta of an individual option is often expressed as a positive number, even though almost all options lose value with the passage of time.

Table 7.4 expands Table 7.1 to include thetas as well as the effects of 10 days of time decay. In this example, the thetas are quite stable over the 10-day time period. They would be less stable if the option were shorter dated. Table 7.4 shows considerable theta variation as the underlying price is changed. As was the case for gamma, an option's theta is usually greatest when the underlying price is close to the strike price. In this case, the 120-day theta peaks with the futures near 100.45.

As with delta and gamma, there is a temptation to over rely on a theta calculation. Often, changes in underlying price or in IVs will have a

TABLE 7.4 Effect of Futures Price on Theta for a European-Style Call on an Index Futures Contract

Strike price = 100.00
Implied volatility = 16
Interest rate = 0%

Futures Price	120 Days		110 Days	
	Option Price	Theta	Option Price	Theta
90.00	0.54	0.0075	0.47	0.0073
92.00	0.87	0.0097	0.77	0.0097
94.00	1.33	0.0118	1.21	0.0121
96.00	1.93	0.0135	1.80	0.0140
98.00	2.71	0.0147	2.56	0.0154
100.00	3.66	0.0153	3.50	0.0159
102.00	4.78	0.0151	4.63	0.0157
104.00	6.07	0.0142	5.92	0.0147
106.00	7.50	0.0128	7.37	0.0132
108.00	9.07	0.0111	8.96	0.0113
110.00	10.74	0.0093	10.65	0.0093

substantial impact on theta or will produce profits or losses that overwhelm the effects of theta.

VEGA

In the options business, we encounter a variety of Greek letters and other terms for the "delta of implied volatility." The most common of these is *vega*. By vega, we mean

$$\frac{\text{Change in option price}}{\text{Change in implied volatility}}$$

for an incremental change in implied volatility with all other variables held constant. The units of vega can be points per IV point, ticks per IV point, or dollars per IV point. European-style calls and puts always have positive vegas since these options are worth more if the underlying price is expected to be more volatile.

Table 7.5 expands Table 7.1 to include vegas as well as to show the effects of higher implied volatilities. As for gamma and theta, we find that the vegas are highest when the option is about ATM. We also find that, with the futures near 100.00, vegas don't change much as implied volatilities change.

TABLE 7.5 Effect of Futures Price on Vega for a European-Style Call on an Index Futures Contract

120 days to expiry
Strike price = 100.00
Interest rate = 0%

Futures Price	IV = 16		IV = 20	
	Option Price	Vega	Option Price	Vega
90.00	0.54	0.117	1.05	0.145
92.00	0.87	0.149	1.50	0.170
94.00	1.33	0.179	2.06	0.193
96.00	1.93	0.204	2.76	0.211
98.00	2.71	0.221	3.60	0.223
100.00	3.66	0.228	4.57	0.228
102.00	4.78	0.226	5.69	0.227
104.00	6.07	0.214	6.93	0.220
106.00	7.50	0.195	8.30	0.208
108.00	9.07	0.171	9.79	0.192
110.00	10.74	0.144	11.37	0.172

That is consistent with the comment in Chapter 6 that it is a good rule of thumb to think of the relationship between price and IV for ATM options as linear.

The sensible use of vegas involves dealing with many of the limitations discussed for delta, gamma, and theta. In addition, vega presents an additional problem for risk analysis of cumulative positions. Generally, deltas, gammas, and thetas are additive. For options on the same underlying instruments, the underlying price usually moves by the same amount for all options. Furthermore, a time change for one is usually a time change for all. Implied volatility changes are different, however. We cannot count on all options on a given underlying instrument to change by the same number of IV points. We can't even count on them to change in the same direction. There is a lot of theory about relative IV movement. The truth is that the IVs of different options can be related, but, within broad limits, each one can have a life of its own. Cumulating vegas can be very dangerous.

LOOSE ENDS

Table 7.6 presents an overview of the sensitivities of option model outputs (call price, delta, gamma, theta, vega) to various levels and changes in model

WHAT KIND OF GREEK LETTER IS VEGA?

If you thought Vega was either the name of an old car or a star in the constellation Lyra, but not a Greek letter, welcome to the "illiterate 80s." Remember, the 1980s was the decade in which the financial world adapted to such terms as "risk arbitrage" (an oxymoron in the civilized world) and "hedge fund" (a term applied to a fund that is likely to do almost anything except hedge).

In the 1970s, most option traders worried more about changes in underlying price and time than about IV changes, and they didn't feel much of a need for a "delta of implied volatility." There was, however, some use of the Greek letter omega in this role. At least it was a real Greek letter. As bank dealing rooms entered the business in the 1980s, the term *vega* became popular, and it stuck. Its use is not universal, however. Quite a few organizations use *kappa,* and I have observed sporadic use of other Greek letters and even of letters from other languages. In this book, we'll stick with *vega,* but with some chagrin.

inputs (underlying price, time, implied volatility). Output data is presented for all combinations of five underlying prices (92, 96, 100, 104, 108), three times to expiration (120, 60, 30 days) and two implied volatilities (16, 20). Most good, experienced traders have well-developed intuitions for these sensitivities. Table 7.6 might help you understand them better. Here are some observations to get you started:

1. As time passes, different kinds of options experience different patterns of price decay. For example, with IV = 16, the ATM option price decays from 3.66 to 2.59 to 1.83. This is clearly slower than linear time decay. In fact, a good rule of thumb is that, for ATM options on forwards or futures, the option's value is about proportional to the square root of time. Hence, whether the IV is 16 or 20, the 30-day price is about half the 120-day price.

   In contrast, options that are significantly OTM tend to lose their value more rapidly as time passes. With the futures at 92, and IV = 16, the option price decays from 0.87 to 0.29 to 0.06. Compared to the ATM case, this is not a lot of time decay if measured in *ticks* (OTM options have lower thetas), but this decay is faster than linear.

   For an extreme ITM example (futures at 108, IV = 16), the parity ingredient (8.00) has no time decay, but the volatility premium decays

TABLE 7.6   Greek Letter Sensitivities for a European-Style Call on an Index Futures
Contract

Strike price = 100.00
Interest rate = 0%

Futures Price	IV = 16					IV = 20				
	Call Price	Delta	Gamma	Theta	Vega	Call Price	Delta	Gamma	Theta	Vega
				120-Day Calls						
92	0.87	19.4	3.26	0.0097	0.149	1.50	25.2	3.02	0.0140	0.170
96	1.93	34.5	4.18	0.0135	0.204	2.76	38.3	3.46	0.0175	0.211
100	3.66	51.8	4.34	0.0153	0.228	4.57	52.3	3.47	0.0191	0.228
104	6.07	68.2	3.74	0.0142	0.214	6.93	65.5	3.09	0.0183	0.220
108	9.07	81.2	2.72	0.0111	0.171	9.79	76.7	2.47	0.0158	0.192
				60-Day Calls						
92	0.29	10.5	3.05	0.0090	0.071	0.61	16.2	3.28	0.0152	0.094
96	1.02	27.5	5.36	0.0173	0.131	1.56	32.2	4.60	0.0233	0.140
100	2.59	51.3	6.14	0.0216	0.162	3.23	51.6	4.91	0.0270	0.162
104	5.11	73.8	4.83	0.0184	0.139	5.68	70.0	4.12	0.0245	0.147
108	8.39	88.9	2.71	0.0111	0.087	8.71	83.9	2.79	0.0178	0.109
				30-Day Calls						
92	0.06	3.6	1.90	0.0055	0.023	0.17	7.7	2.74	0.0126	0.040
96	0.46	19.3	6.22	0.0201	0.077	0.79	24.7	5.73	0.0291	0.088
100	1.83	50.9	8.68	0.0308	0.114	2.29	51.1	6.95	0.0384	0.114
104	4.51	81.0	5.69	0.0216	0.083	4.86	76.2	5.19	0.0309	0.093
108	8.09	95.6	1.90	0.0076	0.032	8.25	91.5	2.52	0.0160	0.050

faster than linearly (1.07 to 0.39 to 0.09). Of course, the volatility premium would be expected to have the characteristics of an OTM put.

2. In all cases in Table 7.6, higher IVs mean higher prices. As described in Chapter 6, ATM option prices are almost directly proportional to IV (their vegas do not change much as IVs change). OTM and ITM options have lower vegas, but their prices can seem to explode at higher IVs. Higher IVs produce higher vegas for these options. (Notice for 30-day calls with futures at 92, vega jumps from 0.023 to 0.040 as IV increases from 16 to 20.)

3. As time to expiry is shortened or as IVs are reduced, OTM options get lower deltas and ITM options get higher deltas. Of course, with not much time until expiration and with low IVs, OTM options seem "hopeless" and an extra 0.01 in the futures price doesn't help much.

Under those same circumstances, ITM options lose most of their volatility premium and begin to act a lot like futures. Hence, their deltas approach 100.

In contrast, with more time and higher IV, these options feel more at-the-money, so the low deltas get higher and the high deltas get lower.

4. The highest gamma situation is where the futures are close to 100, time is very short, and IV is low. As we get *very* close to expiry, ATM gamma can be extremely high but very unstable. We usually regard high gamma situations as quite risky since gamma measures the instability of an important risk management tool (delta).

   The highest theta situation is the ATM, short time, *high* IV case. The $\sqrt{t}$ function gives a high theta to *short*-dated ATM options, while high IVs provide more premium to erode.

   Vega is highest for *long*-dated ATM options. IV doesn't matter much.

5. None of these "Greek" letters are as sensitive to futures price change when IV is high and there is a long time until expiry.

6. For ATM options, there are a lot of approximate $\sqrt{t}$ relationships. For both IVs, vega seems proportional to $\sqrt{t}$, while gamma and theta seem inversely proportional to $\sqrt{t}$. For example, with IV = 16, ATM gamma, theta, and vega change from 4.34, 0.0153, and 0.228 in the 120-day example to 8.68, 0.0308, and 0.114 in the 30-day example.

7. Similarly, ATM option price is not the only output that responds "linearly" to IV change. In each ATM case, theta seems directly proportional to IV and gamma seems inversely proportional to IV.

CHAPTER 8

Thinking about Option Risk

Any approach to analyzing or managing option risk should deal directly with the basic character of options: they are *multidimensional* and *nonlinear*. Traders, hedgers, and institutional investors often feel a need to have simple units of risk (How many gallons of risk do we have today? What's our "value at risk"?) Unfortunately, option risk is not that simple. We have a lot of *different* risks in the options business. We can't afford to ignore any of them, and we can't find a way to competently quantify them *in the aggregate*. We need to look at them one at a time. We need to ask whether *each* risk is appropriate.

For analytical purposes, it can be useful to think of option risks in two categories: *everyday risks* and *remote risks*.

EVERYDAY RISKS

Risk analysis must include some measures of our exposure to routine market events. We must be conscious of how much we might lose as a result of a "typical" daily move in the underlying price, or of a "typical" daily change in implied volatilities, just as we should be aware of our exposure to some short-term time decay.

Usually, the "Greek letters" give us good indications of our everyday risks. That is, our exposures to everyday events are usually sufficiently linear that our deltas, gammas, thetas, and vegas will do an adequate job of warning us (although we must keep in mind the Chapter 7 warning about cumulating vegas).

REMOTE RISK

In my trading career, I have had many option positions—some simple, some complex. There have been a lot of winners and a lot of losers. Some of the losses seemed big, and I felt like the market had beaten me up. The big losses came about in different ways, but *none of them ever happened because of an incremental change in anything.* Big losses happen because of big changes in one or more option variables. The underlying price might make a big move, or a lot of time might go by, or there might be a big change in implied volatilities. Often, we are affected by big changes in two or more variables.

Greek letters do not tell us much about exposure to discrete (i.e., not incremental) changes, nor do they tell us much about exposure to changes in more than one variable. As described in Chapter 7, a Greek letter looks only at an incremental, one-dimensional piece of option exposure. To look at remote risks, we need to specify remote events in option model terms, calculate our financial exposure to them, and decide if the exposure is appropriate.

Scenario 1 of Example 1 is a simple case of one-dimensional change (i.e., only £ moved). Our P&L for the position would be

$$(\$.0064 - \$.0564) \times 10,000,000 = -\$500,000$$

Notice that only 40% of this loss was "predicted" by our delta exposure of $20,000 per 0.0100 move. We lost much more than the delta would

---

EXAMPLE 1

European-Style Option on the British Pound Sterling

59 days to expiry
£ forward at $1.6000
IV = 9
i = 5.8%

Position: Short £10,000,000 calls ($1.65 strike)

Option price = $0.0064/£ ($64,000)
Delta   = 20 ($20,000 per 0.0100 move)
Gamma   = 4.82 deltas per .0100 move
Theta   = 0.000136 ($1,360 per day)
Vega   = 0.00186 ($18,600 per IV point)

Scenario 1: Immediate Sterling Price Move to $1.7000
        No Change in t, IV, or i

Option price = $0.0564
Delta   = 79
Gamma   = 4.50
Theta   = 0.000136
Vega   = 0.00196

indicate because the delta was unstable—it changed from 20 to 79 over the $0.1000 move in the underlying price.

Notice also that the gamma did not fully explain the change in delta. At £ = $1.6000, our gamma was 4.82 deltas per 0.0100 move in £. If this gamma were stable, we would have had a delta of about 68.2 with £ at $1.7000. In fact, the gamma was only 4.50 at $1.7000, but it was higher as the pound passed through the strike price.

Scenario 2: Immediate Sterling Price Jump to $1.6500
            IV Increase to 11
            No Change in t, i

   Option price = $0.0288
   Delta   = 50
   Gamma   = 5.40
   Theta   = 0.000240
   Vega   = 0.00262

Scenario 2 presents a case of two-dimensional change. Our P&L would be

$$(\$.0064 - \$.0288) \times 10,000,000 = -\$224,000$$

The delta of 20 "explains" $100,000 of this loss while our vega of 0.00186 explains $ 37,200. In reality, none of these "Greek letters" are very helpful here since their calculation assumes that other variables are fixed and since the action is neither one-dimensional nor incremental.

Scenario 3: Thirty Days Pass
            Sterling Price Increase to $1.6300
            IV Decrease to 7
            No Change in i

   Option price = $0.0053
   Delta   = 27
   Gamma   = 10.26
   Theta   = 0.000183
   Vega   = 0.00155

The Scenario 3 case of three-dimensional change can be pretty confusing in "Greek letter" terms. Our P&L calculation shows a profit:

$$(\$.0064 - \$.0053) \times 10,000,000 = +\$11,000$$

Our original theta of $1360 per day might indicate a $40,800 profit.

Our original vega of $18,600 per IV point might indicate a $37,200 profit.

Our original delta of $20,000 per 0.0100 move might indicate a $60,000 loss.

It really doesn't matter whether ($40,800 + $37,200 − $60,000) is close to $11,000. Clearly, in anticipation of such a case of discrete changes in three variables, we should forget the "Greeks" and test directly for the discrete changes that might concern us.

The Option
Dealing Business

Neutral Spread Dynamics

In the 1970s, there was great debate among stock option traders about the "right" way to trade options. The big question was: Should you trade options with a "view" on the direction of the underlying stock, or should you try to be *delta neutral* and to take advantage of "mispricing" in options while "minimizing" your exposure to stock price moves?

The advocates of directional trading argued that you could really make good money by "catching" a stock price move, and that *neutral spreaders* (sometimes scornfully referred to as "delta boys") were destined to struggle for small profits that may or may not result from obscure and uncertain edges. The neutral spreaders (later known as *volatility traders*) often spoke the cant of perfect market theory. They usually didn't believe that anyone could predict stock price direction with much consistency. If a trader made money on a directional bet, they assumed he was just lucky. In contrast, they believed that there was plenty of opportunity in trading mispriced options. They liked the idea of using the Black-Scholes model, and they reveled in their understanding of such "sophisticated" concepts as volatility, delta, and curvature. It was 1977 when I first heard a CBOE market maker say "We don't trade stocks; we trade *volatility*." Even then, it was probably an old expression. It was also a gross oversimplification of a complicated strategy.

In retrospect, both sides of the argument were ridiculous. Can you build a career out of using options to make directional bets? Of course you can—if you're good at direction-picking, if you manage the risk well, and if you're careful not to give away too much option edge. I've met a lot of traders who thought they were good at forecasting the direction of a financial instrument's price. Many of these traders were wrong—their skills were imagined, or there was a change in the market conditions that enabled them to succeed. There are, however, some traders who seem to have made money on direction-picking with reasonable consistency over a period of years. Most of these traders don't have magic formulas or extrasensory perception. They have skills, they develop techniques, and they use common sense. Their edges can be as real as the edge in roulette, although they can be harder to explain. If you have this kind of ability, there is no reason that it shouldn't be part of your option trading strategy. One warning though: It is not easy to get from a directional trading edge to a comprehensive strategy that will *make money with reasonable risk* over time.

In the options business, however, a directional view is not the only source of edge. The multidimensional, nonlinear nature of options, along with the power and uncertainty of our mathematical models, can provide plenty of opportunity for traders to search for mispriced options or option relationships. Usually, such option pricing edges do not offer risk-free profits. Typically, as in roulette, the perceived opportunity is statistical. A trader must manage the risk and live through some intermediate ups and downs. In the long run, *if* the edges are real, they will be reflected in the *average* profits rather than in the P&L of any particular position.

In the options business, most professional dealers focus on option pricing edge, rather than on the edge of a directional view. In the course of managing the risk of their positions, these dealers usually would like to minimize the impact on their P&Ls of the short-term price changes in the underlying instruments. Consequently, they frequently work with *delta neutral* positions—that is, positions for which the sum of all of the deltas of their options positions, their positions in the underlying instrument, and their positions in related derivatives is approximately zero.

Different neutral spreads can have different characteristics, providing a variety of profit opportunities and risk characteristics. Example 1 shows a simple FX options situation that is typical of many dealer positions. (Please note that, throughout this book, I have chosen to express Euro prices in "cents per Euro" in contrast to the conventional "dollars per Euro." This has been done to make various tabular presentations easier to read.)

EXAMPLE 1

European-Style Options on Euro (€) Futures

   Futures at 100.00 (i.e., 100.00 cents per Euro)
   83 day call (100.00 strike) at 2.23

   Implied volatility = 12.0
   Interest rate   = 10%
   Delta   = 50

Position: Long 1 futures at 100.00
           Short 2 calls at 2.23

TABLE 9.1 Call Theoretical Data

Strike price = 100.00
Interest = 10%

| Futures Price | 83 days | | | | 76 days | |
| | IV = 11 | | IV = 12 | | IV = 12 | |
	TV	Δ	TV	Δ	TV	Δ
98	1.20	35	1.37	36	1.28	36
99	1.58	42	1.77	43	1.67	43
100	2.05	50	2.23	50	2.14	50
101	2.58	57	2.76	57	2.67	57
102	3.19	64	3.36	63	3.28	64

Table 9.1 is a display of theoretical value (TV) and delta (Δ) sensitivities for the option in Example 1.

EXPOSURE TO FUTURES PRICE CHANGE

For this position, assuming no change in implied volatility (IV), Table 9.2 applies the data in Table 9.1 to demonstrate today's sensitivity to futures price movement. Initially, the position is delta neutral—that is, the net delta of the long futures contract and the two short calls is zero. Hence, we would expect that, for a very small futures price increase of 0.02, the price of each short call would increase by about 0.01 and we would not have a significant net profit or loss.

As the price of the futures contract rises, the delta of the futures contract remains 100, the option's delta increases, and the position becomes net short. These delta dynamics are gradual. For example, at 100.15, the

TABLE 9.2 Spread Dynamics: Futures Price Sensitivity

| | P&L for Various Futures Prices | | | | |
	98.00	99.00	100.00	101.00	102.00
Today's Exposure (IV = 12)					
L1 Futures at 100.00	−2.00	−1.00	—	+1.00	+2.00
S2 Calls at 2.23	+1.72	+0.92	—	−1.06	−2.26
	−0.28	−0.08	—	−0.06	−0.26
Net Delta	+28	+14	—	−14	−26

option's delta is about 51 and the position is about 2 deltas short. Even at that point, however, the position loses a little bit of money with every futures uptick, and every uptick makes the position even shorter. As shown in Table 9.2, when the futures price has moved to 101.00, the option's delta has increased to 57, making the position 14 deltas short. The 1.00 profit on the futures position is less than the 1.06 loss on the option position [2 × (2.76 – 2.23)]. The position has lost 0.06, and every uptick is more expensive than the previous uptick.

Clearly, there is no limit to this position's loss potential as the futures price continues to rise. For a very large price increase, each option's delta would become almost 100, and the position would act much like a short futures position.

If the futures price were to move down from 100.00, we would see a similar pattern of losses. The delta neutral position would become net long as the delta of the short calls declined. With the futures at 99.00, each call would have "lost" 7 deltas and the 0.46 profit per call would not quite negate the 1.00 loss on the futures. As the futures price decline continued, the position would continue to get longer, it would lose money on each tick, and each tick would be more expensive than the previous tick. As the call delta approached zero, the position would act more and more like an unhedged futures position. For all practical purposes, the loss potential would be unlimited. It would be constrained only by the inability of the futures to trade below 0.00.

Is this a ridiculous position? Is it foolish to put on a position in which we lose money if the underlying price increases, we lose money if the underlying price decreases, and our exposure is unlimited? If we operated in a one-dimensional world in which underlying price changes were the only determinants of our P&L, we would not consider such a position. In the options business, however, we are normally subject to two other major dimensions of exposure: *time* and *volatility.*

EXPOSURE TO THE PASSAGE OF TIME

Table 9.3 expands Table 9.2 to demonstrate the effects of 7 days of time decay, assuming no change in implied volatility (the impact of interest on cash flow is ignored).

In 7 days, with no change in futures price or implied volatility, each call's price would "decay" from 2.23 to 2.14. The position would have a profit of 0.18 and it would still be delta neutral. If, on the other hand, in 7 days, the futures price changed, the negative gamma dynamics would reduce—or even overwhelm—the 0.18 time-decay profit.

TABLE 9.3 Spread Dynamics: Sensitivity to Futures Price and Time

	P&L for Various Futures Prices				
	98.00	99.00	100.00	101.00	102.00
1. Today's Exposure (IV = 12)					
L1 Futures at 100.00	−2.00	−1.00	—	+1.00	+2.00
S2 Calls at 2.23	+1.72	+0.92	—	−1.06	−2.26
	−0.28	−0.08	—	−0.06	−0.26
Net delta	+28	+14	—	−14	−26
2. Exposure in 7 days (IV = 12)					
L1 Futures at 100.00	−2.00	−1.00	—	+1.00	+2.00
S2 Calls at 2.23	+1.90	+1.12	+0.18	−0.88	−2.10
	−0.10	+0.12	+0.18	+0.12	−0.10
Net delta	+28	+14	—	−14	−28

With this position, if we knew there would be no change in implied volatility, our P&L in 7 days could be thought of as a relatively simple tradeoff between time-decay profits and price movement losses. This two-dimensional analysis is an oversimplification, but it can stimulate some important observations about the options business. For example:

1. The dynamics of Table 9.3 are often described in terms of theta profits and gamma losses. I prefer to identify this as a *time decay/curvature tradeoff,* since we are looking at discrete variable changes instead of the incremental dynamics described by the Greek letters.
2. Generally, neutral option positions that make money on time decay tend to have negative curvature and vice versa. Sometimes, traders spend much effort trying to find a position with both positive gamma and positive theta. Forget it! Even if you think you've found one, you probably have a position in which both gamma and theta are unstable. You are also likely to have a disproportionately large exposure to some other variable, such as implied volatility.
3. Roughly speaking, we use the term *actual volatility* (see Chapter 6) to describe the combination of the passage of time and underlying price movement. In this example, we would expect to make money if future actual volatility were low, but to lose money in the event of high future actual volatility.

4. In Table 9.3, 7 days of time didn't have much effect on the delta. As described in Chapter 7, at-the-money gamma increases as time gets shorter, but that effect isn't very noticeable when we move only 7/83 of the time to expiry.

5. In practice, you might not keep this position in its current form for 7 days. Perhaps, in 2 or 3 days, the futures price would decline to 99.00. At that point, you would have made some money on time decay and lost some because of curvature. In total, you might be a little ahead or behind. For sure, you would have a long delta position and you might want to do something about that risk. Perhaps, you would adjust by selling 14% of your futures position. This adjustment wouldn't have an immediate effect on your P&L (except for transaction costs), but it would enable you to look forward with a delta neutral position with characteristics that are similar to those of your initial position.

With no implied volatility changes, the practice of frequently adjusting the delta of this position produces a P&L that is roughly the sum of a series of dynamics that resemble the dynamics of Table 9.3. In the real world, however, the elements of profit and loss would involve a variety of increments of both time decay and underlying price movement.

EXPOSURE TO IMPLIED VOLATILITY CHANGE

Table 9.4 expands Table 9.2 to demonstrate the effects of an instantaneous change in implied volatility. In Table 9.4, we see only the effect of a fortunate implied volatility decrease to 11. Of course, in the real world, implied volatility might increase and give us some very ugly P&L numbers. With no change in futures price, a quick IV decline from 12 to 11 produces a profit of 0.18 (2.23 − 2.05) per call with no significant effect on the delta. As in Table 9.3, this 0.36 profit could be reduced or overwhelmed by the effects of a futures price move. Of course, if some time had passed before the IV change, the time decay would have improved the profit picture.

VERTICAL SPREADS

The purpose of Table 9.3 and Table 9.4 is to provide some insight into the three-dimensional nonlinear dynamics of this neutral spread. This position is one of a broad category commonly known as *vertical spreads*. Within the options business, the definition of vertical spreads varies. In

TABLE 9.4   Spread Dynamics: Sensitivity to Futures Price and Implied Volatility

	P&L for Various Futures Prices				
	98.00	99.00	100.00	101.00	102.00
1. Today's Exposure (IV = 12)					
L1 Futures at 100.00	−2.00	−1.00	—	+1.00	+2.00
S2 Calls at 2.23	+1.72	+0.92	—	−1.06	−2.26
	−0.28	−0.08	—	−0.06	−0.26
Net delta	+28	+14	—	−14	−26
2. Today's Exposure (IV = 11)					
L1 Futures at 100.00	−2.00	−1.00	—	+1.00	+2.00
S Calls at 2.23	+2.06	+1.30	+0.36	−0.70	−1.92
	+0.06	+0.30	+0.36	+0.30	+0.08
Net delta	+30	+16	—	−14	−28

this book, two categories of neutral option spreads are considered to be vertical spreads:

1. Spreads that do not include any long options
2. Spreads that consist of two options with the same expiry date in which the holder has more short contracts than long contracts.

Category 1 includes the Example 1 position. An example that fits in Category 2 is described in the "Loose Ends" section that follows.

Among the common characteristics of all vertical spreads are:

■ Unlimited (or practically unlimited) risk
■ Limited potential profit
■ Negative gamma (i.e., a big underlying price move hurts)
■ Positive theta (i.e., time decay helps)
■ Negative vega (i.e., IV decrease helps, but IV increase hurts)

It is worth noting that vertical spreads are *"internally consistent"* with respect to volatility. That is, they usually do well if IV decreases and also if future actual volatility is very low. Usually, increases in IV and high future

HOW ABOUT APPROXIMATELY NEUTRAL?

In the options business, we frequently talk as if a position either is or is not *delta neutral*. One problem with this language is that, as described in Chapter 7, the concept of delta can be a limited and sloppy tool. A delta is not a clear and known characteristic of an option. It is model dependent and variable dependent. Hence, precise delta neutrality is more of an intellectual concept than a reality.

A second problem is that, often, a position that is "almost" delta neutral acts enough like a neutral position that it is useful to think of it as neutral.

A third problem is that, generally, the attractiveness of delta neutrality is that it can enable us to "minimize" our exposure to underlying price movement. However, since a delta describes only *incremental* exposure, we might find that a delta neutral position does not leave us indifferent regarding the direction of the next *significant* move in underlying price. In other words, we might reasonably feel long or short despite our incremental neutrality.

There is no universal answer to the question "What is neutral enough?" but it might help to prioritize your hopes and fears. If a few ticks of underlying price movement in a particular direction would make you particularly happy or sad, maybe you are not neutral enough.

---

actual volatility produce vertical spread losses. This kind of "internal volatility consistency" is not universal in the options business.

It is also worth noting that the vertical spread of Example 1 is quite symmetrical with respect to underlying price changes. That is, the P&L and Greek letter behavior looked about the same for futures price increases as for futures price decreases. In contrast, Example 2, described in "Loose Ends," involves an asymmetrical vertical spread.

BACKSPREADS

What if we did the opposite of the vertical spread of Example 1? That is, what if we were long the calls and short the futures? Clearly, we could then describe the dynamics simply by changing all of the signs in Table 9.2, Table 9.3, and Table 9.4. This kind of neutral spread is commonly called a *backspread*. It is what you wind up with when your counterparty does a vertical spread. Hence, a backspread's characteristics include:

- Limited risk
- Unlimited (or practically unlimited) potential profit
- Positive gamma
- Negative theta
- Positive vega

BACKSPREADS AND VERTICAL SPREADS AS BUILDING BLOCKS

It is useful to think of backspreads and vertical spreads as basic elements, or building blocks, of a neutral option position. Sometimes, a trader will, purposely or accidentally, assemble a backspread or a vertical spread that includes many different option contracts. Other times, he might have something simple, such as the spread in Example 1. Often, for analytical purposes, a trader might decompose a complex position into a collection of backspreads and vertical spreads. This kind of analysis can shed a lot of light on the position's multidimensional dynamics and their potential evolution over the position's life.

LOOSE ENDS

While all vertical spreads share the general characteristics of the spread in Example 1, there can be significant differences in their feel and behavior. Example 2 presents a different kind of vertical spread.

EXAMPLE 2

European-Style Options on Euro (€) Futures

Futures at 100.00
83-day call (100.00 strike) at 2.23; $\Delta = 50$, IV = 12
83-day call (104.00 strike) at 0.84; $\Delta = 25$, IV = 12
Interest rate = 10%

Position: Long 1 call (100.00 strike) at   2.23
          Short 2 calls (104.00 strike) at <u>0.84</u>
          Net debit   0.55

In Example 1, the data in Table 9.1 were used to make calculations to demonstrate spread characteristics in Table 9.2, Table 9.3, and Table 9.4. For Example 2, Table 9.5 contains data comparable to that of Table 9.1, and Table 9.6 demonstrates spread characteristics. Consider the following five observations:

1. In the discussion of Example 1, five characteristics were specified as common to all vertical spreads. All five are apparent in Table 9.6:
   a. *Risk is unlimited.* For a very large futures price increase, this 1 by 2 spread would begin to act like a short futures position.
   b. *Potential profit is limited.* A fantasy scenario for this position would be for it to remain untouched until the options expired with the futures at 104.00. Then the long call price would be 4.00, the short call price would be 0.00, and the profit would be 4.00 – 2.23 + 2 (.84) = 3.45.
   c. *Negative gamma.* The long ATM option's gamma is overwhelmed by the negative gamma of the two short OTM options. This might seem strange since, as discussed in Chapter 7, an option's gamma tends to be the highest when the underlying price is close to the strike price. Certainly, in Example 2, the initial gamma of one call

TABLE 9.5 Call Theoretical Data

Interest = 10%

| Futures Price | 83 days | | | | 76 days | |
| | IV = 11 | | IV = 12 | | IV = 12 | |
	TV	Δ	TV	Δ	TV	Δ
Strike Price = 100.00						
98.00	1.20	35	1.37	36	1.28	36
99.00	1.58	42	1.77	43	1.67	43
100.00	2.05	50	2.23	50	2.14	50
101.00	2.58	57	2.76	57	2.67	57
102.00	3.19	64	3.36	63	3.28	64
Strike Price = 104.00						
98.00	0.33	13	0.44	15	0.38	14
99.00	0.49	18	0.61	20	0.55	19
100.00	0.69	23	0.84	25	0.76	24
101.00	0.95	29	1.11	31	1.03	30
102.00	1.27	36	1.45	37	1.36	36

TABLE 9.6 Three-Dimensional Spread Dynamics

	P&L for Various Futures Prices				
	98.00	99.00	100.00	101.00	102.00
1. Today's Exposure (IV = 12)					
L1 Call (100.00 strike) at 2.23	−0.86	−0.46	—	+0.53	+1.13
S2 Calls (104.00 strike) at 0.84	+0.80	+0.46	—	−0.54	−1.22
	−0.06	—	—	−0.01	−0.09
Net delta	+6	+3	—	−5	−11
2. Exposure in 7 days (IV = 12)					
L1 Call (100.00 strike) at 2.23	−0.95	−0.56	−0.09	+0.44	+1.05
S2 Calls (104.00 strike) at 0.84	+0.92	+0.58	+0.16	−0.38	−1.04
	−0.03	+0.02	+0.07	+0.06	+0.01
Net delta	+8	+5	+2	−3	−8
3. Today's exposure (IV = 11)					
L1 Call (100.00 strike) at 2.23	−1.03	−0.65	−0.18	+0.35	+0.96
S2 Calls (104.00 strike) at 0.84	+1.02	+0.70	+0.30	−0.22	−0.86
	−0.01	+0.05	+0.12	+0.13	+0.10
Net delta	+9	+6	+4	−1	−8

with a 104.00 strike would be lower than the gamma of the ATM call. It is more than half as great, however, and this is a 1 by 2 spread. Chapter 7 also described the concept of *percent curvature*. That concept can be useful in thinking about the aggregate gamma of neutral spreads. When the long and the short have the same number of deltas (but not the same number of contracts) the spread's gamma will be dominated by the option whose delta changes fastest in percentage terms.

  d. *Positive theta.* 83 days of time decay (with the futures price unchanged) would make both options worthless and produce a 0.55 loss. In Table 9.6, however, we see that 7 days of time decay would produce a 0.07 profit. While the theta of an ATM option can be expected to be greater than that of an OTM option, the difference here is small and the 1:2 ratio produces an initial net positive theta. Of course, with a negative gamma for this spread, we would expect a positive theta.

  e. *Negative vega.* As was the case for gamma and theta, the 1:2 ratio enables the total vega of the OTM calls to dominate the spread vega, even though an individual option's vega tends to be greatest when the underlying price is close to the strike price.

2. The spread in Example 2 is *asymmetrical.* It is delta neutral, but this neutrality (or directional indifference) applies only to *small* futures price moves. A *big* immediate down move would produce a loss, but the loss would be limited to the 0.55 debit of the spread. At 98.00, with deltas of 36 and 15, the spread is 6 deltas long, but further futures price declines can't make the spread much longer because (unlike in Example 1) the long side of the spread has a positive gamma. Similarly, at a lower futures price, the other Greek letters "disappear."

  On the other hand, for an increase in futures price, the spread can really "blow up." Clearly, the delta can get very negative and the loss potential is unlimited. Also, as the futures move toward the 104.00 strike, we find the gamma, theta, and vega of the short side growing as the gamma, vega, and theta of the (now ITM) long side shrink.

3. Generally, the net P&L and delta numbers in Table 9.6 seem quite small compared to the comparable numbers in Example 1. In fact, in some instances, minor rounding errors become significant (e.g., today's exposure at 99.00 is not really 0.00. With more precision in Table 9.5, it would be between −0.01 and −0.02).

  For the most part, the spread in Example 2 just wouldn't have much short term action compared to the spread in Example 1. That is partly because the gamma, theta, and vega of the short OTM options in Example 2 are somewhat smaller than the comparable Greeks for the short ATM options of Example 1. Even more important in Example 2 is the fact that most of the vertical spread characteristics of the short OTM calls are negated by the backspread characteristics of the long call.

4. In Chapter 7, there was much discussion about ways in which a delta is a "soft" number, since it is model dependent, variable dependent, one dimensional and incremental. Table 9.6 illustrated some of that "softness." For example, with this spread:

    a. We would be indifferent to the direction of small moves, but not of big moves.

    b. With no change in futures price or implied volatility, the position becomes 2 deltas long in 7 days.

    c. With no change in futures price or time, a lower IV makes the net delta become positive (as the OTM delta declines and the ATM delta stays about the same).

5. These observations might be easier to understand if the position is analytically "decomposed" into a vertical spread (long ½ futures, short 2 OTM calls) and a backspread (short ½ futures, long 1 ATM call). In this example, the two building blocks "add up" to a small asymmetrical vertical spread. Of course, in a different example, a backspread and a vertical spread might "add up" to a backspread or to a spread that didn't fit in either category.

CHAPTER 10

Comparative Strategy Analysis

Chapter 9 presented an introductory view of the dynamics of vertical spreads and backspreads. If you carefully examine the Chapter 9 data, you find a lot of tradeoffs. Every backspread and every vertical spread has both attractive and unattractive features. In general, each good or bad aspect of a spread is offset by a countervailing aspect that necessarily comes with it. It is not unusual for a trader's mind to think about these tradeoffs in distorted ways.

Often, a trader or a manager has a personal preference for a particular kind of spread. Sometimes, one spread feature seems so important that it overwhelms a businessman's sense of balance. For example, the limited risk feature of a backspread can look so good to a manager that he might not want his traders to have any vertical spreads. Other times, a trader's experiences of winning and losing in certain kinds of positions might lead to inappropriate generalizations about "what works." For example, a trader whose experience has been mostly in quiet markets might think vertical spreads are "the answer."

What is the right answer? Is a vertical spread a good idea or a bad idea? How about a backspread?

If you're looking for a simple, universal answer, it would be a good idea to reread the last part of Chapter 3, the discussion of *price orientation* and *trade orientation*. You might then conclude that in a profit center options trading business it is a weakness to have a trade orientation in favor of backspreads or vertical spreads or any other category of spreads. You should be prepared to do either side of the futures/calls spread, but only if the price is right.

As Chapter 3 also explained, for any position we should consider both profitability and risk, and we should require that both be acceptable. In Chapter 10, however, we will focus first on *profitability*. We will ask what kinds of edge might justify a simple neutral spread, what business or market conditions (or skills) might be necessary for us to sensibly pursue each kind of edge, and what trader behavior would be necessary.

EXAMPLE 1

European-Style Options on Euro (€) Futures

> Futures at 100.00 (i.e., 100.00 cents per Euro)
> 83 day call (100.00 strike) at 2.23

> Implied volatility = 12.0
> Interest rate = 10%
> Delta = 50

Position: Long 1 futures at 100.00
Short 2 calls at 2.23

Example 1 again shows the futures/calls vertical spread that was the subject of much of Chapter 9.

If you were a manager and one of your traders had this position, what kind of explanation might be acceptable to you? Surely, you would require that the position fit in some defined strategy. You would also require an expectation of profitability as well as reasonable risk. In the options business, strategy definition can be difficult, and a strategy can have many variations. However, of the sensible neutral strategies that I have observed, most can be described in terms of three broad categories.

STRATEGY 1: MARKET MAKING

In its simplest form, *market making* is a process of trying to make the bid/offer spread. A market maker would make a two-sided market (bid/offer) and would be prepared to deal on either price. For the option in Example 1, the market might have been 2.18/2.23. If the market maker had no substantial position, he would be theoretically indifferent between buying and selling. He would simply want to deal on his price. Of course, if he sold some calls at 2.23, it would be fortunate if the next customer would sell to him at 2.18.

Making the 0.05 spread with this simple approach is neither easy nor risk free. It requires skill, good information, and perhaps a sales program. Most important, it requires extremely rapid turnover since this 2.18/2.23 market is not likely to be realistic for long. If, in a few minutes or hours, the underlying futures price moved to 100.50 or 99.50, the price of this 50 delta option would probably change by enough to make the 0.05 spread insignificant.

A typical options market maker would be concerned about the effects of underlying price movement on his short term P&L ups and downs (i.e., risk, as described in Chapter 3). This concern would probably lead him to trade from a delta neutral position. In the current example, if a customer took his offer of 2.23, he might buy enough futures to be neutral and find himself in the vertical spread of Example 1. If, instead, the customer had hit his 2.18 bid, the market maker would probably sell enough futures to be neutral, thereby winding up with a backspread. In either case, he wouldn't be very concerned about a 0.50 change in the futures price. The gamma for this position is low enough that the P&L effect of this change would be small compared to the bid/offer spread.

It is a common practice for market makers to quote options in "ticks" or "cents per Euro" as described here. However, it is also common to *think about* quotes (and sometimes to *make* quotes) in terms of implied volatility (IV). In the current example, the option's IV is about 12.0 with a price of 2.23 and about 11.7 with a price of 2.18. Hence, the market maker's quote can be thought of as 11.7/12.0 in IV terms.

The Basic Steps

This oversimplified form of market making can be summarized as follows:

1. *Sell the call on the offer (or buy on the bid).* Presumably, the market maker doesn't care whether he sells or buys.
2. *Buy (or sell) enough futures to become delta neutral.* Deciding how many to buy is easy with the 50 delta of this option. In another example, we would have to deal with the delta uncertainties discussed in Chapter 7.
3. *Continue to quote a two-sided market of IV 11.7/12.0.* For now, that means prices of 2.18 and 2.23 with the underlying futures at 100.00. But, for example, if the futures price rose to 100.20, the option quote would move with the 50 delta (at 100.20, the delta would have increased insignificantly to slightly over 51). Then, the price quote would be 2.28/2.33.
4. *Close out the futures position when a customer hits the bid (or takes the offer) to close out the option.* If the futures are then at 100.00, the profit is the 0.05 bid/offer spread. If the futures are at 100.20, the calls are closed out at a 0.05 loss (2.23 – 2.28), but there is a 0.20 profit on half as many futures. Thus, for modest futures moves, the delta neutrality protects the position.

Noise

In this example, it seems that the market maker will make the bid/offer spread (0.05) if someone takes his offer and someone hits his bid. It's not quite that simple, however. While he is waiting for his position to be closed out, some option dynamics could take place, affecting his P&L. These dynamics, which might have nothing to do with buying on the bid and selling on the offer, are often called *noise*. They are best described in terms of the three principal option variables:

1. The underlying price might make a big move. Then, the curvature effect (shown in Chapter 9, Table 9.2) might overwhelm the 0.05 bid/offer spread.

    In the current example, this would be *bad* (or unlucky) noise because the position is a vertical spread. If the first customer had hit the bid, the position would be a backspread and this would be *good* (or lucky) noise.

2. Some days or weeks might pass before the position is closed.

    In this vertical spread, this noise, by itself, would be *good*. It is likely, however, that keeping the position for a while would expose it to more *bad* price movement noise.

    As discussed in Chapter 9, we can combine the passage of time and the underlying price movement into a single concept: *actual volatility*. In this vertical spread example, high *future actual volatility* would be likely to produce *bad* noise, but, of course, future actual volatility might be low.

3. Implied volatility might change. In this vertical spread, higher IV would mean *bad* noise; lower IV would be *good*.

One of the frustrations of the options business is that there always seems to be noise. Rarely, do we get to make a "pure bet." In fact, our exposure to noise often changes over the life of a position, and we frequently find ourselves struggling to keep our "bets" reasonably "pure."

In this example, it is possible that a quick change in underlying price or in IV could produce enough noise to overwhelm the P&L of the market making "bet." Most likely, however, this wouldn't happen in the first day or two. If the position is turned over in that time, there is a good chance that the 0.05 bid/offer spread will dominate the P&L. In a week or so, I'd expect one of the noise dynamics (I don't know which one) to be material. Then, it's not a business; it's mostly luck.

Required Conditions

For market making to be a sensible business, it *requires:*

1. *Good order flow.* Orders must come frequently and there must be a reasonable balance between buys and sells. This permits the rapid turnover that is necessary to build good profits and to minimize the risk that the P&L will be dominated by the noise.

    Orders also must be reasonably small. If a market maker builds up too much inventory, he can't continue to make the 11.7/12.0 IV market. Clearly, this requirement of small size is related to the requirement for order balance.
2. *A good market in the underlying instrument.* The market maker must be able to get in and out of the underlying instrument quickly and with very low transaction costs (including bid/offer spread). In some markets, market makers are frequently able to "do the delta" with the same customer who trades the option.
3. *Good market information* regarding the bids and offers for the option, for related options, and for the underlying instrument.

In addition, it would be *helpful* if there was enough external market liquidity for the market maker to occasionally reduce his inventory without losing a lot of money.

What Might Happen?

In a good market-making business, turnover is usually rapid and the market maker usually makes a significant fraction of his bid/offer spread. Sometimes, the customer "knows something" and the market maker is lucky to break even. Sometimes, order flow is very one-sided and the market maker gets caught with the wrong inventory as IVs move.

Occasionally, through laziness, luck, or lack of discipline, a market maker does not turn over his position very rapidly. If he holds the position in Example 1 for a week or so, he might be lucky. The futures might not move much, IV might decline to 11.0 or even 10.0, and he might make a lot of money on the noise. His profits might make him proud of this position, but he should be ashamed. Remember, he made a two-sided market. He became short options by accident, didn't execute a market making strategy, and made money on the noise.

Often, of course, the noise isn't so favorable.

STRATEGY 2: BETTING ON IMPLIED VOLATILITY CHANGES

In the simple market-making example of Strategy 1, the market maker found himself in the vertical spread of Example 1 by accident. He got it as the result of making a two-sided market. Alternatively, a trader might put on the same position on purpose. He might do it because of an opinion that the option's implied volatility is likely to come down. That is, he might have an *implied volatility forecast* that is less than 12.0.

If the trader makes an IV forecast of 10.0, and if the IV in fact goes to 10.0, will he make money? How much?

Perhaps the IV would go to 10.0 immediately with no change in underlying price. Then, the new option price would be 1.86, and the trader could unwind the position at a profit of 0.37 cents per Euro.

Most likely the life of the position would be more complicated.

The Basic Steps

Sensible implementation of this kind of strategy involves:

1. *Sell the call.* This time the call does not necessarily have to be sold on the offer. It is necessary to receive a good price based on the implied volatility forecast, not compared to the bid.
2. *Buy enough futures to become delta neutral.* The purpose of being neutral is the same as in Strategy 1. It is to reduce the P&L's exposure to the movement in the underlying price. In Strategy 1, a single act of becoming neutral might "protect" the P&L for the life of the position because we expect rapid turnover. In Strategy 2, it is probably unreasonable to expect the IV to change from 12.0 to 10.0 in a day or two. More likely, the position will live for a week—or even a month. During that time the position's delta is likely to change, probably because of underlying price movement (as described in Chapter 9), but maybe because of time or IV change.
3. *Adjust delta as necessary.* In this simple example, we'll assume the adjustment is a futures trade. There are more complex alternatives.
4. *Take the position off if the IV changes as expected or if forecast changes make the edge insignificant or negative.* A *price orientation* requires a position in this strategy to have a *current implied volatility* that is significantly (and favorably) different from the *implied volatility forecast*. When that edge disappears, there is no justification for continuing to take risk.

Noise

As in Strategy 1, this vertical spread is exposed to the noise of time decay profits and curvature losses. Because of its longer life expectancy, a Strategy 2 position is likely to experience a larger P&L effect from the imbalances between "lucky" and "unlucky" noise. However, Strategy 2 can tolerate more noise imbalance because it is "playing for" more profit. In this example, the market maker in Strategy 1 is "playing for" only 0.05 while the IV bet is initially for 0.37.

Also, as in Strategy 1, this vertical spread's P&L is affected by changes in implied volatility. In Strategy 2, however, this is not noise. It is the bet.

Required Conditions

Strategy 2 requires:

1. *A good implied volatility forecast.* It is not the case that every professional options trader is good at guessing future implied volatility, just as it is not true that every bond trader is good at guessing future interest rates. In Strategy 2, the only source of edge is the quality of the forecast. If you are a good IV forecaster, you might be good at this strategy. If you are not a good IV forecaster, try a different strategy.
2. *A liquid market in both the options and the underlying instrument.* If the position is not easy and cheap to enter, adjust, and exit, the edge will slip away.
3. *Reasonable turnover.* For a week or two, it is unlikely that the noise imbalance will be material compared to the edge. As time goes by, however, the noise imbalance is likely to become substantial, while the option's vega decreases (see Chapters 6 and 7). As a rule-of-thumb, I suggest turning over IV bets in the first one-third of their lives.

What Might Happen?

One possible scenario is that the IV will quickly change to 10.0, there won't be much noise, the trader will take off the position, and the profit will be approximately equal to the 0.37 cents per Euro edge. This is not very likely. Even if the trader is "right" on his forecast, the position will probably live for a while, there will probably be some noise imbalance, and the vega will change so that the trader is no longer "playing for" 0.37 when the position comes off.

A second possibility is that the IV might start to increase. After a while, the trader might decide that his IV forecast is "wrong." He would probably "stop the bleeding" and take the position off at a loss.

A third possibility is that the trader might keep the position for a long time. If he keeps it until 7 days before expiration, the IV then decreases to 10.0, and he takes it off, he might think he was "right." Consider, however:

- In the 76-day life of the position, the noise imbalance is likely to be substantial.
- If the futures stay reasonably close to the strike price, the daily increments of noise are likely to increase as gamma and theta increase (see Chapter 7).
- With 7 days to go, the trader is no longer "playing for" much money because vega is so low. With 7 days left, even with the futures at 100.00, the option doesn't have much IV sensitivity. An IV move from 12.0 to 10.0 would change the option's price from 0.66 to 0.55. Then, he's "playing for" 0.11 instead of 0.37, and he's had to live through a lot of noise to get it.
- As time goes by, the futures might move away from the strike price. If that happens, the daily increments of noise would probably decrease, but the IV bet would become insignificant since short-dated options have very little vega unless they are close to the strike.

In other words, the trader *wasn't* "right." He wound up with a position whose P&L had very little to do with the bet (i.e., IV change), and was subject to a lot of noise.

A fourth possibility is that the trader might put on the position because of a view on IV change, and then just "manage the delta" until expiration. Of course, this is very amateurish. The trader has managed the position in a way that *none* of the P&L has anything to do with what he was betting on. It's all noise. This is a blunder that is very common among option traders. Most of us have done it more than once. When *you* do it, you should feel totally humiliated. If you do it with your employer's money, you should feel like a criminal when you cash your paycheck. The good news is that, unless your boss is unusually competent, he won't figure it out. If *you* are a boss, see Chapter 13.

STRATEGY 3: BETTING ON ACTUAL VOLATILITY

Even if a trader had no *implied volatility forecast,* the vertical spread in Example 1 might make sense if he thought the option price was too high in light of the likely *future actual volatility* of the underlying price. That is, the position could be justified by an *actual volatility forecast* that is substantially lower than the *current implied volatility.*

Perhaps, the trader's forecast for the next 83 days is for an actual volatility of 9.0. Then, the option, with an IV of 12.0, would seem to be inefficiently priced. If we knew that the future actual volatility would be only 9.0, we would know that the option would be (statistically) worth about 1.67.

Looking back at Chapter 9, Table 9.3, it should be clear that a vertical spread is likely to do very well if the underlying price stays quiet.

The Basic Steps

1. *Make an actual volatility forecast.* As was discussed in Chapter 6, such a forecast is difficult to make, frustrating to live with, and subject to large expected errors. There is no "correct" way to make such a forecast, but it can be useful to try.
2. *Establish criteria for adequacy of the edge.* There is a lot of uncertainty in betting on actual volatility. What kind of forecasting error can we expect? What about noise?

   You probably wouldn't want a 12.0 IV vertical spread if your forecast was 11.5. How about 12.0 versus 9.0? Does the time to expiration matter?

   In this example, we'll assume that the position has enough edge, but this assumption certainly is debatable.
3. *Sell the call if its price meets your criteria.* This time the call price should look good compared to its value with the trader's actual volatility forecast of 9.0. It doesn't have to look good compared to the bid or in relation to an implied volatility forecast.
4. *Buy enough futures to become delta neutral.*
5. *Adjust delta as necessary.* Since there is no reason to think the edge will soon disappear, the trader should expect to live through many periods of time decay profit, and quite a few experiences of curvature losses. The delta adjustments usually come after curvature losses, "locking them in," but providing a neutral position for the future.
6. *Take the position off if the edge disappears.* The edge might disappear because the IV comes down to the 9.0 forecast for actual volatility. If this happens, there is no reason to keep the position (and its risk) for no edge. Of course, if the trader has a reason to lower the actual volatility forecast, maybe it isn't yet time to get out.

   Usually, when the IV comes down to the forecast, the position has made good money. It is possible, however, that, by the time the IV comes down, the curvature losses would be so large and the time decay profits so small, that the vega profits wouldn't put the position into the black. Nevertheless, with or without a profit, if the edge is gone, it's time to get out.

Another way that the edge might disappear would be through an increase in the trader's actual volatility forecast. For this to happen, there would probably have been some high recent actual volatility. This is not a happy scenario.

Noise

Strategy 1 was subject to noise, both from the level of actual volatility and from changes in implied volatility. In Strategy 2, the "bet" was a change in implied volatility, but the level of actual volatility was still noise. In Strategy 3, the level of actual volatility is the "bet." Noise can come from changes in IV or from other sources that become material because of the position's long life expectancy.

1. *Implied volatility might change.* The basic steps of Strategy 3 do not include forecasting changes in IV. Nevertheless, over a position's life there can be many significant IV changes. An increase (or decrease) in IV is real noise that produces a real loss (or profit). However, this noise is different from other kinds of noise discussed in this chapter in that it can be *temporary.* Because there is usually no great urgency to close out a Strategy 3 position, the trader might wait until the option's vega becomes small. Then the noise of IV wandering would be insignificant.

   There are two important implications of the *temporary* nature of this noise:

   a. When a trader is fortunate enough to have some very favorable temporary noise, he should take the position off, thereby making the noise permanent. If he keeps the position, this lucky profit will become irrelevant as the dynamics of time decay and curvature take over.

   b. A trader using Strategy 3 must plan for unfavorable noise. He must avoid exposure to situations in which he is "forced out" of positions because of normal IV wandering. This means his boss must understand and approve the dynamics of the strategy. It also means he must be careful to keep his position size from getting too big.

2. *The trader might have good or bad adjustment luck.* There seems to be a lot of short term luck in adjusting deltas. For example, in a vertical spread, it sometimes seems that to adjust is to buy "tops" and sell "bottoms." If this happens enough, a position might lose money even though, over its life, actual volatility is quite low.

   It is also possible to have good adjustment luck (traders often call it skill). For example, the underlying instrument might be quite volatile, but if it is "choppy" and seldom moves far enough to require an adjustment, the trader's P&L looks no different than if the underlying instrument had been quiet.

3. *The effective size of the position might change.* If the position's delta is simply adjusted with futures trades, it is likely that its gamma and theta will be unstable over the position's life. If, for example, 7 days before expiration, the underlying price is close to the strike price, the gamma and theta would be very large. Then, the position's P&L would depend heavily on the actual volatility and adjustment luck over its last week.

In contrast, if, earlier in the position's life, the underlying price were to move far away from the strike price, the P&L would be more heavily dependent on the actual volatility and adjustment luck during the days before the gamma and theta shrank.

Required Conditions

Strategy 3 requires:

1. *A good actual volatility forecast.* It might not be necessary to forecast a specific number (e.g., 9.0). A range of expectations might be good enough. It is important to remember, however, that, in this strategy, there is an edge only if the current implied volatility is out of line with reasonable expectations for future actual volatility.
2. *A procedure for sensitivity testing of the edge.* The edge in an option position might look great given our mathematical model and the variable inputs that we "use." But, how sensitive is the edge to the assumptions of the model? How sensitive to the values of the model variables (especially volatility)?

    There is no universal approach for dealing with these kinds of uncertainty, but it can help to address them in a systematic way.
3. *A reasonable attempt at size management.* It is not possible to keep gammas and thetas at the same level throughout the life of the position, but it is necessary to be vigilant to keep them from getting out of hand.

What Might Happen?

One possibility is that, in one day, the IV might drop to 9.0. Then, with no remaining edge in the position, it would probably be closed out at a large profit.

This kind of instant gratification happens rarely for Strategy 3 traders, but it does happen. It is the kind of event that can leave a trader feeling pretty proud of himself. As he counts his profits, it might not occur to him that he made all that money on luck. He might have forgotten that he put on the position on the basis of a 9.0 actual volatility forecast, and that no one will know how accurate that forecast was for another 82 days. It can be hard to face up to the fact that the entire profit came from the noise of the IV decline. In fact, by now, the trader might really think he intended to use Strategy 2, and his forecast was for future implied volatility.

A second possibility is that the IV might stay at 12.0 until the option expires. In that case, the position would experience a long series of profits and losses. For every day without much movement in the underlying price, there would be a small time decay profit. Whenever the underlying price made a big enough move to significantly change the delta, there would be a loss that would be "locked in" by the *risk management* need to adjust the delta. The ultimate P&L would be the net of all of these time decay profits and price movement losses.

Will the trader come out ahead or behind? Of course, it depends:

- What actual volatility will the underlying price experience over the life of the position? If it is very quiet, there will be a lot of time decay profits and not many price movement losses. Then, he'll probably make money. If future actual volatility is very high, the price movement losses will overwhelm the time decay profits.
- What kind of adjustment luck will the trader have? Exceptionally good or bad adjustment luck can cause the P&L to be much different than you might guess by comparing the initial IV to the actual volatility over the life of the position.
- Will size changes (i.e., changes in gamma and theta) distort the P&L picture?
- How much money will the trader "spend" on bid/ask spreads and other transaction costs?

If the trader doesn't spend much on transaction costs, if the noise of adjustment luck and size changes doesn't come to much, and if the future actual volatility matches the 9.0 forecast, the position's profit should be close to the initial edge of 0.56 cents per Euro (2.23–1.67). If the future actual volatility matches the 12.0 original IV (with little net noise), the position should come close to breaking even. Of course, future actual volatility might be 20.0, in which case the P&L will probably be very ugly. It is also possible for the future actual volatility to be 4.0. Then, the trader would be likely to make an enormous amount of money. He probably doesn't "deserve" it, though. His 9.0 forecast wasn't very accurate, but, luckily, the market, with its 12 IV, put him into a winning trade.

A third possibility is that there could be significant changes in implied volatility, but no response by the trader. That is, he might continue to "manage the delta" until the position expired or became insignificant. In that case, there might be considerable P&L swings as the IV changed, but the ultimate result wouldn't be much different than if the IV never changed. IV changes might induce the trader to adjust his delta differently, producing better or worse adjustment luck, but, on average, the wandering IV would not help or hurt much.

A fourth (and most likely) possibility is an odd mixture of dynamics. There would probably be a period of time decay profits and price movement losses that would depend on actual volatility and adjustment luck. Their net could be masked by the P&L effects of short-term IV wanderings. Eventually, either the position would become insignificant as price movement diminished the Greek letters, or the position would be taken off because of changes in the IV and/or the forecast.

STRATEGY OVERVIEW

These three broad categories of strategies, while oversimplified here, provide a useful framework for planning and managing a trading program. The strategies are very different, but all are viable. None are particularly good or bad. Each strategy can be part of a sensible option trading business if, and only if, the required conditions are in place and the basic steps are executed.

It is worth noting that the three strategies look the same on your position sheets. If you have the vertical spread in Example 1, your risk manager probably can't tell which strategy you are working on. Maybe, your boss can't tell. Too often a trader doesn't know, either—especially with old positions.

For responsible management of an options trading business, it is important to continually justify positions. We should ask: What excuse do we have for carrying the position? Are the requirements of the strategy being satisfied? In practice, of course, our behavior and our positions are seldom as clean and simple as described here, and we frequently operate in the gray area between strategy categories. Still, the questions need to be asked, even if we'd rather just wish and hope for a while.

A common mistake of human weakness is to semiconsciously slip from one strategy to another. That is, a market-making position becomes an IV bet which eventually becomes a bet on actual volatility. Occasionally, legitimate forecasts can justify such behavior, but more often this happens because of lack of discipline. Sometimes, colorful excuses are passed off as justifications.

As you read this chapter, it should become obvious why so much of Chapter 6 was focused on distinctions among different kinds of volatility. In Figure 10.1, we repeat Figure 6.1 of Chapter 6. Our discussion of the three

FIGURE 10.1　Volatility category matrix.

	Historical	Future	Forecast	Current
Actual				
Implied				

strategies called attention to several different squares in this volatility category matrix. In Strategy 1, we looked only at *current implied volatility.* There was no volatility forecast of any kind. It was assumed that the position would be turned over before IV changed and before future actual volatility mattered.

Strategy 2 required an *implied volatility forecast.* The position's edge came from the difference between that forecast and the *current implied volatility.* We hoped to make money on the difference between the *future implied volatility* and the current IV. We expected some noise related to the *future actual volatility.* Since we did not make an *actual volatility forecast,* we knew we needed to get out of the position in a reasonable period of time.

Strategy 3 did not require an implied volatility forecast, because we could out-wait the temporary nature of the IV noise. We did, however, need an *actual volatility forecast* and the edge came from the difference between that forecast and the *current implied volatility.* We hoped to make money on the difference between the *current implied volatility* and the *future actual volatility.*

Notice that, in this chapter, there has been no reference to either kind of historical volatility. In the context of these strategies, the *historical actual* and *historical implied* volatilities are just hints. They might help us forecast actual or implied volatility, and they might help us decide how much edge is adequate for a position.

One final note: Example 1 displayed a vertical spread and that spread was used to explain all three strategies. The use of this example does not imply a preference for vertical spreads, nor does it imply that these strategies are best executed through the use of vertical spreads. A backspread example would have worked just as well.

A FIREFIGHTER'S MENTALITY

When I left the corporate life to become an independent CBOE market maker in 1977, I considered myself to be a real adventurer. I wasn't going to spend my career as a cog in a big wheel, and I wasn't going to depend on other people for my success. I was going to be a modern-day Attila the Hun. I was heading for the trading floor to make my own opportunities.

It didn't take long for me to figure out that I had the wrong idea. On the trading floor, I couldn't make anything happen. My chance to prosper was completely dependent on finding inefficiencies in option prices, and I had nothing to do with any of the prices becoming inefficient. Instead of a man of action, I had to become a *man of reaction*. I had to hustle and be alert for any apparent edges that might appear, and then I had to execute positions, manage the risk, and hope the apparent edges were real.

Rather than modeling myself after Attila, I began to try to think more like a firefighter. A firefighter must fight fires when the fires decide to appear. If he's on duty, he can't just choose to fight them when he's in the mood, and, presumably, he can't start one when he feels like some action.

Too many traders and organizations tend to overtrade when opportunities are slim or to shy away when they should be active. The strategies described in this chapter all require market inefficiencies. It is important to remember that the market doesn't "owe you" inefficiencies in any particular strategy. Even if it gives you some available edges, they don't have to suit your personal *trade orientation*. Likewise, if this is a business, when the "fire" starts, you have to be professional enough to participate, even if, at the time, you don't have an appetite for that kind of action.

LOOSE ENDS

The three categories of strategies discussed in this chapter were described in simplistic ways. Many variations are common.

For example, in Strategy 1, it is unusual for a market maker to quickly buy back exactly the same option that he sold. What happens if he instead buys an option with a slightly different strike price and/or expiration date?

FISCHER BLACK'S VOLATILITY ESTIMATES

For almost all of the first 10 years of listed option trading, Fischer Black conducted a business of calculating and selling a variety of information related to the stock options business. Most notable and popular were his volatility "estimates" which he published monthly for each stock for which options were listed in the United States.

In some of his published papers, Dr. Black indicated that these "estimates" were attempts to forecast the *actual volatility* of stocks. I relied on them for that purpose and, while my expectations for forecasting accuracy were low, I was quite satisfied with the results. Other traders were less satisfied, largely because they were in the business of market making or of betting on changes in *implied volatility* (IV). For years, I had the impression that Dr. Black struggled with the difficulty of providing a single "estimate" that would be applicable for any strategy. At the time, his dilemma would have been very difficult for anyone with a strong academic bias in favor of efficient markets. If markets were efficient, we wouldn't need a *volatility category matrix*. For each stock, there would be a single "correct" volatility number for any given expiration period.

Eventually, Dr. Black seemed to make some methodology concessions to pacify his broad customer base. He indicated that he increased the weighting that he gave to *current implied volatility* in calculating his estimates, but still, uncertainty and doubts persisted. It seemed that the most common question I was asked on the CBOE floor in the early 1980s was "What volatility are you using now in IBM?" I never knew what to say because I never knew what business the other person was in. Maybe he didn't know either. Maybe he just wanted me to give him any number so that he could use it for any purpose and he wouldn't be at fault if he lost money.

Finally, in 1984, Dr. Black left MIT to work for Goldman Sachs and he dropped the volatility estimating service. I was sorry to see it disappear, but I'm sure he was glad to be rid of the headaches. Before he left, I called him to ask whether he would use his estimates or the IVs in calculating deltas. He said he'd probably use the IVs. I said I thought he was underrating his estimates.

Most likely, he winds up in an option/option spread that has exposures (in both Greek letters and remote events) that are trivial compared to the bid/offer spread. This is because, with 83 days until expiration, options with slightly different terms can have very similar dynamics.

It is possible, of course, that as expiration approaches the underlying price will be close to one of the strike prices and the option/option spread will have significant risk. In most cases, *diversification* is a good solution to this risk management problem.

Another variation of Strategy 1 involves the nature of the edge. In this chapter, it has been assumed that Strategy 1 makes sense only if the bid/offer spread is wide enough to provide enough edge to justify the risk. In fact, in many competitive markets, bid/offer spreads are so narrow that market makers don't see them as offering edge. Often, traders justify dealing in such markets by pointing to the benefits of order flow information. That is, by making competitive markets they might expect to make money, not on the bid/offer spread, but on the *next* trade. That trade might, for example, be a Strategy 2 trade in which the order flow information was useful in making an implied volatility forecast.

A variation of Strategy 2 is the *relative implied volatility* bet. The "Loose Ends" section of Chapter 9 demonstrated the characteristics of a call/call vertical spread. In that example, both options began with a 12 IV. Now, in Example 2 below, we have a similar spread, except that the options have different IVs.

Maybe a trader would put on this position to bet that the IVs of these calls might move closer together (or he could do the opposite trade and bet that the IVs would move farther apart).

Clearly, in the absence of noise, the trade would make money if both IVs moved to 11.0 or 12.0 or somewhere in between. It should also be clear

---

EXAMPLE 2

European-Style Options on Euro (€) Futures

    Futures at 100.00
    83-day call (100.00 strike) at 2.05; delta = 50; IV = 11
    83-day call (104.00 strike) at 0.84; delta = 25; IV = 12
    Interest rate = 10%

Position: Long 1 call (100.00 strike) at   2.05
            Short 2 calls (104.00 strike) at <u>0.84</u>
            Net debit   0.37

that, as described in Chapter 9, this vertical spread has less exposure to time decay and underlying price movement than the position in Example 1. There are, however, some additional noise elements in this call/call spread, including:

- In addition to exposure to relative IV changes, this position has some exposure to the general level of IV. For example, if the IVs of both options moved to 20.0, the position would be a big loser.
- Since this spread has both long and short options, its Greek letters are likely to be unstable. Through time and underlying price changes, there is the real possibility that its net Greek letter exposure will change, not only in magnitude, but also in sign.

Often traders make relative implied volatility bets by spreading options that have different expiration dates. These can be sensible positions, but they also frequently suffer from exposure to the general level of IV and from radically changing Greek letter exposure.

A variation of Strategy 3 would be to use the position in Example 2 to bet on low future actual volatility. This position has all of the characteristics shown in Chapter 9, but it has a better price. Hence, if our low actual volatility forecast turns out to be a good one, the result should be even better than if both options had 12.0 IVs.

From an IV edge point of view, this position does look good. The problem is the noise. In Strategy 3, it is helpful to have reasonably stable gamma and theta. In this case they might vary too much.

In Strategy 3, the relative attractiveness of the futures/ATM call spread and the call/call spread presents a common dilemma. One spread is more manageable and is likely to have less noise. The other has an edge that seems more attractive in IV terms because of the IV differential, but its changing characteristics make it harder to manage and introduce more uncertainty of results.

CHAPTER 11

Position Management

The multidimensional, nonlinear character of options often seems like a mixed blessing to option traders. Certainly, it provides multiple opportunities to find some edge. That is, there are plenty of ways that an option (or an option combination) can be inefficiently priced. In Chapter 10, we looked at three potential inefficiencies and at simple strategies that might be used to try to take advantage of them.

Strategy 1 sought profit from a bid/offer spread that was wide enough to provide some edge. Strategy 2 looked for its edge from an option's implied volatility (IV) that appeared to be unreasonable compared to a sensible expectation for future implied volatility. Strategy 3 was designed to take advantage of an implied volatility that seemed inappropriate in light of expectations for future actual volatility. This multiplicity of opportunities (and there are many more) is the good part.

Then, there is the difficult part. It is in the nature of option dynamics to make the planning of each of these strategies seem complicated and frustrating. But, it gets worse. During the life of a position, the P&L dynamics, the edge, the noise, and the many aspects of risk can develop in ways that confuse our retrospective view of what has happened as well as our position management decisions.

This chapter explores issues faced by neutral option traders as they live with their positions. It will be assumed that a trader has initiated the position in Example 1 on the following page, which is identical to Example 1 of Chapter 10.

Next, it will be assumed that two weeks have passed, no further trades have been made, the futures have declined to 99.00, and the implied volatility has increased to 12.5. That is, the trader now has the position in Example 2.

SHORT-TERM P&L DYNAMICS

So far, the position has been a winner of 0.14 cents per Euro (of futures). The 1.00 loss on the futures position has been more than offset by the option

EXAMPLE 1

European-Style Options on Euro (€) Futures

Futures at 100.00 (i.e., 100.00 cents per Euro)
83-day call (100.00 strike) at 2.23

Implied volatility = 12.0
Interest rate   = 10%
Call delta   = 50

Position: Long 1 futures at 100.00
          Short 2 calls at 2.23

profit of $2 \times (2.23 - 1.66) = 1.14$. We might think of this profit as the result of changes in the three most important option variables: underlying price, time, and implied volatility. It might be analytically useful to try to attribute part of the P&L to each variable. Here is a crude, but useful, approach.

First, we might assume that two weeks passed with no change in either underlying price or implied volatility. Next, we might imagine that, on the fourteenth day, the futures declined to 99.00. Finally, we might think of the IV increase as coming after (maybe because of) the sudden 1.00 futures price decline.

Effect of Time Change

We can think about the effect of time decay by using our model to reprice the option with:

- 69 days until expiration
- The futures at 100.00
- IV at 12.0

EXAMPLE 2

Long 1 futures at 99.00
Short 2 (69-day) calls at 1.66
IV   = 12.5
Call delta = 43

Under those circumstances, the option price would be 2.04. Hence, the "natural" time decay in the option over that two-week period would be 2.23 − 2.04 = 0.19. Since the position has two short options, we can think of 2 × 0.19 = 0.38 as the effect of the time change on the position. That is, if two weeks had gone by, with no change in futures price or IV, the profit would have been 0.38 cents per Euro.

Effect of Underlying Price Change

If we imagine that, with 69 days until expiration, the futures price dropped from 100.00 to 99.00 with IV still at 12.0, we can reprice the option with:

- 69 days until expiration
- The futures at 99.00
- IV at 12.0

Under those circumstances, the new option price would be 1.58. The P&L effect of the 1.00 futures price decline would be:

- A 1.00 loss on the futures
- A 2 × (2.04 − 1.58) = 0.92 profit on the options

This is a loss of 0.08 cents per Euro due to underlying price change.

Effect of Implied Volatility Change

If, in our example, two weeks had gone by and the futures price had moved to 99.00 with no IV change, the new option price would have been 1.58, the position's P&L would have been

$$(99.00 - 100.00) + 2 \times (2.23 - 1.58) = +0.30$$

and we could think of this 0.30 profit as consisting of a 0.38 time-decay profit and a 0.08 futures price movement loss. In Example 2, however, the IV has increased to 12.5. Hence, the option price is 1.66 instead of 1.58. Since the position has two short options, the IV increase has a P&L impact of

$$2 \times (1.58 - 1.66) = -0.16$$

The position shows a total profit of 0.14 cents per Euro, and we can think of this P&L as having three components:

- A 0.38 profit due to time decay.
- A 0.08 loss due to underlying price change.
- A 0.16 loss due to implied volatility change.

A Few Observations

This is a rough calculation, based on the assumption that all of the passage of time occurred first, all of the underlying price movement next, and finally the IV change. In practice, many different sequences are possible, each producing a somewhat different allocation calculation.

In this example, the time variable dominates the calculation. The 0.38 time-decay profit overwhelms the losses associated with the other two variables. Of course, a trader who put on such a vertical spread and planned to keep it untouched for two weeks would know that this calculation would produce a 0.38 profit. He would also know that a significant change in underlying price would have a negative effect, but he wouldn't know the magnitude (clearly, if the futures price had moved up or down by 10.00 the price movement loss would have overwhelmed the effects of the other two variables).

As for the effect of IV change, the trader couldn't know whether the change would be an increase or a decrease. He also wouldn't know if the change would be big or small. Hence, the effect of IV change could be a profit or a loss, and it could be relatively small (as in Example 2) or it could be quite large and could dominate the P&L.

In practice, for long-dated options, we usually have relatively high vegas and low gammas and thetas. Then, we often find a spread's P&L to be dominated by the effect of IV change. For short-dated options, the reverse is true.

In Example 2, the trader might have initiated the position to employ Strategy 3, as described in Chapter 10. That is, he might have an actual volatility forecast of much less than the 12.0 IV. In that case, after two weeks, he would feel that, so far, he's been "right." Since the time-decay profits have overwhelmed the price movement losses, the futures price has probably not been very volatile. His profits have been reduced by the noise of the IV increase. Of course, if he keeps the position for a while this temporary noise can be expected to become less important.

In contrast, the trader might have initiated the position to employ Strategy 2. He might have expected the IV to decrease. In that case, he might have mixed feelings about the two-week results. *He was wrong.* The implied volatility increased and this increase cost him some money. But the IV effect was overwhelmed by the lucky noise of low actual volatility. At this point, how many of us would have the intellectual discipline and introspection to recognize what really happened? How many of us would think (or tell the boss) that this was a smart trade because it worked?

THE DECISION TO GET OUT

After some experience, most traders seem to become comfortable with their position selection processes. Even if they are a little sloppy, they learn what kind of inefficiencies (or what kind of edges) they like to look for, and the positions go on without a lot of doubt or second guessing. Usually, the decision to get *out* of a position is not as smooth. Sensible, decision-making criteria are less obvious, emotions can be strong, and a trader's mind can be cluttered by recent expectations, experiences, hopes, and the evolution of position characteristics and edges.

The difficulty of formulating simple, sensible criteria for such important decisions can lead to a lot of nonsense. Some traders think that any objective decision rule is better than allowing themselves some discretion. They might not trust their own judgment or discipline, and they can remember making decisions that didn't work out well. Others might be willing to trust their own "feel," hoping that their "gut" will tell them when to get out. Still others seek out simple rules that have a clever, snappy ring to them. Such rules can give the trader the unspoken rationalization that the result isn't his fault.

Retrospective Criteria

Frustrations associated with deciding whether or not to keep a position can cause an otherwise intelligent trader to seek solace in the fantasy that the position's P&L can make his decision for him. If, for example, a trader had initiated the position in Example 1 as part of Strategy 3, there are at least four ways for him to imagine that his P&L has told him what to do next.

1. *Nobody ever went broke ringing the cash register.* If, after two weeks of simply watching his position, a trader found himself in Example 2, he might use the 0.14 profit as a reason to get out. After all, he's in the business of taking profits, and here's a chance to do exactly that.

   The problem is, if he takes his profit, what is he going to do next? Maybe he is making a mistake if he thinks his job is to "take profits" or "make winning trades." If Strategy 3 is part of his business, then it is his responsibility to *have good positions*. If this is a good position (in terms of edge, exposure, and alternative uses of risk capacity), then he should have it. The 0.14 unrealized profit is irrelevant.

   Is this a good position? It probably is. If the original position was justified by the difference between a 9.0 actual volatility forecast and a 12.0 IV, what's different now? The IV (at 12.5) looks more attractive. Is it time to raise the forecast? Probably not. If the futures sat still for two weeks and then dropped by 1%, the *historical actual volatility* over the period was about 5.1. Absent some unusual political, economic, or market situation, it's hard to think of a good reason to walk away from the remaining edge in the position.

2. *Let your profits run. You're playing with the house's money.* If, after two weeks, with the futures at 99.00, the IV had declined to 8.0, the position would have made a lot of money. Could the big profit be a reason to keep the position, even at this apparently unattractive IV?

   Many traders would have a hard time parting with this position. It has treated them well. It is working. It's their friend. When it goes against them, then they'll take it off.

   In some trading strategies (e.g., trend following), recent profits might be predictive of future profits. Strategy 3 is not necessarily one of them. In a multidimensional, nonlinear world, with different kinds of volatility, too many things are changing: forecasts, edges, position dynamics. The use of the present tense here (it *is* working) can be a real trap.

   Even if a trader is "playing with the house's money," it's real money and it could be his. Why risk it for no edge?

3. *Take your losses fast.* Maybe, after two weeks, with the futures at 99.00, the option price would be 1.76 (IV of 13.0+) instead of 1.66. Then, the position would have a loss of 0.06 instead of a profit of 0.14. Would this loss be a reason to get out? Has the position proven you wrong?

   In many trading rooms, the practice of taking losses quickly is a fundamental part of the culture. It keeps small losses from becoming big losses, and it eliminates wishing and hoping by traders who become emotionally weak under adversity. Besides, if you're wrong, shouldn't you get out?

   While this practice might be appropriate for a trader who does big size in spot FX or in bond futures, it can be a wasteful luxury in an option strategy. In options, the cost of quickly giving away the bid/offer spread can be a significant percentage of the position's edge. Furthermore, in Strategy 3, it is not at all clear that a short-term loss is an indication that the position has no significant edge.

   With the futures at 99.00 and the option at 1.76, has the market proven you wrong? What were you betting on? You were betting that the *actual volatility* of the futures would be less than 12.0 over an 83-day period. After 14 days, it's hard to know how right or wrong that forecast will turn out to be.

   In deciding whether to take off the position, does it really matter whether you were right or wrong 14 days ago? Probably not, since taking the position off won't erase the losses. What matters is what the future actual volatility is likely to be for the *next* 69 days and whether, by comparison, the new IV of 13.0+ seems unreasonable.

In Strategy 3, if we don't "take our losses fast," how can we deal with the problem of small losses turning into big losses? The simple answer is to be careful not to get too big. A small position with a good theoretical edge can have better profit expectations than a large position with the same option pricing but with a requirement for expensive risk management actions.

4. *I deserve a better fate.* It is not uncommon for a position like that of Example 1 to lose some money and, at the same time, have its edge disappear. For example, the underlying price might be very volatile for a few weeks and the trader might experience some bad adjustment luck. Then the time decay profits would be overwhelmed by the futures price movement losses. If the IV didn't change much, the position would be a big loser. Would a 12.5 IV still provide an edge? Not necessarily. If the trader is responsible about making actual volatility forecasts, the recent high actual volatility might require him to raise his forecast to about 12.5. Then, the edge would be gone.

At this point a responsible trader would get out. He wouldn't continue to take risk without an edge. Many of us, however, would hang on. We might feel that we put on a responsible position, we deserve to make money, and the losses aren't real if the position is still open. This kind of stubbornness is rarely expressed publicly. We all know how silly it is. Internally, however, we can think of plenty of excuses or distractions that give us a chance to wish and hope for a while.

Prospective Criteria

One of the few traders' slogans that I am willing to seriously utter is "Every day is a new day." Go ahead and laugh! It's not particularly brilliant and, like most slogans, it doesn't solve your decision-making problem. Its benefit is to focus attention on the present and the future—what events might happen, what forecasts are appropriate, is there an edge, what are the risks, what are the alternatives? Sometimes it can be difficult to avoid thinking about old forecasts, old IVs, and old P&Ls, but they should be viewed primarily as distractions. A good trader wants a good position *looking forward.* He must justify it as it is *today,* with today's prices, today's forecasts, today's risks, and the risks that might develop over its life.

It might help to think of "Every day is a new day" as applying to four different decisions:

1. *Should you have a position in the Euro?* Is there really an edge? Sometimes a trader is expected to have a position in a particular financial market. It's his job. He might even be mentally addicted to it and feel

uncomfortable without some exposure. On the other hand, if you're taking risk without some kind of substantial, definable edge, you're not in a business. Please go back to Chapter 3.

2. *What should the long side be and what should the short side be?* The fact that you were long futures and short the 100.00 calls for the past 14 days doesn't make the position a part of your body. Positions in liquid markets are not marriage partners. They are vehicles of convenience. Conceptually, we ought to go to the one that makes us happiest every day—or every minute.

Of course, in practice, execution difficulties and transaction costs limit our ability to switch positions, but we should be continually aware of where we'd like to be and how we might get there.

3. *What should the ratio be?* If a position starts out 1-by-2, we might build our expectations and hopes around the dynamics that go with it. Forget it. Get the ratio that looks the best going forward from here.

4. *What should the size be?* Option traders often exhibit some "size stickiness." Oddly enough, this stickiness is often in the number of contracts held, the number of deltas, or some other measure that might not consistently reflect exposure. If a trader initiated the position in Example 1 100-by-200, there could be many reasons why, later, some other size might be appropriate. For example:

- The Greek letters or the remote risks might have changed by themselves. For example, if, 3 days before expiration, the futures were back to 100.00 and the position back to 100-by-200, the P&L might be good, bad, or insignificant. We can't tell without knowing the delta adjustments. However, we do know what has happened to the position's theta and gamma. They have become much larger and the 100-by-200 position is probably too big.

- The edge might have changed. It's not easy to quantify the appropriate relationship between size and edge, but, somehow, positions with great edges ought to be bigger than positions with ordinary edges. Please note that this concept does not justify the practice of automatically adding to losers.

- The trader's overall portfolio imbalance might have changed. For example, he might have originally put on the vertical spread in big size because he had backspreads in other currencies, and was having trouble finding good vertical spreads. If the portfolio has changed, it might be hard to justify the 100-by-200 size.

- The trader's risk tolerance might have changed. For example, a prudent trader might reduce a position after a big loss, not because the position is no good, but because his (or the organization's) appetite for risk has changed. Note that a big loss is not a reason to get rid of the position entirely. Normally, he shouldn't do that unless he's not satisfied with the current edge.

As sensible as it might be to think "every day is a new day" to help focus on the present state and the future possibilities, the utility of the slogan has limits. For example, if you get carried away, you might say, "If every day is a new day, my criteria for keeping a position should be the same as for initiating it." Then, with an actual volatility forecast of 9.0, if you required a 12.0 IV to put on a vertical spread, you might find yourself taking it off when the IV drops to 11.5. That won't work. Good edges are hard to find and it's not easy to put on good positions. You'll never make much money if you grab every little bit of temporary noise. Somehow, in an options business, the decision to keep a position has to be based on different criteria than the decision to initiate it. Still, it must address the same question: Does the remaining edge justify the risk?

What Should You Do?

While there doesn't seem to be a useful formula for the decision to liquidate a position, it is important to systematically go through a checklist of considerations that address edge and risk. This list should look a lot like the list of considerations that justified the initiation of the position. It might include:

1. *What are the risks?* As Chapter 8 discussed, there are no simple units of risk in the options business. Traders must think through a variety of *everyday risks* and *remote risks*.
2. *How uncertain is the forecast that provides the basis for the edge?* This uncertainty can be a function of the unpredictability of the underlying instrument, the time to expiration, and special market circumstances (e.g., an important political event).
3. *How diversified is the portfolio?* In a well-diversified portfolio, it can make sense to take individual position risk for a relatively small edge. With little or no diversification, the same kind of position risk should require more edge.
4. *How unbalanced is the portfolio?* Portfolio balance is difficult to deal with in the options business because correlations among financial instruments are unreliable (especially for remote events) and because the multidimensional nonlinear dynamics of different positions change in different ways. Nevertheless, the question must be addressed. A trader with all backspreads usually should bias his decisions to favor initiating and keeping vertical spreads.

5. *How good is the edge?* Usually, for simple backspreads and vertical spreads, the edge can be adequately quantified in terms of the ratio between the current IV and the forecast. For other spreads, edge quantification is more complex.

After putting on the vertical spread of Example 1, what would have to happen for me to decide to get out? With a 9.0 actual volatility forecast and a requirement of a 12.0 IV for a new vertical spread, I'd normally think about getting out at about a 10.0 IV with a couple of months to expiration. I might be more aggressive about getting out for a less orderly underlying instrument, for a shorter dated option, or in a market environment where vertical spreads were easy to find. I might hold out for a lower IV if my portfolio really "needed" this kind of spread.

THE DECISION TO ADJUST THE DELTA

In the options business, the delta adjustment process is a source of much trader frustration, dismay, self-pity, foolish ideas, irresponsible behavior, and second guessing. While it might seem to new traders that delta adjustment decisions should be guided by simple mathematical calculations, practitioners often rely more on subjective considerations.

Chapter 10 introduced the concept of adjustment luck as a kind of noise that could be especially important in Strategy 3. While, in the long run, we might expect our good and bad adjustment luck to approximately negate each other, the effect of this noise can be quite significant for a short time, or even over the life of a spread. It can be difficult for a trader to accept his lack of control over this noise. He might feel that it is his responsibility to adjust his delta before the risk becomes excessive, but also that he should be able to avoid taking a quick loss on an adjustment trade. In practice, that is a lot to ask.

Why Adjust?

A delta adjustment is a *risk management* action. For example, if a trader put on the position in Example 1 100-by-200, and if two weeks later he found himself in the situation of Example 2, he would be delta long. Ignoring for the moment the uncertainty and instability of the delta calculation of 43, it seems sensible to sell 14 futures contracts to reestablish the position's delta neutrality. Adjusting to neutrality seems sensible for the same reason that the original 1:2 ratio seemed sensible—because it leaves the position with the most acceptable risk profile we can think of while retaining the edge in the 200 options.

Notice that the adjustment does not simply *reduce* the position's risk. In our multidimensional nonlinear world, there are many kinds of risk. In this case, the adjustment reduces exposure to small moves in underlying price, but it actually increases exposure to a very large increase in underlying price. In some cases, a look at the overall risk profile might lead a trader to prefer the risk of a position that is not delta neutral.

Occasionally, traders use the delta adjustment process to restructure a position or to increase or decrease it. Normally, however, these considerations are minor. *Risk management* is usually the dominant good reason to adjust. Most traders cannot help thinking about whether the adjustment trade itself is likely to make or lose money (just once or on average), but the primary purpose of the trade should be defensive, not offensive. It should be based on unfavorable events that *might* happen rather than on what the trader expects.

Why Not Adjust?

To a casual observer, the next trade might seem obvious for a trader employing Strategy 3 with a 100-by-200 position in the situation of Example 2. He should sell 14 futures. After all, the sale would leave him with a position with the same edge and a more favorable risk profile. A real trader, however, might find many reasons to do nothing. Some reasons might be good, some not so good. Here are some bad reasons:

1. *The trader is bullish on the Euro.* This might seem like a good reason to hold back on adjusting. Why sell if the Euro is going to go higher? In practice, however, there are some real problems in letting a directional view interfere with a delta adjustment decision. For example:
   - *Credibility.* In this example, the trader has had the position for two weeks and everything has gone well until today. Now, in the face of some adversity, he wants to try a different strategy (direction picking) and use the same old position. His manager should be suspicious that this new "view" is mostly an excuse to wish and hope. He might observe that this is not a normal position for a bullish trader since the long deltas disappear if he is "right" and blow up if he is "wrong." Of course, the trader might come up with the explanation that his view is more complicated than a simple directional view, and that, given his volatility expectations, the current position is just right. What a coincidence—both the structure and size of an old

position could turn out to match the needs of a new, more complicated, strategy.

■ *Allocation of risk capacity.* Few organizations are very sophisticated
at quantifying and allocating risk capacity, but it is clear that, if the
trader is allowed to keep this long delta exposure, some other position's risk should be restricted. This is especially troublesome if the
organization has other directional traders.

■ *Edge versus risk.* A well-run trading business allows traders to take
significant risk, but only if some reasonable edge comes with it. The
trader might argue that the quality of his directional view provides
an edge, but how good is it? How does it compare with the edge in
the 12.5 IV options? Maybe, if there is some spare risk capacity, the
trader should sell more options and get neutral.

■ *Cost of the directional view.* Did the development of the directional
view use up any time or expense? Maybe the trader could handle
some additional assignments.

■ *Keeping score.* Strategy 3 and direction picking are very different
businesses. At a minimum, there should be two separate accounts so
these businesses can be monitored and managed.

2. *The trader is afraid of "whipsaw."* A classic example of whipsaw
would occur if the trader adjusted by selling 14 futures only to watch a
quick rally back to 100.00. At that point, he would be delta short, he
would buy back the same number of futures and he would be miserable.

The mathematics of whipsaw are normally less spectacular than
most vertical spreaders believe. In fact, in the present example, where
gamma changes very little over a 2.00 or 3.00 move in underlying price,
the trader who has adjusted at 99.00 should be almost indifferent between a quick whip to 100.00 and a further decline to 98.00. Nevertheless, mostly for psychological reasons, vertical spreaders can be
terrorized by whipsaws. Some would have you think it happens almost
every time. It doesn't, but sometimes it happens several times in succes-
sion. Then, in their frustration and humiliation, they might forget that a
much bigger financial pain would come from not adjusting and watching the futures continue to slide to 98.00.

3. *The trader can think of excuses to delay action so he can wish and hope
for a while.* Bureaucratic duties, personnel matters, complaints about
current liquidity, and personal priorities are but a few of the many categories of distracting excuses that can buy some time for a trader who
doesn't want to face reality. Often, these distractions are perceived to
be more urgent than making the adjustment, even though they are less
important.

There are also some *good* reasons to hold back from adjusting. Among them are:

1. *Maybe the delta doesn't convey a good picture of the exposure.* Chapter 7 included a warning about the danger of regarding a delta as an "equivalent underlying position." A delta is merely a calculation of exposure to *incremental* underlying price movement assuming the other variables are known and fixed. In some cases, delta calculations can be very "soft." That is, they can be so sensitive to small changes in option variables that they don't provide much risk information. If, for example, the delta showed us 14 contracts long with IV = 12.5, but short with an IV of 14 or 11, we might conclude that the delta didn't mean much as a description of our exposure to underlying price movement. Similarly, if, in a more complex position, the net delta were neutral at 100.00, 14 contracts long at 99.00, but 40 contracts short at 98.80, we might conclude that our exposure to a further futures price decline was not a substantial risk. In fact, in such a case, the risk of whipsaw really would be greater than the risk of not adjusting.

   In the present example, however, the option's 43 delta is not particularly soft. It is not very sensitive to time or IV and the gamma is quite stable over normal futures price moves.

2. *Transaction costs might be material.* Transaction costs come in several forms. Usually, for a neutral spread adjustment, commissions, fees, back office expenses, capital charges, and credit line costs don't have much impact on the ultimate profitability of the position—unless there isn't much edge or the adjustment involves a very complicated trade. Often, the most expensive transaction cost is the bid/offer spread. This cost can be minimal in some markets and very large in others. Sometimes traders try to avoid it by offering to sell on the offer. That ploy can save a little money when it works, but it can be costly when the market moves away. It doesn't solve the problem.

   Transaction costs come right out of the position's *profitability.* When they are material, they are a legitimate, but not necessarily conclusive, reason to hold back on an adjustment. Furthermore, for a spread with high anticipated transaction costs, an extra edge requirement should be incorporated into the initial position selection process.

3. *The adjustment might require option trades that have negative edge.* In the present example, the adjustment can be handled with a futures trade. In some cases, however, a futures trade might be inappropriate and the trader might have to consider buying an overvalued option or selling one that is undervalued. For such a trade, the negative edge

reduces the expected profitability of the position and, therefore, must be considered in the decision to adjust.

The Decision Process

The first step in developing a sound approach to delta adjustment decisions is to view them as routine risk management steps. For a vertical spreader, they are often unpleasant since they usually have the effect of locking in recent losses. But the P&L is just a distraction. The adjustment decision should be forward looking. Adjusting can be viewed as quitting and starting over. The focus should be on getting the best possible position for the future.

Normally, a delta adjustment involves a *make money/manage risk* trade-off. That is, our adjustment gives us a more acceptable risk profile at the expense of some edge reduction. The edge reduction usually comes in the form of transaction costs (especially bid/offer spreads), and sometimes as negative-edge option trades. Consequently, if we adjust the delta frequently, we find ourselves with more predictable, but lower, expected profits. Of course, if the results are more predictable maybe we can afford to start with a bigger position.

A make money/manage risk trade-off has no common mathematical units for comparison. Profitability is a single number. Risk is a long list of different kinds of exposures as discussed in Chapter 8 and Chapter 12. The trader must make a judgment as to whether the costs of adjusting are justified by the potential improvement in the risk profile. Clearly, then, there is no ideal adjustment point. Rather there is a range of futures prices (in the present case, perhaps 98.00 to 99.50) within which the adjustment point could reasonably be chosen. Unless the size of the position is exceptionally large, 99.00 is probably as good as any, but with a wide futures bid/offer spread, it might make sense to wait a little longer.

Because adjustment decisions are not always simple, and because there is room for some discretion, it is a useful practice to select adjustment prices while the position is still neutral. For most traders, the level of emotional interference increases as a net delta becomes larger. As another defense against your own weakness, it helps to tell someone where you're planning to adjust. When the time to act comes, the risk might not be enough to overcome your inclination to wish and hope, but maybe the threat of personal humiliation will do the trick.

In planning adjustment points, it can be useful to identify more than one. For example, you might identify 99.00 as a "routine" adjustment point. At 99.00, the position is unarguably long, but you shouldn't be too nervous yet. At 99.00 you can treat the adjustment as a routine event. You don't have to take the easiest available trade and you don't have to place a market order. You almost certainly don't want to leave a *stop order* at 99.00, since the effective bid/offer spread on a stop order can be very expensive.

In most cases, if you identify a routine adjustment point for a vertical spread, and if you act responsibly when the underlying price gets there, the adjustment gets made. Later, about half the time the underlying price reverses its movement and you wish you hadn't adjusted. Also about half the time, the underlying price continues in the same direction. Then, the adjustment has saved you some money, but you're still not happy because you are looking at more curvature losses. It seems that vertical spreaders never get to celebrate the success of their adjustments.

It is possible, of course, for a trader to find himself in a situation where the underlying price has moved well beyond the routine adjustment point but no adjustment has been made. This can happen because of a gap in the underlying price, a failed execution attempt, or (most likely) a failure of discipline. In anticipation of such an event, it is a good idea to select a "panic" adjustment point. At the panic adjustment point, it is the trader's responsibility to panic. That is, he should get neutral quickly, without much concern for transaction costs or even for position structure. After getting neutral, he should go to work at restructuring the position or at building a new position.

In many cases, a trader with an unadjusted position finds the underlying price to have moved beyond his routine adjustment point but short of his panic adjustment point. For example, with a routine adjustment point of 99.00 and a "panic" adjustment point of 97.50, the futures might be at 98.50. He still needs to adjust. In this case, only a slight panic is appropriate since the futures are closer to 99.00 than to 97.50.

A Common Misconception

Many vertical spreaders have a mental model for the delta adjustment process that assumes they are going to lose on adjustment trades. They can remember buying tops and selling bottoms and, as described earlier, they never got to celebrate the adjustment trades that really saved them money. They see a vertical spread as an attempt to "earn" the premium on the sold option, and they accept adjustment losses as the "cost" of earning the premium. Sometimes, they keep score of the P&L of the adjustments separately from the original position's P&L.

Chapter 10 and Chapter 11 have utilized a much different mental model. Here we see the price movement (curvature) losses as occurring *between adjustments,* not because of them. On average, adjustment trades do not tend to be losing trades. Some lose, some win. It doesn't really matter. What does matter is whether the money that is lost *between adjustments* exceeds the money that is made on time decay.

With this view, the "costs" of adjusting are the transaction costs and the negative edge in option trades. Losses on adjustment trades are not considered costs. In fact, keeping track of adjustment P&Ls can be a useless, or even distracting, activity.

Backspreads

In Chapter 11, as in Chapter 10, a vertical spread example has been used to discuss a process that could as easily be applied to a backspread. If the initial position had been

Long 200 Calls at 2.23
Short 100 Futures at 100.00

the position would have had a *short* delta of 14 futures with the futures at 99.00 after 14 days. Then, the delta adjustment would have been "locking in" the "gamma profits" resulting from the futures price movement.

This kind of adjustment is not really very different from the vertical spread adjustment. It is still a risk management step. This time its purpose is to deal with the risk that the futures will move right back to 100.00. The trader is still tempted to hold off so he can wish and hope. This time he is likely to fantasize about spectacular profits from a continued decline in the underlying price. At 99.00, the adjustment is probably "routine" since the price movement risk is moderate. At 97.50, it might make sense to stop celebrating and make a "panic" adjustment, since some big profits could disappear quickly in a futures rally.

Some backspreaders imagine that they can beat the bid/offer spread by placing limit orders. They usually can't. An order to buy at 99.00 might be the bid for a while, but when it gets hit, the trader is probably just buying on the new offer. At that time, it is likely that he doesn't know where the market's real bid is.

In summary, the decision process for adjusting the delta of a backspread is much like the process for a vertical spread. It involves a make money/manage risk trade-off in which a trader might choose to "quit and start over" with a better risk profile if he is willing to incur the transaction costs and possible negative edge of the adjustment trade. As in the case of the vertical spread, the backspread adjustment should be forward looking and defensive. It is not made because of recent profits or because of the expected result of the adjustment trade. It is made because it leaves the trader in the position he wants for the future.

CHAPTER 12

Framework for Risk Management

An option dealing business is exposed to most of the risks that are part of many trading businesses. Information and valuation systems can fail; counterparties can default; traders can lose control or even defraud employers. A trader might accommodate a counterparty with a large trade and, before the position can be turned over or hedged, there can be a dramatic market event.

While all of these risks are important, this chapter addresses only the risks that are specific to the options business. These are the risks that result from the multidimensional and nonlinear character of options, as described in Chapter 2 and Chapter 8.

Addressing these option risks is not a simple matter. In most option trading organizations, much of the analytical work is handled by a computer—a long series of calculations is made and action is taken if a particular kind of exposure is excessive. This activity, however, is not enough. There is still a need in our business for skilled, experienced professionals who, with the help of some electronic computing power, can "smell out" potential problems that might not be found by screening programs.

Even though senior management teams and risk management groups cannot be aware of every possible risk, it is important for them to monitor some of them. This chapter will explore some approaches to measuring everyday risk and remote risk, suggest some specific steps to be taken in risk management, and offer some general comments on the process of establishing and administering risk guidelines.

The chapter will begin by addressing the relatively simple case of managing the risk of a position with a *single* underlying instrument. Later, we will deal with some issues related to option portfolios with *multiple* underlying instruments. For further simplicity, we will assume that all options on an underlying instrument will have the same implied volatility. In the real world, of course, different options on a single underlying instrument can have very different IVs, and, as pointed out in Chapter 7, each option's IV can, within limits, seem to have a life of its own.

EVERYDAY RISK MANAGEMENT WITH A
SINGLE UNDERLYING INSTRUMENT

Because different risks become important for different kinds of positions, Example 1 includes alternative positions.

In this example, the units of gamma are *deltas per 1.00 futures move* (so with the futures at 86.00, we would expect the call (85) delta to be about 60). The units of theta are *ticks per day* (so, 3 days of time decay should reduce the call (85) price to about 1.61). The units of vega are *ticks per IV point* (so at a 12.5 IV, we would expect the call (85) price to be about 1.72).

It was suggested in Chapter 8 that the "Greek letters" usually give us good indications of our everyday risks. Then, we might want to use Greek letters to establish risk limits and be reasonably confident that complying positions will not lose too much money as a result of a "typical" daily change in underlying price, time, or implied volatility. Chapter 7 pointed out that, in a multidimensional, nonlinear world, a Greek letter gives us

---

EXAMPLE 1

European-Style Options on Euro (€) Futures

Futures at 85.00
60-day put (80 strike) at 0.20
60-day put (85 strike) at 1.65
60-day call (85 strike) at 1.65
60-day call (90 strike) at 0.25

All implied volatilities = 12.0
Interest rate   = 0%

	Price	Delta	Gamma	Theta	Vega
Position 1					
Long €100 million call (85)	1.65	51	9.64	1.37	13.7
Long €100 million put (85)	1.65	49	9.64	1.37	13.7
Position 2					
Short €200 million call (90)	0.25	12	4.97	0.71	7.1
Short €200 million put (80)	0.20	10	4.30	0.61	6.1
Position 3					

Both Position 1 and Position 2.

only a one-dimensional, incremental view of our exposure. Nevertheless, for a "typical" one-day change in a variable, we can often ignore some of the potential effects of nonlinearity.

In Example 1, we might decide that we aren't willing to be exposed to more than a $100,000 loss as a result of a "typical" one-day move in any single variable. Then, we'd have to check our exposure, variable by variable.

Exposure to Underlying Price Movement

For a move in underlying price, Position 2 would cause the most concern. As a first approximation, the exposure would be a function of the position's delta, its gamma, and the magnitude of the one-day move that we choose to think of as "typical." With option deltas of 10 and 12, Position 2 is initially short a delta of €4 million [i.e., our put delta would be (.10 × €200 million) and our call delta would be (−.12 × €200 million)]. With gammas of 4.30 and 4.97, we would expect these deltas to change to about 6 and 17 if the futures were to increase to 86.00. At that point, the position's delta would be about €22 million net short. On average, over the 1.00 move, we would have been net short about €13 million (the average of 4 and 22). With no change in any other variable, our loss would be about 1.00 cent × 13 million = $130,000.

If we thought a 1.00 futures price move would be "typical," the position would exceed our desired exposure limit of $100,000. But maybe we should not look at such a big move in assessing our everyday risk. Chapter 6 addressed the relationship between our volatility units and a one-day, one standard deviation change in underlying price. If we are willing to let the options' 12.0 implied volatility be our indicator, we could use the simple mathematics of Chapter 6 to estimate a one-day, one standard deviation move. We could simply divide the annualized volatility by the square root of the number of trading days in a year (presumed to be 250) to calculate a one-day move of 0.759%. With an underlying price of 85.00, this calculation would give us a one-day move of about 0.65.

About how much would we lose if the futures moved to 85.65, with no change in time or IV? With a total gamma of 9.27 (200 million times) the change in delta would be

$$0.0927 \times 0.65 \times €200 \text{ million} = €12 \text{ million}$$

Thus, over the 0.65 move the delta would have changed from €4 million short to €16 million short. The average delta would have been about €10 million short and the exposure would be

€10 million × 0.65 cents per € = $65,000

which would be within the $100,000 limit.

These calculations can easily be generalized as follows:

> If AD = Aggregate delta = The sum of (the underlying size times the delta divided by 100) for each position component
>
> AG = Aggregate gamma = The sum of (the underlying size times the gamma) for each component
>
> TM = Typical move = Underlying price (in dollars per Euro) times IV times 0.01 divided by the square root of the number of trading days in a year, and
>
> L = Everyday risk limit (in dollars)

then $(TM \times AD) + (TM \times TM \times AG)/2$ is the position's exposure to a "typical" increase in underlying price, and it must be better than L for the position to be in compliance. $(-TM \times AD) + (TM \times TM \times AG)/2$ is the position's exposure to a "typical" decrease in underlying price, and it also must be better than L for the position to be in compliance.

In this example,

$$AD = -200,000,000 \times .12 + (-200,000,000) \times (-.10)$$
$$= -4,000,000$$
$$AG = -200,000,000 \times 4.97 + (-200,000,000) \times 4.30$$
$$= -1,854,000,000$$
$$TM = \frac{0.8500 \times 12 \times .01}{15.811} = 0.006451$$
$$L = -100,000$$

and the position's exposure to a "typical" *increase* in underlying price is

$$(TM \times AD) + \frac{(TM \times TM \times AG)}{2}$$

$$= 0.006451 \times (-4,000,000) + \frac{.006451 \times .006451 \times (-1,854,000,000)}{2}$$

$$= -25,804 + (-38,577) = -64,381 \text{ dollars}$$

which is better than –$100,000.

Also, the exposure to a typical *decrease* in Euro price is

$$(-TM \times AD) + \frac{(TM \times TM \times AG)}{2} = 25,804 + (-38,577) = -12,773 \text{ dollars}$$

In some cases, trading organizations choose to monitor gamma separately (apparently assuming the aggregate delta will be insignificant). In that simplified approach, it is only necessary for

$$\frac{(TM \times TM \times AG)}{2}$$

to be better than L. Then, AG may not be more negative than $(2 \times L)/(TM \times TM)$, which, in this example is $-4,806,000,000$.

It is worth noting that, as is typical of risk calculations, this arithmetic has been somewhat crude. For example, we ignored lognormality in calculating TM, and we assumed gamma didn't change over the TM change in underlying price.

After wrestling with these calculations, I expect most readers to be frustrated with their complexity and with their failure to provide intuitive common sense. Don't despair. It is not really necessary to think in the terms of these calculations. While many organizations use delta and gamma units to measure the everyday risk of price movement exposure, I prefer to measure it in *dollars of exposure to a "typical" move*. In Position 2, as is normal, we have two such exposures, $64,381 for a price increase and $12,773 for a price decrease.

Exposure to Time Decay

For a change in time to expiration, Position 2 would not be a problem. It is a vertical spread which would benefit from the passage of time. However, the backspread of Position 1 would be exposed to time decay losses. For everyday risk management, we could use an aggregate theta limit to monitor this exposure.

If our concern is exposure to the time decay of one calendar day, the calculation is simple. Each option in Position 1 has a theta of 1.37 ticks per day. Hence, we can estimate our exposure as $0.000137 \times 100,000,000$ for the call (85) and the same exposure for the put (85). If our exposure limit is again $100,000, the calculation of $2 \times \$0.000137 \times 100,000,000 = \$27,400$ indicates that the position is in compliance.

This approach might seem satisfactory when the next calendar day is a trading day. The thought process gets clumsier when weekends and/or holidays are involved. For a normal weekend, should the time exposure limit be only ⅓ of that permitted for a normal weekday? There is no obvious mathematical solution to this problem (which is not anticipated by most models). One reasonable approach is to use a trading day theta instead of a calendar day theta. Assuming there are 250 trading days in a year, the trading day theta would equal the calendar day theta times 365/250 (or 1.46). In our example, each option would have a trading day theta of 1.46×1.37 ticks per day which is about 2.00 ticks per day. Then our calculation would give us an everyday time exposure of $40,000 per trading day.

Exposure to Implied Volatility Change

In Example 1, we need to worry about IV change for both Position 1 and Position 2. For small IV changes, we can probably rely on the options' vegas to indicate our exposure to everyday events. There is, however, a problem in trying to establish a sensible exposure calculation. The difficult question: What is a "typical" daily change in implied volatility?

A few considerations seem important in addressing this question:

- What is the underlying commodity? Some commodities seem to exhibit more IV stability than others. But, can we count on this stability in the future?
- What is the current IV level? Usually, we expect an option with a 50 IV to have bigger absolute daily IV changes than an option with a 7 IV. Often, it seems to make sense to think of IV changes in percent terms. That is, a change from 50 to 55 might be thought of as comparable to a change from 7 to 7.7.
- How much time remains until the option expires? We usually expect bigger IV changes in shorter dated options. Many traders use an "inverse square root of time" rule. For example, they expect a 10% increase in the IV of a one-month ATM option to be accompanied by a 5% increase in the IV of a four-month ATM option.

A risk manager's idea of a "typical" daily change in IV must be somewhat arbitrary. For Example 1, we might assume that a 0.5 IV change might be "typical." Then we might use the vegas to estimate exposure as follows:

For Position 1, 13.7 ticks per IV point × 0.5 IV points indicates an exposure of $0.000685 per Euro in the price of each option. Then the exposure to a "typical" IV change is $2 \times 100,000,000 \times \$0.000685 = \$137,000$.

If our limit of exposure to a "typical" daily change in a variable is still $100,000, this position would not comply. In contrast, if we guessed that a "typical" daily IV change would be only 0.3, the exposure would be only $82,200 and the position would comply.

For Position 2, the comparable calculations are:

- ■ $(-200,000,000) \times \$0.00071 \times 0.5 + (-200,000,000) \times \$0.00061 \times 0.5$ = exposure of $-\$132,000$, which also exceeds the limit, and
- ■ $(-200,000,000) \times \$0.00071 \times 0.3 + (-200,000,000) \times \$0.00061 \times 0.3$ = $-\$79,200$, which complies.

To generalize these calculations,

If AV = Aggregate vega = The sum of (the underlying size times the vega times the tick size) for each position component
  TC = Typical IV change = An arbitrary estimate of a "typical" one-day IV change
  L = Everyday risk limit

then AV × TC is the everyday risk of IV exposure, and it must have a lower absolute value than L for the position to be in compliance.

For Position 2,

$$AV = (-200,000,000 \times 7.1 \times \$0.0001) + (-200,000,000 \times 6.1 \times \$0.0001)$$
$$= (-\$142,000) + (-\$122,000) = -\$264,000$$
$$TC = 0.5$$
$$L = \$100,000$$

The IV exposure is $-\$264,000 \times 0.5 = -\$132,000$.

Notice that, as in the case of price movement exposure, "Greek letters" are used to measure IV exposure, but the units of exposure are not expressed in vegas, but rather in *dollars per "typical" IV change*.

REMOTE RISK MANAGEMENT WITH A SINGLE UNDERLYING INSTRUMENT

Consider the Greek letter risk for Position 3 in Example 1:

Long €100 million call (85) at 1.65
Long €100 million put (85) at 1.65
Short €200 million call (90) at 0.25
Short €200 million put (80) at 0.20

For this position, exposure to each of the three dimensions of everyday risk seems quite small:

1. For price movement exposure,

$$AD = 100,000,000 \times 0.51 + 100,000,000 \times (-.49)$$
$$+ (-200,000,000) \times 0.12 + (-200,000,000)$$
$$\times (-.10) = -2,000,000$$

$$AG = 100,000,000 \times 9.64 + 100,000,000 \times 9.64$$
$$+ (-200,000,000) \times 4.97 + (-200,000,000)$$
$$\times 4.30 = 74,000,000$$

$$TM = 0.006451 \text{ (as before)}$$

Price movement exposure $= 0.006451 \times (-2,000,000)$
$$+ \frac{0.006451 \times 0.006451 \times 74,000,000}{2}$$
$$= -12901 + 1540$$
$$= -11,362 \text{ dollars of exposure}$$

for an increase in underlying price, and $-(-12,902) + 1,540 = 14,442$ for a decrease in underlying price. Since 14,442 is a positive number there is no everyday risk of a decrease in underlying price. There is, however, a $11,362 exposure to a "typical" underlying price increase.

2. Time exposure $= 100,000,000 \times \$.000137 + 100,000,000$
$$\times \$.000137 + (-200,000,000) \times \$.000071$$
$$+ (-200,000,000) \times \$.000061$$
$$= \$1,000 \text{ time decay per calendar day}$$

3. For IV exposure,

$$AV = 100,000,000 \times 13.7 \times \$.0001 + 100,000,000$$
$$\times 13.7 \times \$.0001 + (-200,000,000) \times 7.1$$
$$\times \$.0001 + (-200,000,000) \times 6.1 \times \$.0001$$
$$= \$10,000 \text{ per IV point}$$
$$TC = 0.5$$

IV exposure $= \$10,000 \times 0.5 = \$5,000$

In summary, using Greek letters to approximate our everyday risk, we find that Position 3 has the characteristics of a very small backspread. It has a small positive gamma (note that the price movement exposure is dominated by the small delta), a small exposure to time decay, and a small exposure to an IV decrease.

If we simply use this Greek letter approach to describe the position's risk, it appears that there is not much exposure, even to large variable changes. For example,

- If the positive gamma were stable, the position would be expected to make money if the underlying price made a big move in either direction.
- At $1,000 per calendar day, the time-decay risk would not seem excessive, even over the entire 60-day life of the options.
- An aggregate vega of $10,000 per IV point might lead us to expect nothing but profits from IV increases and only a $60,000 exposure to a sudden IV drop from 12.0 to 6.0.

There are two reasons why this Greek letter approach does not adequately describe an option position's risk. First, in most situations (including this example) the "Greeks" change as a result of changes in underlying price, time, or IV. For Position 3, this instability is important for all three of the major variables:

1. With time and IV unchanged, an underlying price decline would, initially, be good for the position's P&L. The position would begin with a small, short delta and, for a while, it would get shorter because of the positive gamma. However, as the position moved significantly away from the 85 strike price, the positive gammas from the call (85) and the put (85) would decrease while the negative gamma of the put (80) position would increase faster than the negative gamma of the call (90) position would decrease. Table 12.1 shows the change in option price,

TABLE 12.1 Effects of Large Change in Underlying Price

Option	Futures at 85.00			Futures at 82.50			Futures at 80.00		
	Price	Delta	Gamma	Price	Delta	Gamma	Price	Delta	Gamma
Put (80)	0.20	10	4.30	0.63	26	8.01	1.55	49	10.25
Put (85)	1.65	49	9.64	3.17	72	8.35	5.20	89	4.86
Call (85)	1.65	51	9.64	0.67	28	8.35	0.20	11	4.86
Call (90)	0.25	12	4.97	0.06	4	2.09	0.01	1	0.58

delta, and gamma at 82.50 (about a 3% decline) and at 80.00 (about a 6% decline) with no change in time or IV.

At 82.50, the aggregate gamma has changed from 74,000,000 to −350,000,000. The aggregate delta has changed from −2,000,000 to 0. Early in the futures move from 85.00 to 82.50, the AD becomes even shorter than −2,000,000, but when the gamma becomes negative, the position becomes less short. At 82.50, it is neutral (within rounding) and becoming longer with every downtick in the futures price.

Because the varying AD has been short all the way down from 85.00 to 82.50, the position shows a $60,000 profit at 82.50. Once the futures move below 82.50, however, the P&L becomes less favorable. Not only does the AD become long because of the negative AG, but the AG itself becomes more negative as the futures move away from the 85 strike and closer to the 80 strike. At 80.00, the AD is +18,000,000 and increasing with each futures down tick. The AG is −1,194,000,000 and, except for its delta, the position has the Greek letter characteristics of a large vertical spread. The P&L is −$120,000 which is $180,000 worse than it was at 82.50. In short, the initial delta and gamma conveyed very limited information about the position's exposure to a *significant* underlying price move.

2. The position's initial exposure to time decay is $1,000 per calendar day. However, with underlying price and IV unchanged, the theta of each option would change as time goes by. Table 12.2 shows the change in option price and in theta that would take place in 20 days and in 40 days.

Table 12.2 shows the thetas of the position's long options increasing as time passes while the thetas of the position's short options are decreasing. As a result, the time exposure increases from $1,000 per calendar day to $11,200 per calendar day and then to $37,000 per calendar day. It is no surprise, then, that over the first 20 days (with no futures price or

TABLE 12.2   Effects of Large Passage of Time

Option	60 Days to Expiry		40 Days to Expiry		20 Days to Expiry	
	Price	Theta	Price	Theta	Price	Theta
Put (80)	0.20	0.61	0.09	0.51	0.01	0.22
Put (85)	1.65	1.37	1.35	1.68	0.95	2.38
Call (85)	1.65	1.37	1.35	1.68	0.95	2.38
Call (90)	0.25	0.71	0.12	0.61	0.02	0.31

IV change) the position would lose, not $20,000, but rather $120,000, and that it would lose an *additional* $440,000 over the next 20 days. Hence, the theta conveys very little information about the position's exposure to *significant* time decay.

3. Just as the deltas, gammas, and thetas are unstable and, in Example 1, could lead us to underestimate a position's risk, Position 3's aggregate vega is also unstable and deceptively close to 0. In this case, a large change in IV could produce big losses regardless of the direction of the change. Table 12.3 shows the effect on option price and vega that would result from a large IV change, with no change in futures price or time.

Table 12.3 shows that as IV changes, there is no noticeable change in the vegas of the ATM put (85) and call (85), but there are substantial changes in the vegas of the OTM put (80) and call (90). As a result, for this position, a significant IV decrease produces a large positive aggregate vega and a negative P&L while a significant IV increase produces a large negative AV and also a negative P&L. At IV = 12.0, the AV is +$10,000 per IV point. At IV = 6.0, the loss is, not $60,000, but $780,000 and the AV is +$244,000 per IV point. At IV = 18.0, there is a *loss* of $400,000, and the AV is –$122,000 per IV point.

The second reason why the Greek letters do not adequately describe Position 3's risk is that they do not address the possibility of a change in more than one variable. For everyday risk analysis, this possibility is not usually a major problem. Since the Greeks are likely to be reasonably stable over "typical" daily variable changes, we can usually get a pretty good idea of everyday exposure to multiple variable changes simply by adding the exposures to the changes in individual variables.

The problem of multiple variable changes becomes more serious when we want to consider *remote risks*. Chapter 8 included some simple examples of this problem. Here, we can look at three similar scenarios for Position 3.

TABLE 12.3 Effects of Large IV Change

Option	IV = 6.0		IV = 12.0		IV = 18.0	
	Price	Vega	Price	Vega	Price	Vega
Put (80)	0.00	0.6	0.20	6.1	0.68	9.4
Put (85)	0.82	13.7	1.65	13.7	2.47	13.7
Call (85)	0.82	13.7	1.65	13.7	2.47	13.7
Call (90)	0.01	0.9	0.25	7.1	0.79	10.4

1. In its initial state, Position 3 had a positive aggregate gamma and a positive aggregate vega. However, it was demonstrated in this chapter that, with only one variable changing,

   ■ A futures price decline to 80.00 would produce a loss of $120,000 and

   ■ An IV increase to 18.0 would produce a $400,000 loss.

   What if the futures price dropped to 80.00 *and* the option IVs all increased to 18.0? Then, the option prices would be

Option	Price
Put (80)	2.33
Put (85)	5.68
Call (85)	0.68
Call (90)	0.14

   and the loss would be $980,000. It is worth noting that, not only is an exposure of this magnitude unseen in the Greek letters, it also cannot be found by combining the exposures to large changes in *individual* variables. The magnitude of this risk can only be found by testing the exposure to this particular combination of variable changes.

2. In its initial state, Position 3 had a Greek letter exposure to time decay of $1,000 per calendar day and to IV decline of $10,000 per IV point. Nevertheless, when the position was tested for large changes in a single variable,

   ■ 20 days of time decay would produce a $120,000 loss and
   ■ an IV decline to 6.0 would produce a $780,000 loss.

   If 20 days passed *and* all IVs declined to 6.0, the option prices would be

Option	Price
Put (80)	0.00
Put (85)	0.67
Call (85)	0.67
Call (90)	0.01

   and the loss would be $1,080,000. Once again the exposure to the scenario involving changes in two variables is greater than the sum of the exposures to the changes in the individual variables.

3. It is not always the case that the aggregate effect of two apparently adverse variable changes will be a loss. For example, Position 3 might experience a futures price decline to 80.00 (which, by itself, would

produce a $120,000 loss) and an IV decline to 6.0 (which, by itself, would produce a $780,000 loss). However, the combination of these changes would be profitable since, with the futures at 80.00, the position would have a large negative vega which would become even larger as the IV declined. Under this scenario, the option prices would be

Option	Price
Put (80)	0.78
Put (85)	5.00
Call (85)	0.00
Call (90)	0.00

and the position would show a profit of $1,040,000.

The implication of these calculations is simple. Responsible options risk management *requires* the testing of a position's exposures to a variety of *significant* changes in individual variables and in combinations of variables. This process, which is often called *stress testing,* is necessitated by the *multidimensional nonlinear* character of options.

SOME STRESS TESTING HISTORY: THE LIGHTS OUT TEST

In 1978, I was actively involved in a long-term relationship to give options seminars for the market maker customers of First Options of Chicago. Given the mentality of the time (see Chapter 1), I was concerned that there was too much emphasis on aggressively seeking opportunities, and not enough concern for risk. Generally, traders were willing to make a token attempt at delta neutrality, but they really didn't want to think much about what might go wrong. Fear was for wimps.

In early April 1978, I decided to devote a two-hour seminar session entirely to risk management. I was optimistic enough to think I could give the market makers a broad overview of option risk, put the various risk management tools in perspective, and get some of them to keep their exposures halfway reasonable.

At the time, the options business was caught up in a premium selling mania. The stock market had been in a slow, steady bear market for over a year, almost all of the volume and open interest was in calls (of the CBOE's 95 option stocks, only five had puts), and it seemed that almost all calls were destined to expire worthless. Actual volatility

(continued)

SOME STRESS TESTING HISTORY: THE LIGHTS OUT TEST (Continued)

in most stocks had been very low for as long as anyone could remember. Implied volatilities were about as low as they've ever been—13 to 16 for plenty of blue chip stocks. It was a pretty good bet that most of the people in the seminar room were short calls, short deltas, and very happy with their positions. Their only dissatisfaction was that First Options wouldn't let them leverage their meager capital even farther.

My big innovation for this seminar was the "Lights Out Test." As I recall, I told them that for each vertical spread, they should simulate a stock price gap of 30% of an annual standard deviation move along with a 25% increase in IV. Then they should check to make sure it wouldn't "put your lights out." So, for a $25 stock with a 20 IV they would have to move the stock price by $1.50 and look at the position with a 25 IV. That's a pretty routine event by today's standards, but nobody wanted to look at it. They didn't even want to think about such a possibility.

A few days later the market had what was, for the times, a huge rally. It was about a week before a big expiration, and market maker short gamma was gigantic. We lost about as many market makers as we lost in October 1987. CBOE seat prices collapsed from over $50,000 to $30,000—about the same percentage decline as in 1987.

I'd like to tell you that none of these traders would have been hurt if they had paid attention to the "Lights Out Test" but that's not the case. In truth there weren't many big stock price gaps. For many traders, the problem was the *process,* not the *one-time scenario.* Stocks rallied, positions became delta short, and traders didn't fully adjust, partly because they didn't want to face reality, and partly because they were used to the market going down. As stocks continued to rally, their "dead" out-of-the-money calls came back to life and they found that the positions had gotten bigger by themselves. It was ugly.

The term "Lights Out Test" caught on for a while, and then faded from the language. The testing process lasted. By the mid-1980s almost every options clearing firm was routinely running this kind of test to keep traders from going under. By this time, it was known as "scenario testing." By the late 1980s most big banks were doing it, and in the 1990s, it became known as stress testing.

Once the utility of stress testing for remote risk is recognized, it should be apparent that stress tests could also be useful in managing everyday risk. For example, instead of calculating everyday price movement exposure using deltas and gammas, why not simply change the underlying price by a one-day, one-standard-deviation move, leave time and IVs unchanged, and calculate the change in value of the position. In fact, the Greek letter approach to everyday risk management is just a cruder approach (because it assumes Greek letter stability) to the same calculation.

In practice, the differences between using Greek letters and stress tests to measure everyday risks are usually insignificant, and the choice of methods can usually be based upon calculation convenience or on the mental comfort of the users of the information. For the rest of this chapter, however, it will be assumed that stress tests are used to assess both everyday risk and remote risk.

RISK MANAGEMENT STEPS

For each instrument on which options are traded, the following five actions are necessary for a well-run stress testing program:

1. Decide on levels of remoteness.
2. Select scenarios to match the levels of remoteness.
3. Establish exposure limits by scenario.
4. Monitor prospectively.
5. Enforce the policy.

Some comments are appropriate for each of these actions.

Decide on Levels of Remoteness

If risk is to be managed by monitoring exposure to various market scenarios, a decision must be made about how normal or unusual the scenarios should be. Should an organization worry about exposure to "typical" daily events? Most do, often focusing on Greek letters, an approach which is almost as good as defining once-a-day scenarios and testing for exposure. How about once-a-year events, or once-in-five-years or once-in-twenty-years? Should someone worry about the once-a-century or even the once-a-millenium event? From a practical point of view, most firms should pick three or four levels of remoteness, actively manage their exposures to these levels, and rely on skilled professionals to identify any other undesirable risks.

Within a firm, people with different jobs should be expected to focus on different levels of remoteness. A chief dealer might worry mostly about once-a-day and once-a-year events. A vice president of capital markets might focus on exposures to scenarios that might occur once every five or ten years. Somewhere, there should be a senior executive who would face the reality of exposures to truly remote, but possible, scenarios. The same executive should probably never give a thought to once-a-year events.

This approach leaves some areas of vulnerability. Because of the multi-dimensional nonlinear character of options, it is possible for a firm to have little or no exposure to a once-a-year event or to a comparable once-in-five-years event, but to encounter an "in-between" event that would bankrupt it. Often, it seems, traders (consciously or unconsciously) find these risk management "holes." For this reason, well-run firms have conscientious traders and risk managers who don't simply rely on stress tests.

Select Scenarios to Match the Levels of Remoteness

Even for everyday events, there is no intellectually satisfying way to select scenarios. A little subjectivity is necessary. A "typical" one-day move in underlying price can be based on an actual volatility forecast, but is more commonly calculated using the implied volatility of a short-dated ATM option. For time exposure, it is easy to simply look forward by one calendar day, but some people make adjustments for the weekend and holiday issues addressed earlier in this chapter. Establishing scenarios for IV exposure seems to be the most subjective. What is the *volatility of the IV* likely to be? No one knows, but someone must guess. For sure, it won't be the same for every underlying instrument.

For remote risks, the process is even more uncertain. If we're worried about a vertical spread, what is a once-in-five-years event for the Euro? How about a 5% gap in the spot price accompanied by a 30% IV increase (e.g., from 11.0 to 14.3)? No one knows. A once-in-twenty-years event is even more difficult to estimate. Someone *must* decide on a set of scenarios, however, or the risk won't be managed at all.

For each level of remoteness, a variety of scenarios must be selected. Clearly, a calculation of exposure to the Euro scenario described above would produce some useful information for a vertical spread, but would be useless for a backspread. The backspread would make money if such an event took place. In anticipation of backspread risk, there must be a once-in-five-years scenario of premium shrinkage, such as three weeks of no significant underlying price movement accompanied by a 25% IV decrease. Other scenarios should be designed to address potential problems in more

HOW REMOTE IS REMOTE?

Jim Porter, the current chairman of HyperFeed Technologies, was chairman of First Options of Chicago in 1987. At the time of the October 19 stock market crash, First Options was regularly applying scenario tests to the overnight positions of the many options market makers for which it maintained clearing accounts. These scenario tests enabled First Options to manage its exposure to a potential debit in a customer's account as well as to assess its overall exposure to broad market scenarios.

Despite its extensive efforts in risk management, First Options suffered severe and well-publicized losses (reported in the press to be about $100 million) when the broad stock market declined over 22% in a day.

Later, Jim told me that First Options had run a *risk management* scenario to quantify the firm's exposure to a disaster comparable to the 1929 stock market crash, the worst decline in the nearly 200-year history of the New York Stock Exchange. The calculation indicated that the firm's exposure to such an event (about a 12% broad market decline) was quite acceptable. Jim added, "It never occurred to me to look at something *twice* that big."

This experience presents a classic example of how an exposure curve can "fall off the table"; that is, how, in a multidimensional nonlinear world, extrapolation should not be relied on in addressing remote risk. It also raises several questions that can't easily be answered. Should First Options have looked at double the 200-year event? How about triple? How would a firm decide how much exposure is acceptable for such a remote event? At some level of remoteness, is the exposure irrelevant since the financial system will probably fail? How many industries could survive an event that is twice as bad as the worst event of the past 200 years? In fact, how many nations could survive such an event?

complex positions. For example, it might help to look at the effect of a big gap in underlying price accompanied by a large *decrease* in IV.

The process of establishing these scenarios is uncertain and frustrating. Managers are often tempted to turn over the difficult decisions to statisticians. This is very dangerous. To a manager, it might seem sophisticated to look at a two-standard deviation event, or to a three-, four-, or five-standard deviation event. But, in a particular financial market, how likely is a five-standard deviation event? No one knows, and bell curve mathematics won't help. Historical data doesn't help as much as we'd like. There aren't enough remote events.

Nevertheless, someone has to guess.

Establish Exposure Limits by Scenario

For each scenario for each underlying instrument, management must identify a specific dollar exposure limit. Even for scenarios that are considered equally remote, the limits might be very different. Among the considerations are:

- What business is the trader supposed to be in? If he is a market maker, maybe he shouldn't have to carry big exposure. If he is in a very competitive market, however, he might occasionally take on more inventory than he would like.
- What is the profit budget for options on this instrument?
- For remote events, what are the firm's annual profit expectations?
- For truly remote events, what does the firm's balance sheet look like?
- For a particular remote event, how might the event affect the profit prospects for the firm's other activities?

Monitor Prospectively

At the present time, most organizations seem to calculate exposures daily. As time and technology advance, however, daily reporting seems less satisfactory. Ideally, positions should be monitored continuously, and unacceptable exposures should never be allowed, even for a minute. In that case, especially for market makers, it would sometimes be necessary to provide for expanded (but not unlimited) limits for short periods of time during active market hours.

It should be clear that the purpose of stress testing is to manage *exposure*, not *losses*. It can be difficult for a manager to confront a trader who has been making money, and it is tempting to forgive a violation on a position that worked out well. It must be emphasized that the main focus of risk management should not be on what actually happens to the position, or on what the trader or the organization thinks will happen, or on what might happen on average. Risk management is primarily concerned with what *might* go wrong and how expensive it might be.

Enforce the Policy

Many organizations regard exposure limits as untouchable. If a trader is over a limit, he is disciplined. If he is too far over, he's fired. This is a good approach when managers don't have the skills or the access to traders to be involved in unusual circumstances. It is also a better approach for managing remote risk than it is for managing everyday risk.

Some organizations look at exposure limits not as absolute untouchables, but as calls to action. As a limit is approached, a skilled, active manager might ask if unusual exposure can be justified by an exceptional opportunity (usually, some form of edge), by a sudden, unexpected market-driven change in a position's characteristics, or, for a market maker, by the short term need to take on a large position to satisfy a customer. In such cases, the manager should normally work with the trader to plan and manage the future of the position.

Even for organizations with skilled, active managers, it is important to recognize that *some level* of exposure really should be untouchable.

GENERAL COMMENTS ON STRESS TESTING

1. While it is true that setting stress testing policy is difficult and frustrating, it is also true that there is no single best set of scenarios or limits. What is most important is that the scenarios and limits are assigned and enforced, not that they are perfect.
2. Stress tests (as well as Greek letters) are measures of size, not of quality. It is possible for a very promising position to fail a test, simply by being too big. Likewise, a position with a substantial negative edge might pass the tests if it is small enough.
3. In a large organization, it is important for senior management to be involved in setting risk management policy and in monitoring exposure to *very remote* events. This involvement will probably not be sustained if executives are flooded with details. Consequently, senior people need to receive a very brief report that is designed to permit them to know what it means and to remember what they are supposed to do about it.
4. It has often been the case that responsibility for setting risk management policy and for implementation and monitoring has been delegated too far down in an organization. Sometimes this is done by senior executives who are desperately hoping to retire before they have to learn about options. The result of such delegation can be that no one ever looks at events that are truly remote, but worth worrying about.
5. In establishing exposure limits for everyday events, it can be useful to consider the skill levels, experience, and personal characteristics of trading personnel. Such considerations become less appropriate as more extreme scenarios are considered.
6. Traders sometimes object to having limits imposed for scenarios that include significant passage of time. They argue that they would not let

a losing position decay for very long. The argument is a weak one for a market maker with a large market share. It can also be weak for any trader if the test is for a remote event. Part of the remote risk is the possibility of irrational or undisciplined behavior.

7. After a firm has decided on its maximum exposure tolerances for a set of scenarios, it might want to allocate less than it can tolerate. It can be a good idea to withhold some risk capacity in anticipation of
   - Exceptional opportunities
   - The need to accommodate one or more customers
   - The desire to keep a position after a dramatic event has produced a big loss, or after a market event has changed the position's characteristics.

8. Even a thorough stress testing program addresses only part of a firm's trading risk. Normally, stress tests look at only "one time shots." They aren't concerned with the possibility of a *sequence* of losses or with any other problems in the trading *process*.

9. The biggest mistake that can be made in designing or administering a risk management program is to ignore the possibility of extreme events. The next biggest mistake is to overlook a limit violation because the position made money.

10. One of the problems often associated with a structured risk management program is that traders abdicate responsibility for hard-nosed size analysis. They feel no reason to keep exposure from creeping up as long as they stay within the limits. A related tendency is to let positions take on some unreasonable risks that "fall in the cracks" of the risk management structure.

11. Another problem is the tendency for a structured program to bring about an adversarial relationship between a trader and the risk management system or personnel. Then, instead of feeling responsible for maintaining sensible exposures, a trader's competitive instincts might lead him to take risk for its own sake.

12. Often, senior executives don't want risk management to be this complicated. They would like a single unit of risk, preferably in units they've used (spot equivalent?) or, at least, in simple dollar terms (Value at Risk). They can't have their way if they really want to do their jobs. Even *really important* executives can't make option risk simpler than it is.

RISK MANAGEMENT WITH MULTIPLE UNDERLYING INSTRUMENTS

Example 2 on the following page consists of a portfolio of two vertical spreads for which the underlying instruments are common stocks. Through

---

EXAMPLE 2

European-style options on equities
Each option is for 100 shares
Prices are in dollars per share

Interest rate = 0%; No dividends
Equity 1: ABC at 20.00
60-day ABC call (20.00 strike) at 0.6468 (IV = 20)
Equity 2: XYZ at 80.00
116-day XYZ call (100.00 strike) at 4.12 (IV = 57)

(*Note:* Extra decimal places are added for the ABC call to reduce rounding error.)

| | **Greek Letters** | | | |
	Delta	Gamma	Theta	Vega
ABC Call	51.6	24.6	0.54	3.2
XYZ Call	29.7	1.4	3.83	15.7

Units of theta: Cents per share per day
Units of vega: Cents per share per IV point

Positions: Long 51,600 ABC shares at 20.00
Short 1,000 calls at 0.6468

Long 2,970 XYZ shares at 80.00
Short 100 calls at 4.12

---

a series of stress tests, we can look at the positions' exposures to a variety of everyday and remote events. Although the two vertical spreads have similar characteristics, the stress testing will demonstrate that one spread has more exposure to some variable changes, but less exposure to others. The testing will also demonstrate that, in some cases, the Greek letters do not, by themselves, convey much information about relative exposure. Consequently, the common practice of evaluating portfolio risk by looking at the sum (or dollar-weighted sum) of Greek letters can be deceptive.

EVERYDAY RISKS

First, we might look at exposure to underlying price change. Both spreads are delta neutral, but the ABC vertical spread might seem to have a much higher gamma. Not only does the 24.6 unit gamma look high, but the ABC position also includes more options, more dollars worth of options, more shares of stock, and more dollars worth of stock. Despite all of this, a calculation of exposures to a "typical" daily stock price move indicates that the ABC spread has only about 41% more exposure than the XYZ spread.

Our units of gamma are: "Deltas per $1 move in underlying price." If ABC and XYZ were likely to move by the same number of dollars, the fact that the ABC calls have a higher unit gamma (24.6 versus 1.4) and that the ABC position has ten times as many short options would mean that the ABC spread would be much more exposed to everyday stock price movement. In this example, however, because XYZ has a much higher stock price and a much higher implied volatility, a "typical" daily stock price move should be much bigger (in dollars) for XYZ. With the arithmetic described earlier in this chapter, we might calculate a typical one-day move in XYZ to be

$$\frac{\text{Stock price} \times \text{IV} \times .01}{\sqrt{\text{Number of trading days in a year}}} = \frac{80 \times 57 \times .01}{\sqrt{250}} = 2.88$$

while a comparable move for ABC would be

$$\frac{20 \times 20 \times .01}{\sqrt{250}} = 0.25$$

If both stock prices were to increase by a typical daily move (with no change in IV) the positions would be:

Long 51,600 ABC at 20.25
Short 1,000 calls at 0.7835

Long 2970 XYZ at 82.88
Short 100 calls at 5.03

The P&L for the ABC spread would be

$$51,600 \times (\$20.25 - \$20.00) + (-100,000) \times (\$.7835 - \$.6468) = -\$770.00$$

and for XYZ it would be

$$2,970 \times (\$82.88 - \$80.00) + (-10,000) \times (\$5.03 - \$4.12) = -\$546.40$$

Hence, the ABC spread has only about 41% more exposure to a typical stock price increase. A similar result would occur if we were to test for a typical stock price decrease.

Since the ABC spread has about 41% more exposure to a typical daily stock price move, you might guess that it also has 41% more exposure to a day's passage of time. You would be correct. In looking at everyday time exposure, we don't have to guess how much the variable (i.e., time) changes on a stock by stock basis. We can look at one day's impact on each position. For ABC, with 1,000 short calls with a theta of 0.54, we would expect the passage of one calendar day to be worth about $540.00. Similarly, for the XYZ position, the 3.83 theta would indicate a daily exposure of $383.00 for the 100 short calls.

Although the ABC spread has more everyday exposure to stock price movement and to time, the XYZ spread has more exposure to implied volatility change. At first glance that might not seem to be the case. For ABC, we have a 3.2 vega for 1000 options and we might say our aggregate vega is $3,200 per IV point. For XYZ, the 15.7 vega for 100 options gives us $1,570 per IV point. However, to calculate our everyday exposure, we would have to estimate a typical one-day IV change for each option. We would probably guess that the XYZ option with a 57 IV would change by more IV points than the ABC option with the 20 IV. We might, for example, guess that a typical one-day change would be 3% of each IV (i.e., 1.71 for XYZ and 0.60 for ABC). We could then ask what the P&Ls might look like for ABC with a 20.60 IV (call price = 0.6662) and for XYZ with a 58.71 IV (call price = 4.38). They would be

$$-100,000 \times (\$.6662 - \$.6468) = -\$1,940 \text{ for ABC}$$
$$-10,000 \times (\$4.38 - \$4.12) = -\$2,600 \text{ for XYZ}$$

While these calculations indicate that the XYZ position has more everyday exposure to IV change, there might be some other considerations. One of these stocks might experience exceptionally unstable IVs. Alternatively, the fact that the XYZ options are longer-dated might make us expect their IV to change by less than if they were shorter-dated. While there are no guarantees for IV stability, even for a single instrument, it should be clear that comparing aggregate vegas for different instruments can be very dangerous.

Remote Risks

In managing the remote risk for the spreads in Example 2, it is necessary to assign, for *each* underlying instrument, a set of potentially unfortunate scenarios for a number of levels of remoteness. Not only is it difficult to select these scenarios (since, for example, no one knows what a once-in-ten-years event is for XYZ or ABC), it is also cumbersome and uncomfortable to try to assign equally remote scenarios for different underlying instruments.

We might, for example, decide that a once-in-five-years event for XYZ would be a 25% stock price increase and a 30% increase in implied volatility. For such a scenario, we would want to know what our P&L would be with XYZ at 100.00 and the calls at 16.54 (IV = 74.1). It would be

$$2,970 \times (\$100.00 - \$80.00) + (-10,000) \times (\$16.54 - \$4.12) = -\$64,800$$

Would it also be appropriate, for the *same* level of remoteness, to look at the ABC spread's exposure to a 25% stock price increase and a 30% IV increase? Maybe not! A 25% stock price gap is probably much less likely for a stock like ABC with a 20.0 IV than it is for XYZ. Furthermore, if a 25% stock price gap would be likely to produce a 30% IV increase in a stock with a 57.0 IV, it would probably have a much more dramatic impact on ABC's 20.0 IV. If we were to take the approach that was described for everyday risk, we might use the IVs to guess that a comparable gap in ABC price would be

$$\frac{20.0}{57.0} \times 25\% = 8.77\%$$

and maybe we should look at an 8.77% ABC price increase and a 30% IV increase. With ABC at 21.75 and IV = 26.0 the call price would be 2.0161 and the ABC P&L would be

$$51,600 \times (\$21.75 - \$20.00) + (-100,000)$$
$$\times (\$2.0161 - \$0.6468) = -\$46,630$$

Is this scenario about as remote as the above XYZ scenario? We don't know, but someone has to guess.

It is worth noting that as we look at more remote events, the process of selecting scenarios becomes more subjective. For very common events, current implied volatilities might be good indicators of "typical" underlying price moves and historical implied volatilities might be useful in guessing the magnitude of IV variations. For very remote events, however, traditional statistical methods become much less satisfactory. Substantial judgment is required.

Ideally, for each level of remoteness, an option-dealing organization would establish specific scenarios for each underlying instrument. In practice, some compromises are made. In most cases, it makes sense to divide all traded underlying instruments into three or four categories of instruments that are thought to have similar tendencies with respect to short-term IV wandering and with respect to remote events. Even within each category, however, exposure limits should be assigned individually.

Portfolio Limits

Most risk managers recognize the need to manage the exposure of an entire portfolio as well as the exposure within each underlying instrument. If the behavior of underlying prices and IVs were *perfectly* correlated, it might be simple enough to aggregate the everyday risks and even the remote risks (although, it should be clear from this chapter that simply adding the Greek letters won't work). Likewise, if we could be sure that we know the future correlations among different instruments, the problem would be amenable to a mathematical solution. Unfortunately, in financial markets, correlation is much like volatility—it is not known, constant, or continuous, and its common units don't fit the real world.

Even though correlations among underlying prices, their actual volatilities, and their options' implied volatilities are unreliable (especially for remote events), it is useful to do some portfolio-wide stress testing. The objective should not be to achieve portfolio balance. Not only is this usually impractical because of correlation issues, but it is further complicated by the ways that different positions change characteristics differently as parameters change. Rather, the objective should be to *avoid gross portfolio imbalance.* Limits should be established and tests should be run for both everyday risks and remote risks. Remote events for an entire portfolio should look much different than remote events for an individual underlying instrument. For example, a 15% gap in a stock price is usually considered a pretty big move. For a broad portfolio, it is usually something spectacular.

I have one caveat: After your portfolio has passed all of your stress tests, don't get too comfortable. There are plenty of surprising combinations of scenarios that your risk management reports won't address.

CHAPTER 13

Some Ideas for
Personnel Management

Question: What is a Yuppie Gunslinger?

Answer: A Yuppie Gunslinger is a gunfighter who gets a job in which, if he gets shot, his employer dies.

Chapter 1 described similarities between the option traders of the 1970s and Wild West characters. The comparison is far from perfect. We risked only money, not our lives, and after getting wiped out, it was possible to re-finance and start over. But like the old gunfighters, most of us were pretty much on our own. For many of us, the independence was a big part of the attraction of a trading career—and we were certainly independent. Most of us had no boss, no customers, no employees, and no telephone. Except for risk tolerance conflicts with our clearing firms, no one expressed approval or disapproval of our performance, no one gave us advice or coaching, no one required our cooperation. We risked our own money, and kept whatever profits came along. No one thought about salaries, bonuses, or paid vacations. We had gone to occupational heaven and we thought we would be there forever.

Those days are over. Some time in the 1980s the options business entered the era of the employee trader. The maturation of the industry pushed out the little guy. Now traders learn through apprenticeship, work in groups, receive many forms of organizational support, and risk employers' money. They experience both the benefits and hassles of management, interact with salespeople and customers, deal with bureaucracy and paperwork, and think about career alternatives.

Today's option traders aren't as independent as they might like, and they rarely put their own money on the line, but they still show signs of a gunfighter's mentality. For the most part, that mentality is good. Traders are self-starters, they can live with serious, ongoing financial exposure, and they don't mind taking responsibility for uncertain actions. In fact, they thrive on uncertainty. They can, however, be difficult to manage, partly because of their personalities and partly because of the nature of the business.

This chapter offers some observations, ideas, and opinions related to the management of option dealers. It is *not* a thorough discussion of all personnel management issues. It is presented with the understanding that we do not have a good model for option dealer management, and it will be easy to find traders who think that much of this chapter is nonsense.

The chapter begins by addressing some basic business issues. Next, it offers some observations about some personal tendencies that dealers are likely to exhibit. This is followed by some advice on managing dealers and on the processes of performance evaluation and compensation determination.

BUSINESS ISSUES

What Business Are You In?

A basic question that an option dealing organization must ask itself is to what extent is it in the business of making money from customer order flow versus making it from taking positions. The answer to this question is important in personnel selection, organizational structure, and definition of job responsibilities. It is also important in monitoring trader behavior. For example, a market maker might have very large risk for a very short period of time, but, compared to a positioner, his overnight exposure should be quite small and his trading volume should be large.

P&L Expectations

Profit and loss patterns in option dealing are usually erratic, partly because opportunities do not appear uniformly, and partly because of the dynamics of option positions. Not all managers are comfortable with these patterns. Some believe that a good business should produce steady profits, without big daily, weekly, or monthly ups and downs.

In the options business, the opposite can be the case. A trader whose account shows a profit day after day should be suspected. As Chapter 1 described, it is easy enough to devise a strategy that has a good chance to produce small profits for a long time, but which ultimately has no edge or which has exposure to unreasonable remote risk. Another possibility is that the reported profits are not real, but merely the result of flaws in the accounting system. Many of the well publicized trading disasters of the 1990s included allegations of traders intentionally hiding losses and recording phony gains through mark-to-market abuses. Some very reputable firms, such as Barings and Kidder Peabody reported that they were fooled and devastated by the false appearance of steady profits. Most profits of this nature are less dramatic, however. Many derivatives traders can find some position that will be marked away from the price at which it trades. In a pinch, it is very tempting to trade a few, book a little short-term profit, and face reality later.

Overall Management Style

There is a broad spectrum of management styles that have been attempted by option trading firms. At one extreme, some firms have hired almost every trader who looks promising, given the traders broad discretion in everything except risk limits, and let them know that they will be terminated if losses exceed a certain amount. That is, they have monitored the risk and the financial performance, but have not managed the *people* or the *process*. This approach to the management of traders is common, but weak. In our business, traders need managerial guidance and support. Furthermore, short-term results don't convey enough about the trader, his strategies, or the quality of his decisions.

At the other extreme, a firm can centralize all strategic decision making in a small trading/management team, and assign people to make markets or to execute and manage trades within very specific, narrow constraints.

In most cases, either of these extreme approaches seems like an attempt to avoid treating option trading as a business. In a well-run business, trades, strategies, and risks should be "out in the open." They should be explained and discussed. Managers should be *coaches*. They should work closely with traders so that the traders can contribute and develop, but still receive management guidance and still have to explain their activities, strategies, and tactics, as well as the results. This approach requires the manager to have personal and communication skills as well as analytical and trading skills, and it requires traders to operate without the independence and privacy of a Yuppie gunslinger.

PERSONAL TENDENCIES OF TRADERS

Oversimplification

Young traders often have a tendency to want to master only one part of the business. For example, they might not want to spend the time and energy to really master the fundamentals. Maybe they'd like the complexity of volatility to go away so they could just bet on IV change. Maybe they'd like to go right to "sophisticated" matters such as "exotic" options or complex relative IV bets. Likewise, they might be interested in initiating clever positions, but not in the ongoing analysis and "pruning" that might be necessary during a position's life.

The Trader's Right to Gamble

For a typical option trader, the discipline imposed by his job is a constant irritant. He is likely to resist the need to analytically justify the edges in his positions. Occasionally, he'd like to just go with his feel—or wish and hope for a while. Likewise, he might frequently resent the requirements for limiting his everyday risk or remote risk.

The result of this irritation can be a tendency to think of excuses to "gamble." One such excuse, discussed briefly in Chapter 11, is to imagine that the "rules" don't apply if the trader is ahead and "playing with the house's money." This weak rationalization can be applied to a particular position or to an accounting period. I have heard quite a few dealers, and even some chief dealers, say that, if it's the middle of the month and they are well ahead, it's okay to "roll the dice" a little. I have no idea how they would explain such a concept to a board of directors who thought a trader's job was to have positions that reflected the best possible tradeoffs in terms of edge and risk.

Trade Orientation

Almost every trader is subject to slipping into a trade orientation. As discussed in Chapter 3, this can sometimes be appropriate when risk management is the purpose of option trading. For an option dealer, however, the main reason to trade is to make money and a trade orientation is a weakness.

Often, this tendency is accompanied by comments that utilize the "permanent present tense." For example, a trader might say "buying premium is what works now" or "selling premium is what works now." This means that "this kind of position has been working lately, so it's what I'm betting on for the future." The present tense conveys a fantasy of stability and predictability. It also allows him to think it isn't his fault if he loses money.

A strong trade orientation can also reflect an inclination to "wish away" the multidimensional, nonlinear character of options, and to imagine that the only variable that really matters is the one that the trader is fixated on.

Trader Explanations

Beware of a trader's explanations of his strategies and tactics! He'd probably prefer to have simple, snappy reasons for his decisions (remember "Nobody

TRADE ORIENTATIONS

Excessive trade orientations are most noticeable among two categories of option dealers: compulsive premium buyers and compulsive premium sellers. In both cases, the "disease" can start slowly, and then steadily turn into an addiction. Extremely compulsive traders lose all price sensitivity.

Compulsive premium buyers might be naked option buyers, or they might be addicted to backspreads. Necessarily, they tend to dwell on the potential for spectacular market events. A few traders of equity index options waited a long time for October 1987 to come again.

Compulsive premium buyers sometimes make big "scores," but, more often, they lose money slowly and steadily. Occasionally, they have a disaster, which typically involves exceptionally low actual volatility, accompanied by a collapse in IV. This happened in foreign exchange options in late 1996 when the U.S. dollar came to a near halt against the Pound Sterling, and seemed almost as quiet against the Deutsche Mark and the Swiss Franc. In August 2000, a comparable, but quicker disaster beset premium buyers in U.S. equity options.

Among option dealers, compulsive premium buyers seem to be outnumbered by the compulsive premium sellers. In their case, the addiction could be to naked short options or to vertical spreads. These traders might have noticed that most options expire worthless, and they might have felt like chumps when they bought options and watched them die. In some cases, excessive management focus on short-term results can feed this disease.

Big premium sellers are subject to sudden death, and the spectacular stories of their demises are endless. It seems that, sometimes, they are stimulated by the threat of a horrible remote event. They might tend to tell themselves that disaster won't strike in the *near* future, that they can have the "free money" now, and that they will see the next dramatic event coming or that their adjustments will save them. In Chicago, Joe Ritchie of CRT was generally given the credit for describing such trading behavior a "picking up nickels in front of steamrollers."

As Chairman of First Options of Chicago, Jim Porter spent many years worrying that the irresponsible behavior of his market maker clearing customers would hurt both the customers and First Options. After much observation, and after hearing many creative rationalizations, Jim told me, "You can always spot a compulsive premium seller. In normal times, he'll sell some options to make some money; but when premiums are cheap, he'll sell twice as many so he can make the same amount."

ever went broke ringing the cash register" in Chapter 11?). He'd also like decision rules that are objective enough to relieve him of some responsibility.

In the options business, a trader's decision processes are often more complicated than he realizes. If he really makes decisions that follow silly, simple rules, he's not going to do well. Sometimes, however, a good trader makes decisions for good reasons that he is unable or unwilling to explain, then uses a silly reason (really, an excuse) because it makes him feel good or he thinks it makes him look good.

No Personal Stake in the Risk

In the option trading business, it should be every employer's fear that his trader does not really have a personal stake in the risk. No matter how careful managers are, and no matter how clever the compensation system is, it is almost impossible to perfectly align the interests and priorities of the trader and those of the employer.

Often this kind of incompatibility produces trading behavior that is not what the employer would like. Occasionally, a trader is overwhelmed by the inescapable fact that he has limited personal exposure to a real financial disaster. Then, irresponsible trading can be driven by trader greed (after all, his participation in spectacular profits can be much bigger than in spectacular losses) or by trader desperation (he might need quick profits to avoid being fired, or he might be personally desperate for a big bonus).

A related problem could be that the employee has *too much* stake in the risk. For example, late in the year, a trader or a department might stop trading because there is already enough profit for the year. Additional profits won't help bonuses, but losses might reduce bonuses. In such a case, the trader participates in the downside, but not the upside. Then, stopping trading might make sense to the trader, or even to his boss, but it wouldn't make sense to me if I were a stockholder. If there were good opportunities, I'd want to take advantage of them. I'd also like to know who was responsible for the incentive system.

There is no general solution to problems like these. They require constant awareness on the part of management, and they require supervisors to know their traders and to be alert for their personal crises.

POLICIES AND PRACTICES

What Kind of People?

It is not easy to identify good prospects for positions in option trading. A wide variety of skills, backgrounds, and experiences have produced successful

PERSONAL STAKE IN THE RISK

For many years, O'Connell & Piper has offered a one week seminar program for option traders. Most of the participants have been dealers who had traded on bank option desks for a year or so. Many have been colorful characters.

One of the 1990 programs included a trader from New York named Gary. Gary was quite outspoken, a characteristic that is not surprising for a New Yorker, but is usually a valuable one in a small seminar.

Early in the program, I talked about profitability and risk. I explained that I'd rather not take any risk, but that some is necessary if we want some edge. Then, we spent a lot of time talking about option risk and how we might keep it from getting out of hand.

After a couple of days, Gary had heard enough. With no warning he said "You've got the whole wrong idea. You talk as if risk is bad. Risk is good! When I trade, I try to maximize my risk because if I win, I get a big bonus and, if I lose, it's my employer's problem."

Some of the participants were shocked, but all Gary had done was articulate an attitude that is common, but usually unspoken, among employee traders of all kinds. In fact, it's not limited to traders. Plenty of corporate executives and small businessmen have "bet the business" with similar attitudes.

The Brazilian Spread

In the 1970s, CBOE marker makers used to talk about the "Brazilian spread." Here's how it worked:

A trader would begin by selling calls in IBM (IBM was the glamour underlying instrument of the era). In fact, he'd sell a lot of calls— enough so that a significant IBM rally would put his account into a serious deficit. He wouldn't be naked short, however. He'd hedge the calls by buying an airplane ticket to Brazil. If IBM started to rally, he'd go to O'Hare airport until the end of the day. Then, if IBM had come back down, he'd go home. If it kept going up, he'd get on the plane. In the minds of CBOE traders, this was sensible since the United States didn't have an extradition treaty with Brazil.

I don't know if anyone ever actually did a Brazilian spread in its simplest form, but when someone said he did it, everybody knew what he meant. In the 1980s, the Brazilian spread was reinvented by bank option traders in what we called the "Xerox machine spread." As you'd guess, that spread consisted of putting on a large irresponsible option position, and then heading for the Xerox machine to start copying a resume.

traders. Some strange people have done well. Many solid, intelligent, hard-working people have not.

Although we often think of the options business as being special, it is still a business, and the most important issues in selecting option trading personnel are the same as for professional personnel in any business. You should begin by asking yourself:

- Is he a good person?
- Will he work hard?
- Is he disciplined?
- Does he have broad business perspective?
- Is he intelligent?
- Is he willing and able to be introspective?
- Will he accept his role in the organization?

There are, however, some special considerations in selecting option traders:

- *Math skills.* There are many aspects of the options business that require some mathematical aptitude. However, unless "exotic" options are involved, a trader does not need rocket scientist skills. It is important for an options trader to have a good sense of high school level math, along with basic calculus and statistics. More important, a trader should be *interested* in the mathematical relationships involved in options.
- *Statistical passiveness.* While a trader must be driven by financial performance, he should not be overly concerned about short-term results. If he needs to be "right" every time, this is the wrong business for him. Rather, as described in Chapter 1, he should have the attitude of an insurance underwriter or a casino. He should be interested in making transactions that will be successful *on average over time* while keeping exposure to short-term losses *reasonable.* Not everyone is capable of this attitude, especially if it is not frequently supported by management.
- *Emotional balance.* Traders need to execute strategies on a consistent basis. Most have a tendency to lose perspective occasionally. Often, this is triggered by excessively good or bad short-term results. A good manager will become more involved with a trader whose perspective is being pressured by recent performance.
- *Firefighter's mentality.* Option trading is not steady work and its intensity is not usually determined by the trader or his boss. Activity and opportunities come in bursts. A trader might crave action when it is time to hold back, or he might not feel like participating at a time when inefficiencies abound. He *must* be able to rise above these personal tendencies.

There is no consensus in the options business as to whether it is helpful or necessary for an option trader to have had prior experience trading the underlying instrument. Certainly, some familiarity with the underlying instrument is necessary. Specifically, a trader should have informed expectations regarding the extent to which the instrument's behavior is likely to vary from the assumptions of his mathematical model. However, too much trading experience can be a problem. An old bond trader might unconsciously overrate the relevance of his experience in trading cash bonds, and he might not be able to fully focus on all of the important considerations involved in bond option trading. This is similar to a problem commonly encountered by mathematicians who have to fight their inclination to think that mathematical modeling is the essence of option trading.

Breadth of Trader Responsibility

For many of us old-timers, option trading was a one-person business. We designed our own strategies, established our own policies, made our own forecasts, executed the trades, and managed the positions. Many of us also handled our own administrative and clerical duties.

It is no longer necessary for a single person to handle such a breadth of activities. Careful segmentation of responsibilities can improve a firm's productivity and enable it to utilize people who have narrow skills or limited experience. For example, market making is a specific skill that is not necessarily related to the skill of position management. Many firms find it useful to separate these two functions. In some cases, it makes sense to separate them selectively; that is, to allow some market makers to manage their positions while requiring others to make markets within mandated parameters and pass the positions on to someone else.

Productivity is not the only issue to be considered in allocating responsibilities. Sometimes firms find that narrowing job definitions can inhibit personnel development or make it difficult to attract and keep good people.

Getting Started as a Trader

New traders should be permitted to make real trades *almost immediately.* However, the purpose of these trades should be to learn, not to make material profits. Hence, the trader should be allowed *token size only,* and this restriction should remain long after he has made money and gained some confidence. This discipline is hard to keep since the manager can be as quick as the trader to gain false confidence after a little "success."

Strategy Supervision

Many option traders work in loud, crowded environments, but even these traders can be alone when it comes to their decisions and their emotions. Subtle differences among option strategies and terminology, different mental frameworks for thinking about the business, and the discomfort of being "cross-examined" all tend to reduce option conversations to trivialities. This is not conducive to clear thinking, to professional growth, or to informed personnel evaluation.

It is very useful for every trader to have a regular (perhaps weekly) strategy review with his supervisor. This review should not be adversarial. Rather, it should be handled in a "coaching" mode. The trader should explain his transactions and positions in the context of specific strategies such as those described in Chapter 10. Issues such as volatility forecasts, size, the quality of the opportunities, alternative approaches, expectations, fears, adjustment points, and contingency plans should be discussed.

The knowledge and expectation on the part of the traders that they must be prepared to explain and defend their trading and/or positioning rationales on a regular basis will, in itself, improve their skills and discipline, and provide an important "brick" in the risk management structure.

Initially, these strategy sessions can be uncomfortable. Some traders are likely to be defensive or unable to explain positions. After a few tries, most traders can learn to get their "story straight" and to have positions that are consistent with the story. Then, it's a good idea to have less frequent scheduled sessions and an occasional unscheduled session.

Volatility Forecasting

Chapter 6 pointed out that there is no correct way to make a volatility forecast. The process is frustrating, and expected errors are uncomfortably large. This is true whether we are forecasting actual volatility or implied volatility. Nevertheless, almost all option trading strategies should involve some determination of specific volatility expectations that are crucial to the trader's appraisal of profitability and risk.

At a minimum, managers should require that traders be specific about their volatility expectations. At an extreme, a firm might want to dictate its own forecasts or even its IV standards for position initiation. This approach might work for risk management purposes, but, unless they really like the methodology, "volatility traders" are likely to fight the edge calculations that these forecasts produce.

Most traders can use some organizational help in collecting and presenting the current and historical data that might be useful in making a volatility forecast. Such data can include not only calculations for the trader's underlying instrument, but also for potentially related instruments and indexes. It is not too much to insist that traders be aware of how current IVs and IV relationships compare with historical levels of actual and implied volatilities and of volatility relationships. In addition, they should be willing to defend their forecasts, and they should be realistic about forecast uncertainties. However, in most situations, it *is* too much to ask that traders subscribe to a specific set of mathematical algorithms for volatility forecasting. There is nothing wrong with incorporating a little trader intuition into the process, as long as the trader is willing to openly discuss the forecast and, later, to review its accuracy.

Portfolio Management

Ideally, a firm would trade options on many underlying instruments, allocating risk capacity where opportunities appear to be most attractive, and staying alert for potential portfolio imbalance problems. In practice, many firms assign people to trade options on a single instrument or on a small group of instruments. While there are good reasons for this practice, it can encourage "overtrading" by individuals who don't have many places to "shop" for opportunities.

It requires a special management effort to overlay some portfolio management when traders are operating independently. It is important to assign a senior trader to this activity, to be sure that trading personnel understand that they are constrained by portfolio considerations, and to provide a supervisory environment in which *no position* can sometimes be the *right position*.

PERFORMANCE EVALUATION

At least six considerations are important in evaluating a trader's performance:

1. *How good have opportunities been?* A scalper needs order flow. A "volatility trader" needs some implied volatility aberrations. In most cases, traders cannot create their own opportunities. These opportunities can vary from month to month, from quarter to quarter, even from year to year.
2. *Short-term luck.* Some businessmen like to think they make their own luck, but that's seldom true in options in the short run. Since a single trade or position can often dominate a monthly or quarterly P&L, a decision to ask for a better price, to choose one spread over another, or to

get out of a position early can have a major effect on performance. Similarly, we can be very lucky or unlucky in terms of how the market treats us. For example, Chapter 10 described the possibility that a trader might put on a vertical spread with a 12.0 IV because his actual volatility forecast was 9.0. In that example, if the trader kept the position for a long time, and the future actual volatility turned out to be 4.0, the position would probably fare extremely well even though the trader didn't make the low actual volatility happen and didn't expect it. Later, he might well give the money back through comparable bad luck. This is part of the normal flow of trading activity and the manager should be aware of it.

3. *Did the strategies get executed?* Chapter 10 described requirements for three broad categories of neutral option strategies. Did the trader actually trade in the context of such strategies? Did he know what strategy justified each position, were the required conditions met, and did he take all of the appropriate steps for each strategy (including getting out before the noise took over)?

4. *Appropriate risk behavior.* Did the trader comply with the organization's risk management policies? In addition, did he consistently subject positions to *hard-nosed size analysis.* That is, did he stay "small" when opportunities were less than exciting, saving risk capacity for the most attractive opportunities? Comparably, when really good opportunities seemed to appear, did he step up to big size?

5. *P&L.* Short-term P&L is only one element of performance, but it is an important one, and not just when the trader has complete control of his trades and positions. Equally important is performance when responsibilities are shared. Group evaluation is very useful.

6. *Cooperation.* In most trading organizations, traders can and should contribute to the overall operation of the business. This might involve sharing observations and ideas with other traders, training junior people, and working with sales people to help generate profitable order flow.

COMPENSATION

Most employee option traders receive salaries and annual bonuses. When times are good, a bonus can be a very substantial portion of a trader's income. Consequently, the magnitudes of bonuses, and the processes by which they are determined, can be controversial and even counterproductive.

In the minds of many traders, the concept should be simple. They tend to believe that profits come from their own skills and decisions, and that organizational support has a minor impact. They want a salary plus a large percentage of the profits of their trading. They don't want to participate in any losses (that's beyond the limit of their role as entrepreneurs), they don't want to be subject to supervisory discretion, and they don't want to hear about financial problems elsewhere in the organization. They want the bonus formula to be determined in advance. They certainly don't want a big surprise at bonus time.

An employer might see the situation very differently. The employer might think that the trader's P&L is not a perfect measure of his performance as an employee. He might want to relate the bonus to all six of the performance evaluation considerations identified earlier in this chapter. He might also be constrained by the reality that the capability to pay large bonuses is related to profitability in other areas of the organization.

While this employer's view might make some managerial discretion seem appropriate, it doesn't justify a system that keeps the employee completely in the dark. Before the year begins, a trader can be given an exact list of the criteria to be used in determining his bonus. He also can receive a mid-year review so he knows how he's doing with respect to each criterion.

As the years go by, more bonus systems seem to move toward this employer's view. Some firms still seek out "hired guns," but many firms have business plans that require cooperation among traders within a group, between traders and salespeople, between traders and customers, and so on. Many firms have been unhappy with their experiences with traders who might produce good profits for a while, but then move along to the next high bidder, possibly after collecting some big bonuses and then sticking the employer with some losses. They would rather attract longer term employees, and pay them partly for what they can control (i.e., the *process*). Of course, a hot trader claims he controls the P&L, but he doesn't—he only influences it.

Although this employer's view makes a lot of sense, it cannot always be implemented. When the market for good traders is tight, employers can find themselves offering pay structures that they don't like, simply in responding to competitive forces.

Here are a few more questions relating to trader compensation:

■ *Should trader bonuses be capped? Is it necessary to keep a hot trader from receiving pay that is "completely out of line" with the incomes of senior nontrading people? If a trader really makes a lot of money, isn't it likely that he was just lucky or that he took too much risk?*

Answer: There are two ways to make a trader feel that he has no incentive to make additional profits. One is to cap his bonus. The other is to let one year's successes make future bonuses harder to achieve. Neither is a good idea.

It is not always the case, however, that big profits should be rewarded. Sometimes, very large gains are the result of extraordinary luck. Others result from excessive risk taking. Good managers become very suspicious when results are too good, but capping bonuses is a weak way of managing these circumstances. If a trader takes too much risk, the boss should know about it, and put a stop to it immediately. Later, at bonus time, he should reduce the discretionary part of the bonus. Likewise, if a trader had some extraordinary luck, this event should be known and addressed directly in setting bonuses.

■ *Should consistency of performance be considered in setting bonuses?*

Answer: Generally no. As discussed in *P&L expectations,* a position trader who makes money every day is to be suspected. It is likely that he has been involved in positions or trading patterns that favor frequent profits and ignore long-term average profitability and/or a potential nuclear bomb. It is also likely that he has recorded the profits by finding or causing an imperfection in the accounting process.

■ *What can an employer do about the "trader's option," that is, about the trader's view that he can "roll the dice" because he will participate in big profits, but, with big losses, his only exposure is getting fired?*

Answer: There is no single solution to this problem. The most important steps are managerial, not mathematical. It is important to manage the risk, but also the *people* and the *process.* It would help if the employer could pay bonuses based on longer term performance, as well as on short term performance. If a trader were to get a bonus based partly on three-year results, he might notice that, after he gets ahead, he participates in losses as well as gains. While such bonus plans are not yet commonplace, they could become so as the business continues to mature.

■ *If a trader gets an annual bonus, and incurs losses early in the year, there is an incentive problem. He probably can't make much money unless he "goes for broke." Alternatively, there is a real incentive to quit and start over with another employer. How should this be handled?*

Answer: If an employer really wants to keep a trader in such a situation, it has to be ready to be flexible. It might offer a "reset" with a smaller expected percentage payout. This approach sounds a lot like some of the strike price adjustments that some new high-tech firms made in executive stock options after their stock prices collapsed in 2000 and 2001. It should be used rarely and only for people who seem important to the firm in the *long run.*

Using Options
in a Business

Speculative Trading Principles

To an options neophyte, nothing seems simpler than using an option position to take advantage of a directional view on an underlying instrument. All you have to do is to figure out which way the underlying instrument will go, and then pick out an option position that will make good money if you're "right" and won't lose too much if you're "wrong."

In practice, this kind of use of options involves a complex combination of views and tradeoffs. We'll use a simple example to illustrate a few of them.

EXAMPLE 1

Assume the British pound sterling (£) trades for $1.6000, and 3-month forward sterling also trades for $1.6000. A 3-month call with a $1.6000 strike trades for $0.0300. You could buy the call to take advantage of a bullish view. Alternatively, you could buy the pound forward. If you hold your position for 3 months, you face a simple P&L profile.

P&L at Expiration $

£	Call	Forward
1.45	−0.0300	−0.1500
1.50	−0.0300	−0.1000
1.55	−0.0300	−0.0500
1.60	−0.0300	—
1.65	+0.0200	+0.0500
1.70	+0.0700	+0.1000
1.75	+0.1200	+0.1500

Let's look at a few issues that might be of concern to a buyer of this call.

1. *What will you say to the boss in 3 months?*

If the pound is at $1.70 in 3 months, you will tell the boss that this was a brilliant trade. After all, you've made $0.0700 (a 233% profit on a $0.0300 exposure). On the other hand, if the pound is at $1.50 in 3 months, you will also say it was a good trade. You cleverly took your long position with a call instead of with the £ forward. The option "saved" $0.0700.

This approach to trade evaluation is based on a *double yardstick*. As is often the case in option speculation or hedging, we have two alternative performance measures:

■ How much money did the trade make (or lose)?
■ How did the trade perform, compared to an alternative trade (in this case, £ forward)?

If you wait to pick your yardstick until you have seen the results, you improve your chances of calling the trade a winner (of course, with the pound between $1.57 and $1.63, you lose with either yardstick).

If your boss is exceptionally stupid or if he doesn't pay attention, you might get away with this once or twice. If he goes for it more than once or twice, you might ask yourself if you should look for a better boss.

2. *What will the boss say to you in 3 months?*

If the pound is at $1.70 in 3 months, the boss will tell you it was a foolish trade. If you had just bought forward, you would have made $0.1000. The option trade was a waste of $0.0300. On the other hand, if the pound is at $1.50 in 3 months, the boss will call the trade a complete loser (you lost 100% of your "investment"). The boss can use the double yardstick on you just as easily as you can use it on him.

The double yardstick is one of the many manifestations of human weakness that are so visible in our business. Its overt and covert uses are widespread. It leads to bad trades, and bad relationships. The obvious solution seems simple: Decide on a yardstick before the trade and get everybody to agree. In practice, this can't always be done, especially in organizations that are new to options and in organizations that live with their own external multiple yardsticks. My advice is even simpler: Always remember that the double yardstick is lurking. Be realistic about it. Don't imagine or pretend that there is magic in options that can defeat the fallacy of this kind of thinking.

3. *What is the probability of making money on this option trade?*

It's probably not very good. The pound would have to be above $1.63 in 3 months. Even though you are bullish, you might not put a high probability on such a net positive move (I don't suppose you are always right on your directional views).

4. *What is the probability of outperforming the forward trade?*

Obviously, you would see this probability as being quite low. The pound would have to be below $1.57 in 3 months.

5. *What is the probability of making money on the trade and outperforming the forward trade?*

It can't happen.

6. *What is the probability of losing money on the trade and underperforming the forward?*

What are the chances that the pound will be between $1.57 and $1.63 in 3 months? 20%? 30%? 40%?

REPETITIVE CALL PURCHASES

To buy the call in the above example, a trader accepts:

■ A high probability of losing money
■ A high probability of underperforming the alternative forward trade
■ No chance to perform well against both yardsticks
■ A real possibility of losing against both yardsticks

Does this make him a fool? Not necessarily. Suppose he made the same transaction three different times and the pound finished at:

■ $1.50 the first time
■ $1.60 the second time
■ $1.70 the third time

His results are displayed in Table 14.1.

TABLE 14.1 Buy Call for $0.0300 or Forward for $1.6000

£ at Expiration	Call P&L	Forward P&L
$1.50	−$0.0300	−$0.1000
1.60	−0.0300	—
1.70	+0.0700	+0.1000
	+0.0100	—

In this example, the trader lost money on two of the three trades. He underperformed the alternative forward trade on two of the three trades. In the aggregate, however, he made money and outperformed the forward. Here is a clear example of the distinction that was made in Chapter 1 between a trade that is likely to do well once, and a trade that is likely to do well on average. A statistically passive (see Chapter 1) trader might buy the option and live with the short-term frustration.

One feature of the option trade that seems attractive is its limited loss potential. It is clear that, although this call trade is likely to lose money, it will never lose more than $0.0300—and sometimes it will win big. Likewise, this call trade is likely to underperform the forward trade, but never by more than $0.0300—and it might outperform by a lot. Beware! This kind of exposure profile can encourage a *trade orientation* that can be just as dangerous as the "probability of winning" trap. As discussed in Chapter 3, a trader needs a *price orientation* if he wants to come out ahead on average.

Table 14.2 illustrates the nature of price sensitivity for a speculative trader. In this case, the trader must pay $0.0400 for the call instead of $0.0300. Notice that, as in Table 14.1, the trade is a loser in two out of three instances using either yardstick. You can see, however, that although the extra $0.0100 doesn't have much effect on the probability of winning, its cumulative effect can be to turn a long-term winner into a long-term

TABLE 14.2 Buy Call for $0.0400 or Forward for $1.6000

£ at Expiration	Call P&L	Forward P&L
$1.50	−$0.0400	−$0.1000
1.60	−0.0400	—
1.70	+0.0600	+0.1000
	−0.0200	—

loser. To the trader, this means that the extra $0.0100 probably won't be noticed if the trade is made once, but, in the long term, price can be very important. This is an example of the *short-term invisibility of the edge* that was discussed in the roulette example in Chapter 3.

In Table 14.3, we see the impact of actual volatility on the attractiveness of the option trade. In this case, the call price is $0.0300 as in Table 14.1 but the net changes in the pound price are smaller.

In Table 14.3, as in Table 14.1, the call trade lost money two times out of three and underperformed the forward trade two times out of three. In Table 14.1 the call still performed well on average because the sterling price move to $1.70 produced a $0.0700 profit, and the move to $1.50 produced a $0.0700 outperformance of the forward trade. In Table 14.3, the absence of big underlying price moves made the call a net loser as measured by either yardstick.

How Should You Think about These Three Tables?

If you buy the call once, your evaluation of the results will probably depend mostly on the direction of the pound's move and on the yardstick you choose to use. In contrast, if you are in the business of buying these calls, over time your average result will depend primarily on the *future actual volatility* of the pound. The direction of the moves and the yardstick will probably become less important.

The arithmetic in these tables is simple and well known. Consequently, it is natural to assume that, if most people expect the kind of future actual volatility shown in Table 14.3, then they would not pay $0.0300 for the call and its price would go down. In fact, you might assume that, if the market has priced the call at $0.0300, the market "consensus" must be that we're likely to experience a sterling market that is a little less volatile than the kind of action displayed in Table 14.1. In contrast, if the call price is $0.0400, then "they" must think we're going to see

TABLE 14.3 Buy Call for $0.0300 or Forward for $1.6000

£ at Expiration	Call P&L	Forward P&L
$1.55	−$0.0300	−$0.0500
1.60	−0.0300	—
1.65	+0.0200	+0.0500
	−0.0400	—

more future actual volatility than we see in Table 14.1. Now, of course, we're talking about *current implied volatility* (as discussed in Chapter 6). In a crude way, we're looking at an option price and asking: What kind of future actual volatility expectation would make that price reasonable in a statistical sense?

What Volatilities Matter for This Trade?

The answer depends on whether you are watching the results or making the decision. If you make a series of these call purchases, your results are likely to look good against either yardstick if the future actual volatility of the underlying currency turns out to be higher than the implied volatility of the options when you bought them. However, when you have to make a decision to buy the call, you don't yet know the future actual volatility of the pound. Hence, you should make an *actual volatility forecast* and compare it to the current implied volatility. If your forecast is higher than the current implied, there is an expected profit (in a statistical sense) in the call trade. If your forecast is lower, you would have an expected loss.

It is important to remember that it is the *relationship* between the current implied volatility and your actual volatility forecast that determines your *edge*. You *don't* get an edge by buying an option simply because you expect unusually high future actual volatility. That expectation might already be priced into your option's implied volatility. Likewise, you *don't* get an edge simply by buying an option with an implied volatility that is low on a historical basis (i.e., low compared to *historical actual* or *historical implied*). You should make an actual volatility forecast and compare it to the current implied volatility.

The Transactional Nature of Option Decisions

Options frequently appeal to the natural human tendency to try to get something for nothing. Options are often presented as vehicles to limit your risk without giving up your upside, or as ways to "enhance your income" (implicitly, without giving anything up). Common sense tells us that the markets won't give up something for nothing. Rather, the nature of options is *transactional*. In every trade we get something and we give something up. The key is to recognize the entirety of the transaction and to make sure we get what we need and give up only what we can afford. Thinking clearly about these issues can be much more difficult if we have a weakness for a double yardstick.

DECISION CHECKLIST

Here is a list of considerations for someone who is thinking about buying this call and holding it until expiration:

1. What yardstick? Remember the call will underperform the forward when you are "right" on direction.
2. Are you more concerned about your performance *on this trade* or your performance *on average?*
3. Is there an option edge? That is, is the current implied volatility lower than your actual volatility forecast? Is it *low enough,* in light of the uncertainty in your forecast?
4. If your option edge is positive, you still might be giving up too much in terms of risk. What kinds of P&L variation (based on your yardstick) are likely, and are you willing to accept them to get the edge? It is not easy to make this kind of "apples and oranges" comparison, but you need to address this issue.
5. If your edge is negative, are you getting enough risk management benefits to make the trade worthwhile? You might consider how much "edge" there is in your directional view.
6. Do you have a personal *trade orientation* that is influencing your answer to any of these questions (especially 3 and 5)? Remember, a trade orientation is normally a weakness unless you are using options for risk management and you don't care very much about profitability.
7. What are the risk versus risk tradeoffs and do you like them? In this case, compared to the forward trade, the option reduces your exposure to a sterling price collapse, but introduces a new exposure: time decay. Because these two different exposures have no common units, it is probably not appropriate to think in terms of increasing or decreasing your risk. You've really exchanged one kind of risk for another. Such tradeoffs are very common in the options business.

This last consideration is very difficult for senior corporate executives who like to say things like "We don't use derivatives to speculate. We just use them to reduce risk." Often, their business exposures are much too complex to justify such a simplistic view. If you think about it, you might agree that this one-dimensional view of risk comes from the same kind of fantasizing that can produce a vulnerability to a double yardstick.

A CLASSIC YARDSTICK MESS: CORPORATE PUT SELLING

Suppose you are a senior executive at PQR, a high-growth, high-tech company. Your stock has performed extremely well for the last 10 years, increasing from a split adjusted $1 per share to today's price of $80 per share. It's 55% annualized compound rate of return includes a spectacular move in the most recent 12 months, during which PQR's stock price has doubled. The company has never paid a cash dividend and it has no plans to pay one.

The only negative aspect of the stock price appreciation has involved the firm's employee stock option program. For many years, PQR has granted stock options to key employees. Some of these options have already been exercised, but most are still outstanding. Of the outstanding options, some have been granted in the past year and have exercise prices of $50 to $70, but many more have very low exercise prices. In the past, PQR has been hesitant to dilute its stock by issuing new shares to deliver upon option exercise. Instead, it has purchased shares in the open market. However, as the stock price has risen and the number of outstanding options has grown, management has become increasingly concerned about both the P&L effects and the cash requirements of this approach.

You have heard a lot of talk that firms with similar problems have made a great deal of money by selling puts on their stock. One of your subordinates has suggested that PQR should do the same. Since your stock has been very volatile, it is possible to sell options with IVs in the high 50s. Your subordinate thinks this would be a great way to "monetize the volatility." Specifically, he thinks you should sell some one-year European-style puts with an exercise price of $70. The put price would be $10 per share. In a year, you might be assigned on the puts, but you agree with him that getting assigned to buy some stock at $70 looks attractive right now. Furthermore, he points out that, with a $10 put premium, you would really be buying the stock for $60.

At first glance, it might seem that there are four possibilities here, and they are all good:

1. PQR stock might keep rising, in which case the firm would make $10 per share to reduce the cost of buying stock.
2. In a year, PQR's stock could be between $70 and $80, the put would expire worthless, the firm would make $10 per share, and it could buy its stock for less than today's price.

A CLASSIC YARDSTICK MESS: CORPORATE PUT SELLING (Continued)

3. In a year, the stock might be between $60 and $70 and the firm would effectively buy the stock for $60, less than today's price and less than the price on the exercise date.
4. In a year, the stock price might be below $60. Then, the firm would have bought the stock at $60, which is $20 better than today's price. In addition, this stock price decline would take the pressure off of *all* of the firm's employee stock option exposure, an amount significantly greater than the number of shares involved in this put sale.

A put selling program might seem sophisticated, exciting, and fun, and you might take courage from the knowledge that some really important firms are doing it. You might also notice some troubling issues:

1. Is this a hedge or a speculation? It seems that it is a hedge against the firm's exposure, but if people are boasting about how much money their trades have made, this sounds like speculation. Maybe it is some kind of an exchange of risk—whatever that means.
2. When we talk about this, it sounds like we've found some free money (or riskless profit). We know there's none of that lying around.
3. The truth is that PQR has had short call exposure for a long time, and the stock has moved a long way against the position. Is this an attempt to make the past untrue?
4. The firms that talk about their successes have all made money because their stock prices have risen and the puts have expired worthless. Is this just a disguised directional bet?
5. Selling out of the money options is usually a way to take big remote risk while getting a high probability of a small profit. Is this simply a trade that seems attractive because it works most of the time.
6. So far, no one has said a word about *edge*.

THE DOUBLE YARDSTICK

At a minimum, this kind of put selling program has a double yardstick problem. Certainly, it would not be a surprise for the stock price to increase or decrease by a factor of two in a year. If the stock price doubles again in the next 12 months, the firm will talk about the $10 per share

(continued)

A CLASSIC YARDSTICK MESS: CORPORATE PUT SELLING (Continued)

profit on the short puts and will ignore the fact that it is paying $160 for stock that could have been bought $80 cheaper. If the stock price drops to $40, the firm will not publicly discuss the $20 per share loss on the puts. Instead, it will switch yardsticks and call the trade a success since it resulted in an effective purchase price of $60 per share instead of today's $80.

EXTRA WRINKLES

As is usually the case in real-world multiple yardstick situations, there are a few more things to think about:

1. Part of the rationalization for this trade is that the decision maker would like to buy the stock at 70. But a year is a long time. What if, in the first three months, the firm's business takes a turn for the worse and the stock drops to 70. You might have changed your mind about wanting to buy it there. Too bad! You're short a put with a mark-to-market loss. The position has a lot of risk and not necessarily enough profit opportunity.
2. What if the stock price drops to 60 and then rises to 120? Too bad, again! Because you were short the put, you missed your chance to buy the stock at 70.
3. Is a high actual volatility for the stock good for this program? At first glance, it seems to be because it is likely to produce a high implied volatility which the put sale can "monetize." After a while, this thought process might not seem very good. Suppose after a year, the stock price is $160. Then, the firm has made $10 on the put (and called it a success), but it has to buy the stock for $160 per share. Next, it might sell a new one-year put ($140 exercise price) for $20 per share. After another year the stock price might be $100. Now, even the double yardstick can't save the program. In two years, the stock price has increased by 25%, the puts have shown a net loss of $10 per share (a $10 profit in the first year and a $20 loss in the second), and the firm had to buy stock at $160, instead of the initial price of $80 or the current price of $100. Of course, this series of events might look even worse if the firm increases its size in the second year (based on the first year's "success").

A CLASSIC YARDSTICK MESS: CORPORATE PUT SELLING (Continued)

4. What if the stock price declines so far that employees never exercise their stock options? Most likely, the firm will buy back the puts at a big loss. Maybe, put exercises will force the firm into a major stock buyback at terrible prices. In either event, the result is likely to drain a lot of the firm's cash at a time when it can't spare it.

ONE VIEW OF THE POSITION

It seems that, if it adopts this kind of put selling program, PQR will have hedged some short calls with some short puts. That might not seem like the world's best hedge, and the special situation of PQR makes it even more disturbing. For example, normally, someone who is short a call is happy when the underlying stock price goes down. In this case, however, if it goes down very far, no one at XYZ will be happy. The firm will probably be doing poorly, and the employees will be dissatisfied with their financial situation. The firm won't really have a short call benefit to offset the short put loss.

Think about this position in terms of *everyday risk* and *remote risk* as described in Chapter 8. The put sale does help reduce the everyday risk of a small stock price increase, but it does very little for the remote risk of a large increase. It also adds a new remote risk problem in its exposure to a stock price collapse. Unfortunately, a stock price collapse is already a bad event for PQR, and the put sale adds to it. In summary, from a risk management point of view, the put sale makes sense only if the firm wants to reduce its everyday risk and doesn't want to address its remote risk.

If this risk profile is less than desirable, maybe the firm can still justify put selling on a *profitability* basis. (Remember Chapter 3?) To be consistent with the analysis of the present chapter, this would make sense only if the firm had made an actual volatility forecast and found that it was significantly lower than the put's current implied volatility. (Such a forecast wouldn't necessarily have to be made within the rigid concept of volatility described in Chapter 6, but some view on a probability distribution of stock price movements must be addressed.) I wonder how many corporate put sellers do that. I also wonder how much edge should be enough, given the remote risk problems.

(continued)

A CLASSIC YARDSTICK MESS: CORPORATE PUT SELLING (Continued)

WHAT SHOULD PQR DO?

PQR should recognize that an issued stock option is a nonlinear dilution, and that it is (and should be) a drag on the stock price's upward movement. There is no perfect risk management approach to this situation, and the appropriate action of the firm depends on the profile of outstanding options, the firm's tolerance for everyday risk and for remote risk, and a variety of volatility considerations. For sure there is no free money here, there is no way to negate the value of the outstanding options, and while there might be *some* edge, no trade orientation is likely to produce *consistent* edge.

PQR needs some expert advice that begins with first principles and includes some very specific descriptions of expectations and priorities. While no single hedging structure is "correct," I suggest that, in this example, a good one would be likely to include:

- Some long stock.
- Some short options with exercise prices close to $80.
- Some long options with exercise prices well above $80 and some other long options with exercise prices well below $80.

No sensible structure will produce "option magic." The spectacular "profits" often associated with put selling programs are usually the result of one-way stock markets and/or double yardsticks. However, a sensible structure can produce a little risk management and a modest positive edge. Alternatively, it might produce a little more risk management and a modest negative edge. Notice that the term *risk management* is used here rather than *risk reduction* since, in this multidimensional nonlinear situation, it is likely that there will be some "exchange of risk" in which one or more of the many option risks will actually be increased.

CHAPTER 15

Hedger Motivation and Behavior

In the markets for options on financial instruments, there are two major categories of hedgers:

1. Corporate treasury people who seek to manage the exposure of a firm's assets and liabilities
2. Investors who seek to manage the risk and/or improve the performance of financial assets

The people in these two categories might have different job definitions and different day-to-day concerns. Sometimes they even seem to speak different languages. Often, however, they have much in common in terms of the business issues, management influences, and personal tendencies that affect their behavior. This chapter explores some of these important behavioral influences. Their application to specific trading decisions will be discussed in Chapter 16 and Chapter 17.

BUSINESS ISSUES

Competitive Environment

Many businesses feel the pressure of corporate double yardsticks. They need to produce good profits at reasonable risk for their investors or owners. They also need to outperform their competitors. These needs can produce real conflicts. For example, a competitor might manage exposure in a way that is irresponsible with respect to remote risk, but which is likely to produce good short-term results. In the competitive world of investment management, customers can pay a lot more attention to recent performance than to "loser's talk" about what might have happened. Later, when these customers get hurt, the responsible investment manager rarely benefits.

In the world of corporate hedgers, this particular problem should be less severe. Minor firm-to-firm performance differences seem less dramatic.

For a corporate hedger, the competitive performance focus should be on the possibility that it will underperform by enough to impact its position in the industry. For example, severe increases in crude oil prices in 1999 and 2000 put financial pressure on airlines, for which jet fuel costs are a significant P&L ingredient. Some tried to collect fuel cost surcharges from customers. Others boasted of the savings produced by their hedging programs. But what about airlines that initiated hedges when prices were near their peaks? Later, with lower jet fuel prices, how could they compete with their irresponsible competitors who gambled on price declines and won? Maybe an option hedge would be a good compromise in such a market.

Very Specific Performance Expectations

An equity investment manager might feel that it is extremely important to outperform the S&P 500 index. He might feel that, if he underperforms, he'll lose his customers. If he overperforms, even slightly, he might keep them and attract more. There might be little additional benefit for substantial overperformance. With this frame of mind, there can be tremendous pressure to maximize the probability of reaching the threshold level of profitability. With options there are often ways to maximize this probability at the price of accepting negative edge and/or unreasonable risk. It can be easy to be irresponsible with the customer's money if it gives the firm a chance to be successful.

A comparable example for corporate hedgers would involve the need to meet the consensus earnings forecast of stock analysts. In the late 1990s, it became common for even small negative earnings surprises to produce massive stock selloffs. In this environment, there are plenty of opportunities to be irresponsible with options in order to give the company a chance to meet or beat the consensus number.

General Need for Trading Profits

Sometimes, a business doesn't seem to be profitable enough without a contribution from speculative trading. For a corporate hedger, that might mean "selective hedging" in which it leaves part of an exposure unhedged if someone has a directional view. It might mean "partial hedging" where an option hedge reduces or limits the risk, but leaves some opportunity for profit (or loss). It might also mean finding some option edge in an attempt to add an increment of profit.

A comparable situation for an investment manager would be one in which the returns in his financial assets can't be expected to, on average, produce enough profits. Then, like the corporate hedger, he might need to

I NEED A PROFIT—NOW

I once had a conversation with a friend named Jerry, a sole proprietor market maker in Chicago, who was feeling a little depressed. It was shortly after a major stock option expiration and Jerry had lost quite a bit of money because he had sold some short dated calls and the stock had rallied through the strike price. Jerry said: "I should have known better. They weren't even that expensive, but I figured if I didn't sell them I wouldn't have anything coming in this quarter."

If Jerry could irresponsibly risk his own money in order to meet a P&L target, imagine how easy it is to fall into that trap when you are risking someone else's money. A person who *must* reach a particular financial objective in the short-run might do some amazing things to give himself a chance. Most of these things are not good for his employer or investor.

find some option edge, even if that means taking more risk (against some yardstick). In practice, it is not surprising for a firm to expect too much profitability from options, and then to slip into some of the irresponsible behavior described earlier.

Emphasis on Consistency in Reported Performance

For either an investment manager or a corporate hedger, an aversion to random performance ups and downs can diminish the flexibility to respond to positive or negative edge considerations. Furthermore, the apparent "unfairness" of various accounting rules can actually discourage risk management in cases where sensible trades would be likely to produce erratic short-term reported results.

Options "Imbedded" in the Business

Often, in the normal course of their business, firms have nonlinear exposures that resemble options. Usually, these imbedded option exposures are concave; that is, they resemble short options. A classic example can occur when a firm makes an offer to buy a foreign company in a foreign currency. While the offer is open, the firm is "short" the equivalent of a currency option, and it is probably also "short" the equivalent of an interest rate option. A rarer example of a "long" imbedded option would occur if a firm had production facilities in countries with different currencies and it could easily switch production volumes among them.

Investment managers often deal in nonlinear instruments such as convertible or callable bonds. These are more easily recognizable as *option positions that need to be managed.*

Performance Measurement Problems

A mutual fund might pay its dividends on the basis of *realized* P&L rather than on its total return. Such a practice (which is very common) can put tremendous pressure on managers to maximize the probability of a good *realized* return at the expense of risk, edge, or even *certain* reductions in total return.

A comparable situation for a corporate hedger would take place if a firm put excessive emphasis on the amount of money "spent" for option premium. The hedger might find hedges that produced more risk and a worse edge, but didn't require much option premium "expenditure." In most cases, however, this problem is not a result of the business the firm is in, but rather the result of management policy. Then it would be more properly included next as a problem of management influences.

MANAGEMENT INFLUENCES

It is rare that a hedger receives a clear and consistent statement of management objectives and priorities. Often there are policy documents written with language that doesn't reflect the realities of the process.

Sometimes, management's day-to-day behavior reflects an unstated fantasy that options should provide a way to get something for nothing. Because of the difficulty of communicating in short discussions about options, it is not uncommon for a hedger to feed that fantasy by saying what the boss wants to hear. The failure of that concept can motivate a boss to micromanage the hedging process or to occasionally attack with a double yardstick.

Of course, the opposite can be the case. Good management can establish sensible procedures and limits, measure performance with appropriate yardsticks against reasonable benchmarks, and provide a "coaching" function that can help the hedger make decisions, help him grow in his job, and help him deal with his personal weaknesses.

There are two major areas of concern where a hedger will receive management guidance. This guidance might be formal or informal, clear or

WHO'S THE REAL BOSS?

In a discussion of the double yardstick problem at one of my seminars for corporate option users, a foreign exchange hedger for a large U.S. exporter made the following comment:

> *My direction doesn't come from within the company. It comes from the securities analysts. All of the analysts know that we are big receivers of foreign currencies, and, if the dollar weakens, they expect us to profit from it. On the other hand, if the dollar strengthens, they don't expect us to get hurt.*

Without further information, this might sound like a ridiculous set of expectations, and an invitation to wild gambling. It is not uncommon for hedgers to be put in such a situation. In this case, however, I suggested to the hedger that she might have a single yardstick. Maybe her performance should simply be compared to that of someone who is always long at-the-money puts against her assets.

murky, and consistent or inconsistent. It will be communicated in major meetings, casual conversations, and, especially, in the compensation system.

The Firm's Appetite for Speculation

Some corporates view hedging as a staff function for which the only justification is risk reduction. Others expect sensible risk management, but want some increment of profit (although the word *profit* might not be used). Still others want "profit center" trading. Sometimes, there are sensible performance measures and clear, reasonable tolerances for the risks that must be accepted as the price of getting some edge. In other cases, managements are not able to be statistically passive (see Chapter 1) enough.

One disturbing practice is to assign "budget rates" for individual cash flows that are to be hedged. Although there are some good reasons for this practice, the problem is obvious. When the budget rate is easy to meet, the hedger feels entitled to gamble with the extra money. When the budget rate is difficult to achieve, the hedger feels required to gamble to achieve it. If the hedger worked for me, I'd want him to gamble only when he had substantial edge, and the size of the gamble wouldn't have anything to do with the characteristics of a particular cash flow.

Investment firms are usually more open and straightforward about these issues. They know that they are in the business of speculating, and they know that not every trade will be successful. However, management people sometimes have difficulty understanding the expected returns and performance characteristics of options trading programs. As a result, they can be unaware of the quality of the opportunities that are available during a particular time period. They can also err in promoting their programs and in evaluating the performances of their people.

The Firm's Tolerance for Everyday Risk and Remote Risk

The day will probably come when investors and corporate hedgers will measure option risk with something like the framework and attitude described in Chapter 12 for dealer risk management. In the year 2001, that is still too much to hope for. At the present time, most firms consider themselves to be prudent and sophisticated if they use a *value at risk* (VAR) program. While VAR programs vary, they are usually relatively crude ways of looking at exposure to events that are more unusual than everyday events, but not remote enough to indicate anything about exposure to real catastrophes. In a multidimensional nonlinear business like options, they leave a lot of unaddressed risk gaps, but they are better than nothing as long as the user doesn't really think they solve his risk management problem.

In practice, if a firm has decent mark to market accounting, the problem of communicating everyday risk tolerance can take care of itself. Eventually, management will express its approval or disapproval of the sizes of the day-to-day P&L swings. Hedgers should be able to adapt. The bigger problem is in dealing with remote risk. Even experienced practitioners have trouble coming to grips with remote risk tolerance. Most remote events have unknown probabilities and we don't really know how to decide which ones to worry about or how severely we should limit our exposures to them. Unfortunately, the result of all of this uncertainty is that often remote risk doesn't get managed at all. The examples in Chapter 8 demonstrated that there can be some surprises when unusual events take place, and those examples are quite tame. Management teams that don't squarely address remote risk tolerance will inevitably get a very unpleasant surprise.

Management should specify some sample remote events, identify specific dollar exposure limits to those events, and measure the ongoing exposure on a day-to-day basis. If it doesn't do this (and most don't), its normal day to day behavior is likely to *encourage* people to take big remote risk. Every conversation about performance, every motivational speech, and every expression of confidence in the trader can have the effect of making disastrous events seem less likely and less a matter of concern.

PERSONAL TENDENCIES

For either a hedger or his manager, nothing matches the challenge of dealing with unstated personal biases. Sometimes, these biases come from the hedger's experiences in the market (often, our memories are too long or too short). In other cases, decisions are influenced by personality characteristics that belonged to the hedger long before he made his first option trade. Regardless of the cause, we all have personal tendencies that affect our trading behavior. The more introspective traders can discover them, be embarrassed by them, and deal with them. Some tendencies to watch for are discussed next.

Excessive Trade Orientation

Chapter 3 described the tendency of many traders to gravitate toward favored positions, regardless of the positive or negative edges they might offer. When risk management is the purpose of an option trade, it might make sense to favor the position that best manages the risk, even if the edge is negative. Usually, however, there are alternative positions that offer different edges as well as different risk management characteristics.

For hedgers, there are three major categories of trade orientation:

1. *Long premium.* Some traders are excessively conscious of the possibility of spectacular market events. They prefer to be long options so that their risk is limited, while they retain the opportunity for big profits. If they pay too much for the options, their hedges will be, on balance, losers. Losing on hedges might be acceptable if they are the price of holding a very attractive underlying instrument (there is nothing wrong with carrying a negative edge fire insurance policy on a profitable factory if holding an uninsured factory would be too risky), but hedgers with strong trade orientations aren't always able to be rational about such tradeoffs. They also can be hesitant to look at alternatives.
2. *Short premium.* There is no getting around the fact that most options go down in price over their lives. If you have a hard time being statistically passive (as described in Chapter 1), you can be constantly

tempted to sell options, even if they are cheap. Often, this tendency is accompanied by a feeling (or fantasy?) on the part of the trader that he will see trouble coming before anything spectacular happens. Sometimes traders like to take too much comfort in expiration P&L curves. They see wide ranges of profitability at expiration and imagine that, if the underlying price breaks out, they'll make an adjustment. Of course, if an adjustment is a real possibility, what's the point of looking at the expiration curve?

3. *Zero premium.* In the mid 1980s, it suddenly became popular to hedge exposures with combinations of trades that had no net debit or credit. Typically, a hedger would hedge an asset by buying some out-of-the-money puts, and would "pay for" the puts by selling some calls (usually also out-of-the-money). Originally, this was a rage among foreign exchange hedgers who didn't have cash to spend on options, and, in many cases, were willing to imagine that they were getting something for nothing. Often, the hedge contracts were written to make it appear that there were no options involved. Soon, the popularity of these combinations spread to interest rate hedgers, and finally to equity hedgers. While these trades are not necessarily a bad idea, neither are they necessarily a good idea. They don't always do a good job of managing risk, and they often have substantial negative edges which the hedger might ignore because they are "free."

Concept of the Role of Options

Many hedgers don't want to think about option edges. They might even assume that options are always "fairly" priced. They think their edge comes in their directional view for the underlying instrument, and they use options for risk management only. Other hedgers see options as opportunities to "enhance" returns. Some expect attractive option positions to always be available. They would be better off thinking of edges as market inefficiencies that occur occasionally, but not because the hedger wants one.

Ignoring Remote Risk

While there are hedgers who are excessively preoccupied with remote risk, it seems to be more common for hedgers to be too comfortable about unusual events. Sometimes, they just can't imagine the causes or the dynamics of spectacular events. Other times, their desire for good short-term performance pushes remote risk analysis out of their minds or makes them believe they just can't afford to worry about such things.

Weakness for the Double Yardstick

It is just so easy to feel comfortable with a trade if you can see that, if the worst happens, you'll be able to say: "It's still a lot better than if . . ." Opportunities for this sort of fuzzy thinking are endless.

Fantasy of Getting Something for Nothing

Chapter 14 included a discussion of the transactional nature of options. It would be useful if every hedging decision would be preceded by the listing of "what we get" and "what we give up." Often, hedgers can imagine that they are not giving up anything if they are weak enough to fall back on a double yardstick.

Looking for Ways to Avoid Responsibility

Some hedgers are excessively influenced by sales people or by the "experts" who support them. Others want to do trades that "everybody" does or that seem sophisticated. Some even want to rely on government action to make them safe.

This kind of weakness played big roles for many of the losers in the 1987 portfolio insurance disaster, in the 1992 collapse of the British pound sterling, and in the 1998 Long-Term Capital Management melt down.

Trader's Right to Gamble

Many people are attracted to options because they like the "action" and they enjoy trying out their market ideas with real money. Sometimes they imagine themselves to have (unproven) talents that they should exercise. For many hedgers, there is some frustration in the discipline of their roles, and they are good at thinking of excuses to take more risk than they need to take. Many of these excuses fall into two categories:

1. Playing with the house's money. Hedgers who are doing well on a particular position, or are doing well for a particular accounting period can imagine that the profits don't yet belong to their employers or investors. This provides an opportunity for speculation *without the usual constraints*.
2. Getting back a loss. Some people can't accept the fact that a trading or hedging decision didn't work out well. Sometimes, the boss can't accept it. The loss might have resulted from a bad decision, or from a good decision that wasn't a sure thing (such as the dice example of Chapter 1).

Regardless of the reason, it's easy to imagine that the loss isn't real yet, and that having a chance to get it back is more important than the risk of losing more. This kind of attitude can be a serious distraction from the hard-nosed analysis of profitability and risk that is necessary for a successful options business.

Personal Stake in the Risk

It is almost impossible to structure a job so that the hedger trades as if it were his own money. Employers and investors must be vigilant for situations in which the hedger's personal interest is not consistent with his role as a fiduciary.

CHAPTER 16

Positions for Corporate Hedgers

There seems to be an endless list of ways for a business to hedge financial assets or liabilities. In many hedging situations, there can be alternatives that are very different, but perfectly reasonable. No type of hedge is a good solution to all hedging problems.

This chapter explores several categories of hedges. Its objective is not to itemize every possibility, nor to suggest that there is a best solution for any situation. Rather, it is an attempt to provide a feel for the advantages and disadvantages of the alternatives as well as for the thought processes that hedgers might use in making their decisions.

For simplicity, there will be a single example of foreign exchange exposure to a known cash flow (Example 1). It will be assumed that an option

---

EXAMPLE 1

You are a US$ based firm, expecting to receive a £10 million payment in 90 days.

Spot £ at $1.6000
90-day forward £ at $1.6000

90-Day Option	Price	Delta
1.50 Put	$0.0030	8
1.55 Put	0.0100	23
1.60 Put	0.0300	49
1.55 Call	0.0600	77
1.60 Call	0.0300	51
1.65 Call	0.0100	25

We assume that there is no cost of carry of the options, and that early exercise is not permitted.

---

hedge will be held until the expiration date of the option (although, as discussed in Chapter 18, in many cases this is very inappropriate).

SIMPLE HEDGES

First we will consider five alternatives hedges:

1. Sell 90-day forward £
2. Buy 1.60 put at $0.0300
3. Buy 1.55 put at $0.0100
4. Buy 1.60 put at $0.0300 and sell 1.55 put at $0.0100
5. Sell 1.60 call at $0.0300

Table 16.1 displays, for a variety of sterling expiration prices, the profit or loss for each of the alternatives. Table 16.1 does *not* include any gain or loss in the value of the sterling asset.

If the asset were hedged with a 90-day forward, the aggregate position (i.e., the asset and the hedge combined) would have no profit or loss, regardless of the expiration price of the pound. For the alternative option hedges, Table 16.2 displays the profile of aggregate profit or loss for the same expiration prices as in Table 16.1.

In examining Table 16.1 and Table 16.2, it seems that none of these alternatives is clearly the best or worst. Depending on where the price of the pound goes, any of them might produce a relatively good or bad result. By changing from one to another, you get something and you give something

TABLE 16.1   P&L ($MM) on Hedge Trade (at Expiration)

£	S Forward	B 1.60 Put	B 1.55 Put	B 1.60 Put S 1.55 Put	S 1.60 Call
$1.40	+2.0	+1.7	+1.4	+0.3	+0.3
1.45	+1.5	+1.2	+0.9	+0.3	+0.3
1.50	+1.0	+0.7	+0.4	+0.3	+0.3
1.55	+0.5	+0.2	−0.1	+0.3	+0.3
1.60	—	−0.3	−0.1	−0.2	+0.3
1.65	−0.5	−0.3	−0.1	−0.2	−0.2
1.70	−1.0	−0.3	−0.1	−0.2	−0.7
1.75	−1.5	−0.3	−0.1	−0.2	−1.2
1.80	−2.0	−0.3	−0.1	−0.2	−1.7

TABLE 16.2 P&L ($MM) of Option Alternative Compared to Forward Hedge (at Expiration)

£	B 1.60 Put	B 1.55 Put	B 1.60 Put S 1.55 Put	S 1.60 Call
$1.40	−0.3	−0.6	−1.7	−1.7
1.45	−0.3	−0.6	−1.2	−1.2
1.50	−0.3	−0.6	−0.7	−0.7
1.55	−0.3	−0.6	−0.2	−0.2
1.60	−0.3	−0.1	−0.2	+0.3
1.65	+0.2	+0.4	+0.3	+0.3
1.70	+0.7	+0.9	+0.8	+0.3
1.75	+1.2	+1.4	+1.3	+0.3
1.80	+1.7	+1.9	+1.8	+0.3

up. This is a demonstration of the transactional nature of options described in Chapter 14.

In terms of profitability, it is not easy to decide which alternative looks the best. To guess the "average" result, you'd have to assign some probabilities to different sterling prices. This process might feel a lot like making an actual volatility forecast as described in Chapter 6. It is also not easy to rank these alternatives by the acceptability of the risk, but, even without selecting a yardstick, you might think that alternative 4 and alternative 5 look kind of scary. Each of the option alternatives merits some analysis.

1. Buy 1.60 Put at $0.0300

Expiration Dynamics: This is the classic insurance example. For $300,000, the hedger has passed on the risk of a decline in the price of the pound, but retained the potential for unlimited gain from sterling price appreciation.

Hopes and Fears: This is normally the trade of a bullish hedger. Like his personal life insurance policy, he buys it hoping to lose the premium. Unlike his life insurance policy, however, just losing the premium isn't enough. Unless the pound finishes more than $0.0300 higher, he won't be happy with his hedge.

The fear here is that the price of the pound won't go anywhere. The hedger might say that the put was a risk reduction trade. It really produced an *exchange of risk.* He has gotten rid of his unlimited exposure but has taken on a new risk, that of time decay.

Volatility Considerations: As is normally the case in purchasing a single option, it would help if the put had a low implied volatility. After the hedge, a high actual volatility would help. A big sterling price increase would produce enough profit on the aggregate position that the $300,000 "insurance premium" might seem small. A collapse in the price of the pound would mean that the hedger underperformed the forward hedge by $300,000, but that might not seem like much if the hedge saved $1 million or $2 million of exposure in the asset.

Reasons to Do It: Hedgers have used all of the following reasons for buying puts. You can decide which, if any, are sensible:

- The price is right. That is, the put's IV seems low compared to likely moves in the price of the pound.
- You're bullish, but you can't afford much risk (note that this is a very limited use of the term "risk").
- You need to sleep at night.
- You can't afford to miss the rally (as was the case for the hedger in "Who's the Real Boss," Chapter 15).
- You're "playing with the house's money"; that is, you've been beating your benchmarks and you can "afford" to gamble with $300,000.
- You're behind your benchmark and hedging with the put instead of the forward gives you a chance to catch up.
- Compared to a stop order, a put provides "staying power" for a directional play. You don't have to "cave in" when the market goes against you.

WHAT TRANSACTIONAL NATURE?

The Philadelphia Stock Exchange held its first annual Foreign Exchange Options Symposium in September 1984. It was well attended by bankers, brokers, and even some corporate hedgers. Although almost everyone was new to options, there was a lot of optimism expressed by people who felt both smart and progressive.

One exceptionally enthusiastic speaker was a senior manager at a large New York bank. He was fully committed to FX options. Finally, he said: "We never hedge with forwards anymore. We always use puts, because, with puts, you can have your cake and eat it, too."

I've often wondered what kind of a career in options he had.

■ With a put, you get the best of both worlds—you get protection and unlimited profit potential. (What ever happened to the transactional nature of options?)

Price Sensitivity: Although it seems that the put's IV should be an important consideration, the more desperate or fanciful the hedger's reasoning, the less likely it is that he will be concerned about the option price.

2. Buy 1.55 Put at $0.0100

Expiration Dynamics: While this out-of-the-money (OTM) put "costs" only a third of the price of the at-the-money (ATM) put, from a "worst case" viewpoint, it could be thought of as a riskier trade. If the price of the pound increases significantly, this hedged position will do only $100,000 worse than an unhedged position. On the other hand, for a decline in sterling price, this might not be much protection. The aggregate position is exposed to a possible $600,000 loss, double that of the position with the ATM put hedge.

This is much like "deductible" insurance. Just as you can reduce the premium payments for health or fire insurance by "self-insuring" up to a certain level, the hedger in this example can "reduce" the "cost" of his put by self-insuring the first $0.0500 of the exposure.

Hopes and Fears: Once again, someone using this put for a hedge is probably very bullish on the price of the pound. You would be likely to use this hedge only if you thought that the put price would almost surely go to zero.

Your big fear in this case would be a 90-day $0.0500 decline in the underlying price. Then, there would be a $500,000 loss in the value of the sterling asset, and a $100,000 loss on the "protection" that didn't help.

Volatility Considerations: Generally, you might expect this trade to look best if the pound exhibited high future actual volatility, especially if it came on the up side. However, if the pound moved slowly upward to $1.62 or $1.63 over 90 days, you might feel pretty good about this trade, especially compared to the 1.60 put.

Reasons to Do It:

■ You don't want to hedge at all. This meets the minimum requirements.
■ A decline in the price of the pound is unlikely, but, if it happens, it could be big (this might be the view of a technical analyst).

- You are quite sure there won't be a big collapse in the price, but, if it happened, and you were unhedged, it would devastate the firm (there can be an admirable humility behind this attitude).
- Budget considerations require low "hedging costs." (There really are executives who think nothing of an extra $500,000 of "deductible" exposure, but think of an extra $200,000 in option premium as an irresponsible expense.)

Price Sensitivity: Is this trade a good idea when IVs are low? Maybe. If IVs are low, the option is cheap and you probably aren't very worried about the downside; but, if IVs are low, the 1.60 put is probably cheap and you won't "save" much by self-insuring the first $0.0500.

In practice, this trade is not usually motivated by price sensitivity. The motivations driving it can be organizational or can be related to a perceived edge in your directional view on the pound that can overwhelm the edge in the option.

3. Buy 1.60 Put at $0.0300 and Sell 1.55 Put at $0.0100

Expiration Dynamics: This put *bear spread* is a lot like capped insurance. In buying health or fire insurance, if you don't want to take a deductible, you might reduce your premium payment by accepting a "cap" on the insurer's liability. Then you self-insure for losses in excess of the cap.

Here, the insurance coverage is limited to the first $0.0500 net sterling price decline. If you show Table 16.2 to your boss, he might think this doesn't look like much of a hedge. If you are a schemer, you might show it to him without the top row or two.

Hopes and Fears: Once again, this is a hedge that is likely to be used by someone who is looking for a big increase in the price of the pound. Your *big* fear is probably a sterling price collapse into the self-insured zone, but you have paid $200,000 for this hedge and, after a while, you might notice a time-decay problem.

Volatility Considerations: In this example, with the strike prices relatively close together, the general level of IV is not very important in determining the price of the spread. That is because the vega of the 1.60 put that you are long is not much greater than the vega of the 1.55 put that you are short. However, the data in Table 16.3 demonstrate that the price of the spread is more sensitive to changes in the *difference* in the IVs of the two puts. In this case, the IV is 9.47 for the 1.60 put and 9.04 for the 1.55 put.

TABLE 16.3 Put Prices and IVs

	Example 1 Price	Both IVs = 9.47 Price	Both IVs = 11.30 Price
1.60 Put	$0.0300 (IV = 9.47)	$0.0300	$0.0358
1.55 Put	0.0100 (IV = 9.04)	0.0111	0.0158
Spread	$0.0200	$0.0189	$0.0200

If both options had IVs of 9.47, their prices would be about $0.0300 and $0.0111, and the price of the spread would be about $0.0189 instead of $0.0200. That is, the 0.43 difference in IV was worth about $0.0011 in the price of the spread. Keeping the IVs of the two options identical, an increase in the general IV level would increase the spread price (since, as discussed in Chapter 7, the ATM option has a larger vega). However, since both option prices are volatility sensitive, it takes quite an IV change to produce a spread price change of $0.0011. In this case, as shown in Table 16.3, at IV = 11.30, the put prices would be about $0.0358 and $0.0158, and the spread price would be about $0.0200. Thus, a 0.43 change in the IV of the 1.55 put *alone* had about the same effect on the spread price as a 1.83 change in the IVs of *both* puts.

The analysis of the actual volatility dynamics is much simpler. If there is going to be a lot of future actual volatility, it had better be on the up side, because this position can get pretty ugly if the pound price goes much lower than $1.55.

Reasons to Do It:

- You need protection, but you can't imagine a sterling price collapse.
- If the pound starts to go down, you'll adjust the position (but, as pointed out in Chapter 15, if an adjustment is a real possibility, it doesn't make much sense to look at a table of expiration data).

Price Sensitivity: Since this isn't much of a hedge, you need a very good price. You have given up a lot in risk management to hedge this way. There should be a significant profitability consideration to compensate you.

4. Sell 1.60 Call at $0.0300

Expiration Dynamics: While this short call *is* a hedge in that it will make money if the price of the pound moves in a direction that is a problem for the asset, Table 16.2 shows that it *isn't* much more help than the bear spread. What's more, it leaves the aggregate position with little opportunity for profit in the event of a sterling price increase. As a hedge, this call does help somewhat for everyday risk but is of little value in managing remote risk.

As in the case of the bear spread, your boss might not think of this as much of a hedge, and you might be tempted to limit Table 16.2 to £ prices between $1.50 and $1.70, and maybe to use $0.0250 increments. This kind of presentation won't actually make the remote risk go away.

I prefer to think of this trade, not as a hedge, but rather as something to do instead of hedging. You are selling off your upside potential for $300,000 while keeping much of your risk.

Hopes and Fears: You would probably feel best if the pound closed right at $1.60 in 90 days, but, for the next month or so, you'd probably like to see it a little higher.

If the pound rallied to $1.75 you would have outperformed the alternative forward hedge, but you would probably have some regret about selling off your upside for only $300,000. The real fear is of the down side, where exposure is very large (but never larger than for the bear spread).

Volatility Considerations: It's difficult to justify such a questionable hedge unless the call's IV is quite high in light of your expectations for sterling price movement. After the trade is made, low future actual volatility is your hope, but, especially as time goes by, sterling price direction might be as important as actual volatility.

Reasons to Do It:

- The price is right. This could be a good idea at a high IV. The forecast that supported the trade wouldn't have to be an actual volatility forecast in the strict sense described in Chapter 6. A view that the currency is trapped in a narrow range might be enough.
- The pound is not going down.
- Selling premium worked last time.
- You *need* a profit (or need to enhance the exchange rate) and therefore, you either imagine that the market is giving you the edge because you want it, or you feel that it's OK to be irresponsible about risk to give yourself a chance to meet a profit objective.

Except for the "price-is-right" reason, these reasons can be signals that a trader is desperate or is looking for something for nothing.

Price Sensitivity: It is absolutely essential to be price sensitive if this hedge is to be sensible. If you are to remain this exposed to the remote risk of a sterling price collapse while severely limiting your upside potential, there should be some serious edge. Even if there is some good edge, you might ask yourself whether the firm should do this on the full size of £10 million. When you make this kind of make money/manage risk tradeoff, you are shirking your duty by letting the size of the cash flow decide the size of your speculation.

Unfortunately, premium sellers often have such a strong trade orientation that they pay little attention to price considerations. Remember, a trade orientation might not be a problem if it is leading you to reduce exposures, but if it is leading you to take more risk, it is a dangerous weakness.

ZERO PREMIUM HEDGES

The Chapter 15 discussion of the zero premium trade orientation focused on hedgers' weakness for these trades. Certainly, many hedgers go for these trades instinctively with little thought of what they get, what they give up, and what the alternatives might be. Often, they begin with the attitude (perhaps imposed by management) that they must not pay any premium for their hedge, and that they must put an absolute limit on the "worst case" loss. They might also think that, if they comply with those two requirements, they are hedged and it's okay to speculate.

It is also certainly the case that these hedges are motivated by the normal, but dangerous, human instinct to try to get something for nothing. In fact, these trades are rarely described as zero premium trades. They are almost universally categorized as *zero cost* hedges, a term that I find difficult to use, given my emphasis on the transactional nature of option trading.

Nevertheless, these hedges can be sensible under the right conditions. They require the same kind of analysis of risk and edge as any option hedge. The key question is: if you want put protection and you don't want to pay cash, what are you willing to give up?

We will continue to use Example 1 on page 193, and consider two basic zero premium hedges. Then we will look at some variations. The basic hedges are

1. Buy 1.55 put at $0.0100 and sell 1.65 call at $0.0100
2. Buy 1.55 put at $0.0100 and sell 1.55 call at $0.0600 on ⅙ of the exposure

Table 16.4 (much like Table 16.1) displays, for a variety of expiration prices, the profit or loss for each of the alternative hedges (without considering

TABLE 16.4   P&L ($MM) on Hedge Trade (at Expiration)

£	S Forward	B 1.55 Put S 1.65 Call	B 1.55 Put S 1.55 Call (on ½)
$1.40	+2.0	+1.5	+1.5
1.45	+1.5	+1.0	+1.0
1.50	+1.0	+0.5	+0.5
1.55	+0.5	—	—
1.60	—	—	−0.083
1.65	−0.5	—	−0.167
1.70	−1.0	−0.5	−0.250
1.75	−1.5	−1.0	−0.333
1.80	−2.0	−1.5	−0.417

the change in value of the sterling asset). Table 16.5 (much like Table 16.2) displays P&L information for the aggregate positions.

As for the simple hedges, each of these zero premium hedges merits some analysis:

1. Buy 1.55 Put at $0.0100 and Sell 1.65 Call at $0.0100

Expiration Dynamics: This hedge, often referred to as a *fence,* a *collar,* or a *range forward,* offers the "deductible insurance" of the OTM put. Instead of paying for his downside protection in cash, the hedger gives

TABLE 16.5   P&L ($MM) of Option Alternative Compared to Forward Hedge (at Expiration)

£	B 1.55 Put S 1.65 Call	B 1.55 Put S 1.55 Call (on ½)
$1.40	−0.5	−0.5
1.45	−0.5	−0.5
1.50	−0.5	−0.5
1.55	−0.5	−0.5
1.60	—	−0.083
1.65	+0.5	+0.333
1.70	+0.5	+0.750
1.75	+0.5	+1.167
1.80	+0.5	+1.583

up his profit potential above the strike price of the OTM call. Very often, the price of the underlying instrument finishes between the two strike prices. Then both options expire worthless and the result is no different than if the asset were unhedged. Thus, this hedge gives a trader the feeling that he has the action of an unhedged position, but only within a defined range. Of course, that is the case only if the position is untouched for the full 90 days.

Hopes and Fears: Someone who used this hedge would probably hope for (and predict) a modest rally in the price of the pound. In limiting his potential to profit from a sterling price increase, he would probably say $0.0500 is enough (which might mean he has trouble envisioning a big increase). It is not uncommon, however, for hedgers to think differently after the big increase has occurred and they have found out how expensive their "zero-cost" protection turned out to be. A classic example occurred in 1998, when many Canadian firms used fences to hedge their US$ exposure, only to see the US$ rally to C$0.15 or C$0.20 above their short strike.

Another frustration would be to see the pound rally above $1.65 during the 90 days and then retreat to under $1.60 by expiration. That is when the hedger would notice that even OTM options have deltas and the $0.0500 of "play" in the position applied only on expiration day.

Looking at Table 16.5, it might seem that the hedger should especially fear a slow sterling price decline to $1.55. In practice, a hedger would probably have decided that he had $500,000 to lose and all sizable down moves might be about equally disappointing.

Volatility Considerations: With the underlying price about midway between the strike prices, there isn't much net gamma, theta, or vega to the initial position. Consequently, the initial hedge price (zero) is not very sensitive to the general level of IV, and the position is not likely to be justified by a forecast for either actual volatility or implied volatility. However, it is not unusual for OTM call IVs to be higher or lower than OTM put IVs, and that kind of IV action could affect pricing.

While volatility considerations might not be important with the pound at $1.60, it is likely that, during the position's life, the pound will approach one of the strike prices, in which case, the option that is more ATM will, for a while at least, dominate the volatility and greek letter action.

Reasons to Do It: Maybe the most common, and often unstated, reason is that the fence meets the firm's requirements for a hedge, while leaving the hedger room to gamble on his directional view. Other reasons include:

- You have a directional view, but no volatility view.
- You don't mind selling your asset at $1.65.
- Your budget price for this asset is $1.55, so this hedge enables you to "play with the house's money."
- Your budget price is $1.62, and this hedge gives you a good chance to make it, with limited risk.
- You have a price orientation and you think the call is overpriced because you expect a small sterling price increase. You might also think the put is cheap, because, even though you're bullish, you think a sterling price decline, if it does happen, will be big.
- Everybody does it.
- It's politically easy.
- You don't like to deal with option complexity.

For many hedgers, it seems that their comfort with collars is related to an unstated double yardstick: if the call expires worthless, this was better than paying for the put; if the call doesn't expire worthless, the position shows a good $500,000 profit.

Price Sensitivity: Some hedgers consider themselves to be price sensitive for collars because they insist on a zero debit. In that case, the price sensitivity is in the negotiation over the strike prices. Often a hedger will specify the strike price he wants for the long option (in this example, the put) and ask for a quote as to what strike price he has to sell to do the trade for zero. With the put strike price at $1.55, does it matter much if the call strike price is $1.6450, $1.6500, or $1.6550? As in the call buying example of Chapter 14, you probably wouldn't notice the difference in result if you hedged this way once or twice, but, over an extended period of time, the strike price differences would be likely to become material. This is a different form of the short-term invisibility of the edge, described in Chapter 3.

In practice, many hedgers' trade orientations have put them in a "zero-cost habit" that makes price sensitivity a secondary consideration, at best.

2. Buy 1.55 Put at $0.0100 and Sell 1.55 Call at $0.0600 on ⅙ of the Exposure

Expiration Dynamics: This hedge, often referred to as a participating forward, is somewhat similar to a fence in that the hedger has "paid for" his put by giving up some potential. In this example, he would give up ⅙ of the benefit of the price of the pound finishing above $1.55. Strictly speaking, he would not just be giving up profit potential since the hedge would be a small loser if $1.60 turned out to be the price of the pound on expiration day.

Because the hedger doesn't pay cash for this hedge, there is a tendency to think of it as being neither long nor short options. However, the arithmetic of *synthetic forwards* introduced in Chapter 4 sheds a different light on the hedge's character. If, as described in Chapter 4, a long call/short put combination, with a single strike price and a single expiration time, can be thought of as a synthetic forward, we can look at this participating forward as

Long 1.55 put on ⅚ of exposure and

Long 1.55 put on ⅙ of exposure and

Short 1.55 call on ⅙ of exposure

or

Long 1.55 put on ⅚ of exposure and

Short a synthetic forward on ⅙ of exposure

Therefore, it is apparent that the hedger could have achieved the same P&L profile simply by hedging ⅙ of the sterling asset in the forward market and buying a 1.55 put on ⅚ of the asset. What is the attraction of doing this synthetically through the participating forward? The participating forward includes a synthetic forward that temporarily generates $0.0500 per pound in cash. On expiration day, this cash difference between the real forward and the synthetic forward will be negated. The real short forward would be a commitment to sell the pound at $1.60, while this synthetic forward is a commitment to sell it at $1.55.

Hopes and Fears: A hedger who uses a participating forward is almost surely hoping for a large favorable move in the underlying price. It might be a hedger who had been "burned" by the lost opportunity that was the cost of a fence. He has chosen to give up a fraction of everything above $1.55 instead of keeping everything from $1.55 to $1.65 and giving up everything above $1.65.

As in the case of the fence, Table 16.5 makes it seem that the hedger should fear a moderate sterling price decline, but in many cases, the hedger has decided that the "loss" at $1.55 is tolerable (or is not really a loss, at all).

Volatility Considerations: This is not really much different than simply hedging with the 1.55 put. The price would be attractive at a low IV; that is, you wouldn't have to sell calls on much of the exposure if the IV were low. After the trade, high future actual volatility would be likely to produce a satisfactory result.

Reasons to Do It: The reasons given earlier to hedge the whole position with the 1.55 put also apply to the participating forward. In addition:

■ You don't want to pay for an option hedge.
■ You were dissatisfied with a fence.
■ It seems sophisticated.
■ The budget price is $1.55.

Price Sensitivity: This kind of hedge does, and should, look more attractive if the IV is low (note that, because of the synthetic relationship, there will almost surely be a single IV for the call and the put). In that case, however, you might not expect much price movement and the fence might look attractive. Also, if you don't mind paying cash, a low IV makes the 1.60 put look very attractive, and gives you a much better "worst case."

VARIATIONS ON ZERO PREMIUM HEDGES

The minds of hedgers and salespeople can be attracted to any number of variations of the two basic zero premium hedges. Some examples follow.

1. A Seagull: Modify a Fence by Selling an OTM Put

You might choose to turn the 1.55/1.65 fence into a credit trade by selling the 1.50 put at $0.0030. This $30,000 credit isn't much in light of the position's risk, but, if you're hooked on trades that have a high probability of winning (the Chapter 1 weakness), this hedge trade makes money at any closing price below $1.6530. Of course, the put sale means you are unprotected below $1.50. There are three ways you might rationalize this decision:

■ The price of the pound can't get there (you might be right, but it could be expensive to change your mind).
■ You don't care if it gets there. Maybe you have a yardstick that applies here (e.g., you might have a major competitor who doesn't hedge at all).
■ You are price oriented and the put is too expensive. (You need to think carefully about risk. Is this the right size?)

If you were the boss, would you accept any of these rationalizations?

If you don't need a credit for the trade, you could "use" the $30,000 cash to get a better strike price on one side of the fence. That is, if you sell the 1.50 put, you might be able to do the whole thing for zero premium and get the 1.56 put and have more immediate protection or sell the 1.66 call to have a little more upside potential. Then you could think of the trade as buying an OTM put and "paying for" it by selling a *strangle* (a common term for a combination of an OTM put and an OTM call).

This seagull might seem insane to some hedgers, but it is surprisingly popular in foreign exchange, especially when the currency hasn't made a big move for a while. It seems to be a response to short-term performance pressure, which can push remote risk considerations into the background.

2. Use Multiple Strike Prices

While many hedgers and their salespeople operate with the fiction that there is an ideal option structure for a particular exposure, there usually isn't. From the data in this chapter, it should be clear that the selection of a particular strike price can have a dramatic effect on the result of a hedge. Concentration at a single strike price is not necessary. For example, how about hedging £5 million with the 1.57/1.63 fence, and £5 million with the 1.53/1.67 fence?

3. Do a Debit Fence or a Credit Fence

For example:

Buy 1.60 put at $0.0300 and
Sell 1.65 call at $0.0100

This trade would have an edge if you thought IVs were too low. The worst case for the aggregate position would be −$200,000 and you would have a profit potential of $300,000.

Another candidate would be:

Buy 1.55 put at $0.0100 and
Sell 1.60 call at $0.0300

This trade would have an edge if you thought IVs were too high. It enables you to sell premium, but still have limited risk.

A *warning:* If you consider debit or credit fences, it is necessary to think through everything you are getting and everything you are giving up. There is plenty of opportunity for self-delusion.

4. Ratio Write

For example, if you want a zero premium hedge with a 1.57 put, you might get it by selling a 1.65 call on £20 million. While this looks ridiculous, and usually *is* ridiculous, it happens often. Usually, the hedger rationalizes it with a double yardstick. He might say, if the pound is above $1.65 in 90 days, he'll deliver a different (unhedged) asset when he is assigned on the call. In order to do this, he must leave the second asset exposed without put protection.

This use of the double yardstick to justify ratio writing appears in many forms.

5. Consider Compromises between the Fence and the Participating Forward

In a zero premium fence, the hedger "pays for" the put by giving up *all* participation above the call strike price. In the participating forward, he "pays for" it by giving up a *small fraction* of his participation above a much lower strike price. Another choice would be:

> Buy 1.55 put at $0.0100 and
> Sell 1.60 call at $0.0300 on ⅓ of exposure

With this position, the hedger "pays for" the put by giving up *one-third* of his participation above the *current* forward price.

CHAPTER 17

Use of Options in an Investment Portfolio

The flexibility of options has provided a broad range of applications for investment managers. Among them are:

1. *Alternatives to a position in the underlying instrument.* To the extent that an option position has a significant delta, the position might be considered an alternative to a long or short position in the underlying asset.
2. *An opportunity to enhance returns on an underlying asset.* This enhancement might be an improvement in edge as the term is used in this book. Alternatively, it might involve a tradeoff in which there is no improvement in long-term expected profitability, but rather an increase in the likelihood of a good result *one time.*
3. *Risk management.* Options can be used to reduce everyday risks or remote risks, or to make tradeoffs among different kinds of risks. In some cases, as discussed in Chapter 3, reductions in certain kinds of risks can provide the flexibility to increase the sizes of attractive positions.
4. *Major modifications of underlying positions.* Sometimes, assets can be hedged in ways that change their character and produce speculative positions whose P&L characteristics bear little resemblance to those of the underlying assets.

In most cases, the building blocks for any of these applications are similar to the *positions for corporate hedgers* described in Chapter 16. The mathematics, and some of the motivations, discussed in Chapter 16 are applicable to investors. However, compared to a corporate hedger, there are some significant differences in the role of an investment manager and in the characteristics of his underlying instruments. These differences affect the applicability of certain kinds of positions, the motivations for their use, and the potential for investors to deceive themselves.

Investment managers are quite aware that they manage assets that have expected returns that are greater than a risk-free rate. While corporate hedgers can often meet their risk management responsibilities by simply hedging in the forward market, investors usually need to retain enough of the fundamental exposure of their assets so that their P&Ls will benefit from the assets' performance. In other words, it is part of their responsibility to *have some exposure* to underlying price movement. In many cases, a serious reduction of everyday risk would be irresponsible.

Often, however, exposure to remote risk is quite another matter. In many situations an investor wants the everyday ups and downs that are characteristic of a particular kind of asset, but can't afford to be seriously hurt by a remote event. In such a case, good management of remote risk might make room for *more exposure* to everyday risk provided that it comes with good expected returns.

EFFECT OF HEDGING ON EXPECTED RATE OF RETURN

Chapter 3 introduced the concept of a spread as a risk management technique. In the roulette example of that chapter, it appeared that it was possible to assume positions that were negatively correlated to find a better risk profile, while keeping the edge. In the extreme case of the roulette example, it might be possible to induce players to bet an equal amount on each number, leaving the house with its edge and no risk; that is, a sure thing.

If you are an equity investor, you might be tempted to try to do the same. If the risk-free interest rate is 6% but you think the expected return on equities is 10% (a rate that might have seemed low in early 2000, but more optimistic by early 2001), you might decide that you would be happy to have the 10% but you would like to hedge with options so that the intermediate ups and downs of your P&L would be less severe as you wait to make your 10% in the long run. This is not easy to do.

Assuming a stock's dividend, if any, is known, the ultimate option hedge is a short synthetic (as described in Chapter 4). That is, if you are long PQR at 100.00, you could eliminate your risk for three months by buying a three-month European-style put and selling a three-month European-style call with the same strike price. For example:

Long PQR at 100.00

Short 100 call at 10.00

Long 100 put at 8.50

Assuming no dividend, this position would be riskless. It would be settled by the delivery of PQR at 100.00 in three months. The 1.50 return on the 98.50 investment would assure the holder of receiving the *risk-free* rate, *not* the 10% annualized return expected for equities.

Two important observations can be made from this example. First, no matter what you or "the market" think the expected rate of return on an asset should be, the options are likely to be priced as if that rate is the risk-free rate. Second, in the absence of some other kind of edge (such as an IV edge), an option hedge is likely to change the expected return of a position. The return is likely to move closer to the risk-free rate. As a rule of thumb, the extent of this change in expected return is likely to be about proportional to the delta of the hedge.

These observations should force us to refine the concepts of *theoretical value* and *edge* that were discussed in Chapter 3 and Chapter 4. In those chapters, the theoretical value of an option was described as the long-term breakeven price. This is a simple enough concept in roulette, or even in foreign exchange where the forward price and the expected future price are arguably the same. But, when we have an investment asset, we can think of the option as part of an "asset substitute" position, in which case we might price it with an eye toward the expected return on the asset. Alternatively, we can think of it as part of a risk-free position, in which case it should be priced *as if we expected the asset's return to be the risk-free rate.*

In the options business, we calculate option values as if the asset's expected return is the risk-free rate. This makes sense because of conversion arbitrage, but it leaves us in the troubling situation where the "fair value" of an option is not the long-term breakeven price for someone who buys the option *by itself.* Rather, it is the long-term breakeven price for a delta neutral position that is funded at the risk-free rate and that has the "correct" IV.

Another look at the PQR option position might clarify this. The short call/long put combination has a delta of −100, a price of −1.50, and no IV sensitivity. If, at expiration, the stock price is 101.50 (the price at which it would earn the risk-free rate), the option position would break even. If however, we expect a 10% annual return on equities, the expected price for the stock in three months is 102.50, and this "fairly valued" option position has an "expected P&L" of −1.00.

While this arithmetic might be disturbing to equity hedgers, it certainly doesn't mean that using option hedges to make money and/or manage risk is inappropriate. However, it implies that a few considerations might generally be important:

- ■ If a call sale and/or a put purchase is intended to improve the portfolio's profitability, you need more option edge than you might think, or enough risk management to enable you to responsibly increase your equity position.

■ Fairly valued, low delta options don't have much effect on expected return. Thus, it might be easier to justify option use to manage remote risk than to manage everyday risk.

■ If you'd like to reduce everyday risk and you can't find appropriate options with significant edge, you might be just as well off to sell some stock and invest the cash at the risk-free rate.

PUT PURCHASES

Hedging by buying puts provides the simple P&L profiles described in Chapter 16. In the investment world, put hedges can be driven by a variety of motivations. For an investor with PQR stock at 100.00, we might consider three different put purchases.

1. *Buy the 3-month 80 put at 1.50 (Delta = 12).* This put would probably be considered cheap disaster insurance. It might be cheap in four ways:
   ■ The 1.50 might seem small compared to the profit potential for the stock.
   ■ The option's IV of about 45 might seem low compared to the expected stock volatility.
   ■ The option is so far out-of-the-money that its edge is not so much a function of volatility considerations as of the possibility of a remote event. You might think that, even though PQR's price will probably increase, the chance of a big collapse is substantial (e.g., PQR might be a small company with one major customer who needs refinancing in the next three months).
   ■ Even if the option is fairly valued, a 12 delta put won't have much impact on expected return.
   Alternatively, this put might be considered necessary for remote risk management, either because a disaster is intolerable or because remote risk management enables the investor to responsibly hold more PQR. This kind of *protective put* is commonly, and sensibly used by wealthy individuals or families who have excessive concentration in a particular equity, especially if there are legal or tax reasons that discourage them from selling the stock and diversifying.
   Buying protective puts on stock indexes for remote risk management can make sense for wealthy families who can afford plenty of everyday risk, but aren't willing to take *any* exposure to events that might change their lives. It might also make sense for pension plans for

which large losses are simply intolerable. In some cases this kind of re-mote risk management is absolutely essential if the investor is to have significant equity holdings.

2. *Buy the 3-month 90 put at 4.00 (Delta = 26).* This put might be bought as protection for an old position or it might be bought as a *married put* at the same time as the stock.

An investor might buy this kind of put against appreciated stock to ensure that the gains don't turn into losses. He might feel that, with at least some gain locked in, he is now "playing with the house's money" and, no matter what happens, the position is a success. Normally, I find this to be poor reasoning, especially if this is only one of many posi-tions in the portfolio. Yesterday's gains are history. The investor should have positions that look good prospectively. If the stock is no longer a good hold, sell it. If you have too much of it, sell some unless you can find a hedge with characteristics that are attractive *prospectively.*

A better excuse to buy this put is that it is cheap on a value basis. Re-member though, the put's 26 delta is big enough to reduce the expected return on the position. You might consider selling 15% of the position and buying 80 puts on the rest.

Another good excuse for buying this put is that the stock's apprecia-tion has made it overweighted in the portfolio. Of course, you'd still have to consider alternative ways of lightening up, but this put might be the answer if there are tax or legal reasons to keep the stock, or if you like the chances of an upside explosion. (Is this a high actual volatility forecast that makes you think you have an edge?)

If you are considering buying both the stock and the put at current prices, you are looking at a synthetic call. Maybe you should just buy the 90 call for 15.35 and invest the other 88.65 at the risk-free rate.

3. *Buy the 3-month 100 put at 8.50 (Delta = 43).* Unlike the purchase of the 80 put, which is a remote risk management step, the purchase of the 100 put serves mostly to manage everyday risk. As discussed in Chapter 16, a corporate hedger might often have to take strong steps to manage everyday risk, especially if the asset or liability to be hedged is large. In an investment portfolio, however, we should nor-mally *want* the everyday exposure. That's usually the whole idea of ac-quiring the asset.

If the put's IV is considered to be very low, this might be a good idea. If the idea is to lock in profit or to reduce an overweighted posi-tion, this seems like a clumsy way to do it. 8.50 seems like a lot of time-decay risk. How about just selling some stock?

Of course, combining the put and the stock produces the P&L pro-file of an ATM call. A bullish view combined with a forecast for high actual volatility or higher IV might make this an attractive position. It is important, however, to be sure the position is justified by *both* a directional view and a volatility view.

CALL WRITING

Call writing is probably the most popular form of option hedging for investment assets. It seems to have tremendous appeal for many investors, partly because it seems to offer plenty of opportunity to reduce risk *and* to increase returns. Also, unfortunately, it appeals to people who have a weakness for the *double yardstick,* or who are so anxious to have a winning trade that they might not think about edge or remote risk.

Call writing strategies generally fall into one of two categories: *overwriting* and *buy/writing.* Either can be sensible, but both offer the temptation for sloppy thinking.

Overwriting

Call overwriting typically appeals to an institutional equity investor who has a diversified portfolio of many stocks, and who would like to use short calls to "enhance" returns. The institution might employ a separate options adviser who would sell (write) OTM calls on some or all of the stocks in the portfolio. Alternatively, the adviser might sell OTM index calls, thereby overwriting the entire portfolio.

While the institution might view this as a hedge, it is usually not a hedge for the overwriting adviser. His performance is likely to be evaluated on the P&L of the short calls. In other words, these calls are legally hedged, but he is *operationally* naked short. If the calls expire worthless, he's a hero; if the stocks rally too much, he's in trouble.

For example, the investor might own shares of PQR at 100.00. The overwriter might sell 3-month 120 calls at 3.50 (Delta = 27). If the option expires worthless, the option sale would "enhance" the portfolio's return by 3.50. If comparable results could be achieved for every stock in the portfolio, the quarterly performance would be "enhanced" by 3.5%. (This might be annualized to 14%.)

What considerations might drive the overwriter to sell this call?

- He might think the stock won't go above 120.
- He might think the call is overpriced.
- He might think it's his job to be short calls.

- Even if the call's price looks cheap, it's 20% out-of-the-money, it will probably expire worthless, and it gives him a chance to have a good quarter (remember my friend Jerry in Chapter 15?).
- If the stock price rallies, he can buy back the call, "roll" to another short call with a higher strike price and later expiration, and wait for the new call to expire worthless. (This is a form of trying to use options to make the past untrue.)
- He might sell calls against only ½ of the stock, so, if it goes against him, he can buy back the call and sell twice as many to get the money back.

He might not think about some other considerations:

- He doesn't help the investor's long-term performance by making a lot of winning trades. He can only help by making trades that win *on average*.
- To the extent that there is a difference between the expected returns on the stocks and the risk-free rate, positions in short calls that are "fairly valued" will, on average, lose money.

Is overwriting a good idea? Like most option strategies, it depends. Can everyone involved remember that this is not much of a hedge. Its purpose is profitability, and profitability requires selectivity (that is, a price orientation). Can the investor afford to give up the potential to get very good returns if the market explodes upward? Does the overwriting adviser have a good strategic framework and the discipline to stay within it?

Since shortly after the CBOE opened in 1973, institutional overwriting has experienced waves of popularity, followed by periods in which it has practically disappeared. Naturally, since most OTM options expire worthless, most programs have prospered for a while. During periods of quiet or declining markets, the popularity of overwriting has grown and institutions and advisers have been happy to publicize their results, often reporting the extent of their profit "enhancement" in the present tense instead of the past tense. Noise levels have seemed to peak just before major market advances such as those in 1982 and 1995. It seems that no one quits overwriting because options get cheap. They wait until they lose money.

While overwriting can be troublesome because of its appeal to human weakness and difficult to manage because of the short-term invisibility of the edge (see Chapter 3), it can also be a sensible part of an investment program. The keys are to recognize it for what it is, and to maintain both a *price orientation* and *statistical passiveness*. I don't know what to do about the problem of how to pay overwriting advisers without giving them incentives that encourage dysfunctional behavior.

Buy/Writing

If you are long PQR at 100.00 and short the three-month 100 call at 10.00, you might not know if this is a stock position that is hedged by the short call or if this is simply a different kind of investment. If it is the former, you might be confused about the call's role as an income "enhancer" and its role in risk management. If the stock price drops to 60, the short call would "enhance" your return by 10.00, but it wouldn't do much about your remote risk. As a risk management step, it helps only with everyday risk. If the stock price rises to 140, the call would lose 30.00 (not a very good income "enhancer"), but, in terms of risk management, it wouldn't be too bad since the aggregate position would be profitable. However, except for short periods of time, or in cases where the IV is ridiculously high, hedging an investment asset with an ATM call doesn't seem to make much sense because

- As discussed earlier, a 50+ delta option hedge can materially reduce the expected rate of return.
- In most cases, options seem useful for investors who worry more about remote risk than about everyday risk. If you are very concerned about everyday risk, you are probably overinvested.

On the other hand, if you want to think of the stock and the short call as a single position (often called a *buy/write*), it might be a sensible investment even if, in the short run, it is not likely to have results that look like those of a stock investment.

What considerations might motivate you, as an investor, to select this buy/write investment?

If you are tempted to forget about the transactional nature of options, you might focus only on what can go right. It is quite likely that, in three months, PQR's price will be at least 100.00, the call will be exercised, and you will receive 100.00 in return for an investment of 90.00. Since this 11.1% quarterly return will be yours with the stock price unchanged or better, it is often referred to as "return-if-unchanged" or the "static rate of return." Sometimes it is described in annualized terms, but usually not in compounded terms (that is, an investor would be more likely to say that the annualized static rate of return is 44.4%, rather than the 52.4% you would get from four compounded returns of 11.1%).

You might also focus on the downside breakeven point. In this case, you would at least break even unless the stock price is more than 10% lower in three months. This fact might seem very important to you if you don't think about the short-term invisibility of the edge.

Another possibility is that you might think the position has an edge because your forecast for PQR's actual volatility for the next three months is lower than the current IV of about 47. Alternatively, you might not forecast volatility in the units described in Chapter 6. You might simply decide that PQR's price is likely to trade in a relatively narrow range for a while.

While these reasons are all legitimate considerations, they have one common discomforting characteristic—they all focus on things that are *likely to happen*. This buy/write is a position that will do well if expectations are met and has acceptable everyday risk, but it *can't* make an unusual profit from a remote favorable event and it *can* lose a lot of money from a remote unfavorable event. Maybe some analysis of the probabilities and costs of these events would be important. This might especially be the case since, if there is much focus on static rate of return or downside break even points, you are likely to find yourself with buy/writes only in the most volatile stocks.

In addition to the legitimate considerations just described, you might be tempted to use some less appropriate reasoning. For example:

■ *You don't think PQR can go up much, so you are almost sure to make a profit on the short call.* But if PQR's price is higher in three months, your P&L will be the same whether the price change is large or small. With the buy/write, you should think more about the probabilities of big PQR declines.

■ *You don't think PQR can go down much, so this position is almost a sure winner.* Maybe your expected return would be greater if you just bought the stock and forgot about the call.

■ *You are bullish on the stock. Once again, naked long stock might be a better idea.* By going with the buy/write, you are giving up the upside for a stock you like. Are you more interested in a high probability of a good return than in expected performance (i.e., edge)?

The problems with these weak reasons point to a simple view of a buy/write with an ATM call. It is probably a good idea only if you don't expect a big PQR move in *either direction*. If there is much chance of a big down move, the big losses can overwhelm the smaller gains. If there is much chance for a big up move, you would probably be better off with just the stock.

If you like the stock but think the IV is too high (given your expectations for actual volatility), you might consider a buy/write with an OTM call. For example:

Long PQR at 100.00
Short 110 call at 6.00

OPTION INCOME FUNDS

From late in the 1970s until late in the 1980s, U.S. mutual fund companies attracted quite a bit of retail investment money to option income funds. Most began with equity-based funds, but eventually most of the U.S. Treasury bond-based funds became bigger. These funds offered high current incomes. They paid dividends on the basis of net capital gains from underlying assets, interest and dividends received, and income from expiring or exercised options.

Their investment approach was to put on roughly ATM buy/writes for bonds or for stocks that looked good. If the options were exercised, the profit from the buy/write could be used to pay the dividend. If the options expired worthless, the profit on the option could be used to pay the dividend, even if there was a large unrealized loss in the underlying asset. Thus, no matter what the stock did, there was plenty of realized profit available to pay dividends—at least for the first buy/write.

In the equity-based funds, the problem was obvious. They were paying dividends that could not be sustained by the long-term profitability of the strategy. Some stocks would go up, others down. The winners were called away, but the fund could use the proceeds for new buy/writes that would generate new realized gains. The significant losers, however, became "deadwood." It was difficult to use them to generate option income because the only options with significant thetas had strike prices that were well below the stocks' cost bases.

This wasn't a big problem as long as there was plenty of net investor inflow. Static rates of return were high enough to enable acceptable (and ultimately unsustainable) dividends to be paid as long as the "deadwood" wasn't a large fraction of the fund. Eventually, though, the "chain-letter" dynamics couldn't keep alive the fiction that buy/writes could produce extremely high long-term income. The equity option income funds pretty much disappeared after the 1987 stock market crash. Coincidentally, the bond-based funds, which really couldn't diversify, met their demise at about the same time. When bond prices declined in the Spring of 1987, almost everything in the funds went "under water" and became "deadwood."

In the mid-1980s, O'Connell & Piper did some consulting for a large U.S. mutual fund company that had option income funds. We had a difficult time communicating the reality of the limited expected rates of return for buy/writes. Finally, I compiled about eight years of

---

OPTION INCOME FUNDS (Continued)

---

data comparing the performance of the firm's equity option income fund to that of the S&P 500 index and the firm's money market fund. In every year except one, the option income fund's performance was between the performances of the other two funds (in the other year, the option income fund's performance was the worst of the three). For the entire period, the option income fund's total performance was about 1.3% per year worse than what would have been returned by a 50/50 split between the other two funds. I suppose the 1.3% was about the amount of their transaction costs.

I compiled this data to demonstrate that, even though an individual buy/write isn't likely to have a P&L that is much like that of the underlying asset, its expected return is nothing like its static rate of return. Without significant option edge, a 50 delta option hedge should move the asset's expected return in the direction of the risk-free rate. The edge problem was invisible in the short term, but was unavoidable in the annual performance data.

For this buy/write, the quarterly static rate of return is only $6/94 = 6.4\%$, and the downside break even point is 94.00, but it offers more profit potential on the upside. If the stock finishes at 110.00 or above, your profit is 16.00 on an investment 94.00, or a quarterly "return-if-exercised" of 17.0%. Compared to the ATM buy/write, this position is a little riskier and has a lower probability of profit, but if there is edge in your directional view as well as in the option price, this position might provide a superior expected return.

One last comment on call writing: Often, traders like to justify these positions in part by saying that, if the stock moves against them, they will adjust the position. Chapter 18 will discuss the adjustment process. For now, however, it should be noted that an adjustment is often a sensible risk management step, but it is not a substitute for an edge.

COLLARS

Just as in the corporate hedging example of Chapter 16, it might make sense to hedge PQR with a collar. The collar might have zero premium or it might have a debit or a credit. In any event, it would have the effect of "fencing in" the exposure.

An extreme example of a collar is a short synthetic. If you have

Long PQR at 100.00
Short 100 call at 10.00 (Delta = 57)
Long 100 put at 8.50 (Delta = 43)

there is no exposure and the return will be the risk-free rate.
If you sell the 105 call instead of the 100 call you have

Long PQR at 100.00
Short 105 call at 7.75 (Delta = 49)
Long 100 put at 8.50 (Delta = 43)

and there is a little room for action. If, in three months, PQR is at 100.00 or
below, you have lost 0.75. If it is at 105.00 or above, you have made 4.25.
Between 100.00 and 105.00, the expiration return curve is linear.

Before you become too excited about this position's P&L characteristics, please note that it will cost about 1.50 to carry this position for three
months, so the real P&L range is −2.25 to +2.75.

It should be obvious that this hedged position doesn't look much like an
equity position. For the moment, it is only 8 deltas long, it has no significant
net gamma, theta, or vega (see Chapter 7) and its expected rate of return is
close to the risk-free rate. No doubt you might think of a reason to have this
position, but, for the time being, it wouldn't be an important position.

We could look at the combination of the long PQR stock and the long
put as a long synthetic call. Then, we see that we have a synthetic bull
spread. In fact, the comparable call bull spread would be

Long 100 call at 10.00 (Delta = 57)
Short 105 call at 7.75 (Delta = 49)

and would have the same return characteristics as the collared stock.

An asset hedged by a collar that is very narrow should probably not be
thought of as a hedged asset. Its characteristics have been modified to the
point where it is simply a different kind of investment. As the collar is
widened, however, the position becomes more of a hedged asset. For example, you might decide to have

Long PQR at 100.00
Short 120 call at 3.50 (Delta = 27)
Long 90 put at 4.00 (Delta = 26)

Now the position has some "play" in it, and it might be justified by some of the same reasoning used to justify collars in Chapter 16. If you are not careful, however, you might fool yourself into thinking this position is much better than the foreign exchange position on page 202 of Chapter 16 since, for only a 0.50 debit, you get 20.00 of PQR "play" on the upside, but only 10.00 of downside exposure. There are three considerations to keep in mind:

1. The forward price of PQR is 101.50, so there is really 18.50 of upside and 11.50 of downside.
2. It is the expectation of our models (and often our own expectation) that, at 120.00 the daily moves (in price) of PQR would be bigger than at 90.00. Hence, the likelihood of a large point increase in PQR would be greater than the likelihood of a decline of the same number of points. Thus, we are "giving up more" by selling a high strike option than we are getting by buying a low strike option. This subject is discussed in the "Loose Ends" section of Chapter 6.
3. The expected rate of return on PQR is greater than the risk-free rate.

Of these three considerations, only the expected rate of return is a good reason to favor this position over the foreign exchange position. However, PQR has the expected return advantage even without the hedge.

As the strike prices continue to widen, the hedged position becomes more like an equity position and the expected rate of return becomes closer to the equity rate. Look at

Long PQR at 100.00

Short 140 call at 1.00 (Delta = 10)

Long 75 put at 1.00 (Delta = 8)

Now we have an equity position with protection against some remote risk (the 75 put) which has been paid for by selling off the remote upside potential. I can think of some good reasons to buy the put but, unless IVs are outrageously high, I would think a seller of the 140 call is suffering from a strong zero premium "habit."

LONG STOCK/SHORT STRANGLE

On May 4, 2000, the stock of Oracle Corporation (ORCL) had a closing price of $74.25. The exchange-listed September options had 4 months and 11 days remaining until expiration. Consider the following position:

Long ORCL at 74.25

Short September 90 calls at 7.50

Short September 60 puts at 5.75

If you are an equity investor, this position might seem attractive for many reasons. For example:

- While ORCL has been a volatile stock, enough is enough. You expect it to be between 60 and 90 in September. Even if it's not, because of the 13.25 credit on the options, this "hedge" will be profitable at any closing ORCL price from 46.75 to 103.25.
- You'd be perfectly happy to sell your stock at 90.
- You'd be happy to buy more stock at 60.
- If ORCL is at 90 or higher at expiration, you'll deliver stock at 90 and keep the options proceeds. Your total profit will be 29 on an investment of 61. That's almost a 50% profit in 4+ months.
- The aggregate position will be profitable in September at any ORCL price above 61.

While this position can *seem* attractive—and might *be* attractive—it certainly tempts you to take refuge in a multiple yardstick. There are at least four ways to measure the performance of this position (assuming it is untouched until September 15). You could look at the P&L compared to that of

- No ORCL position
- ORCL stock unhedged
- Twice as much unhedged ORCL stock (since you are saving some capacity to buy at 60)
- ORCL stock unhedged, buying more if it goes to 60, and selling it all if it goes to 90

On September 15, ORCL closed at 78.3125. If you held this position and didn't touch it, your profit was 17.3125 on an investment of 61. That's a 28.4% profit in a little over four months. Are you happy?

- Pick a yardstick!
- Did you really leave the position untouched?

What Really Happened

On May 24, with almost four months remaining on the options, the price of ORCL plunged through 60. At that point, you had lost 14.25 on the stock, but had a slight profit on the options. Markets were chaotic, but the price of the September 90 calls seemed to be about 2.50, while the September 60 puts were at about 9.00. You still might have been unhappy about the options, as there wasn't much more to make on the calls and you could see the puts exploding as the stock went through the 60 strike. Twenty days earlier, you thought you'd be happy to buy more stock at 60. Is that still the case? If you've lost your nerve, you could take the position off, realizing your loss. On the other hand, if you still are happy to buy more stock at 60, you can't. Your short put has used up that risk capacity.

The ORCL selloff didn't last long (but long enough for you to have bought some more stock if you hadn't sold the put). The stock price rallied through 80 in early June and on August 31, it crossed 90. Would you still be happy to sell it there? Sorry, but you probably can't because you are short the September 90 call, which is trading for about 4.00. If you've changed your mind about selling here, you could chase the call. Otherwise, you'll just have to hope ORCL holds 90 for 15 more days.

ORCL held 90 for a few days, but then sold off and closed at 78.3125 on September 15. At that point, you would have to be happy if you didn't chase the September 60 puts when the stock plunged or the September 90 calls when they went in-the-money. What you really wish you did was stick with your original stock attitude, hold ORCL unhedged, buy more at 60, and sell it all at 90. Then, your profit would have been 45.75 instead of 17.3125.

Of course, ORCL didn't have to follow the path that it did. If the stock price's decline had stopped without getting to 60, and if its rally had stopped before 90, the option result would have been by far the best. Waiting to buy at 60 and sell at 90 would have been a frustrating experience. It is worth observing, however, that part of the mental justification for this kind of position is that the investor is willing to trade at those strike prices. The options create two problems however. First, they make it very difficult, and probably expensive, to change your mind. Second, ITM short options turn into stock trades *only at expiration*. By selling them, you have given up the flexibility to make the trade you want if the stock gets to the strike *before expiration*.

HEDGING WITH LONG DATED PUTS

On December 27, 2000, the stock of Oracle Corporation traded at $31.00 (after a 2 for 1 split in October). With the stock well off of its September highs, and with plenty of scary economic news in the air, an individual investor with excess concentration in ORCL might be getting nervous. This might be a particular problem if the investor had a very low tax basis in the stock and/or was an insider with restrictions on the sale of the stock. If you were advising such an investor, you might suggest some long-term remote risk insurance. The 2003 January 20 puts were available for 4.00. These puts would put a limit on the investor's exposure to a life-changing disaster, but 4.00 seems like a lot of money. Perhaps he could begin to "pay for" this insurance by selling OTM calls. The 2001 March 45 calls were trading for 1.00. Consider this position:

> Long ORCL at 31.00
>
> Long 2003 January 20 put at 4.00
>
> Short 2001 March 45 call at 1.00

This position might make the most of a difficult situation but it could create some problems. If the stock doesn't move too far for a few quarters, but the calls have reasonably high IVs, the investor can sell enough calls to make the put seem "free." Of course, if the stock price declines by March expiration, he might not be happy with the strike price he has to sell to generate another 1.00. The bigger problem might be: What if the stock really goes up? If he can, he might be happy to deliver the stock at 45 (and maybe pay some taxes). If he'd *like to* sell the stock at 45, he's going to be frustrated if it goes through 45 and then retreats before March expiration. If he is unwilling or unable to sell the stock, there could be a real problem. At what point does he buy back the call? If he really has a lot of stock and not much else, where does he get the cash to buy it back? He might try to buy back the call and sell the June 50 or 55 calls to avoid laying out more cash, but that might simply extend the problem.

What actually happened? On March expiration day ORCL stock closed at 14. The 2003 January 20 puts closed at 8⅜. Now what?

There is no magic in this approach, but it can make sense for the right investor. Since it involves only remote risk management and since there is potential for severe problems, it might make sense to use it for less than all of the stock investment, and it might also make sense to use several different strike prices and/or expiration dates. Sometimes, it makes sense simply to buy the long-term puts, and to forget about selling the calls. In the options business, if you find yourself trying to get something for nothing, you should worry about yourself. If you are doing it in big size, it's probably a bad idea.

REPAIR STRATEGY

Throughout this book, there have been warnings about the natural tendency of traders to do almost anything to avoid recognizing losses. Often, they make trades that, under certain circumstances, would be perfectly sensible. When driven by human weakness, however, the same kinds of trades can be a bad idea. One of the classics is the so-called *repair strategy*.

If I were to buy PQR stock at $100 per share, only to find the price drop to $80, I might be desperate to break even. I could just wait and hope for a rally. I might also try a ratio call spread. For example, using three-month calls:

Long 1 call (80 strike) at 8.00

Short 2 calls (90 strike) at 4.00

If I assume that I will keep this position until expiration, I will have improved my chances of breaking even. Without the options, I need the stock price to increase to 100. With the options, at any expiration stock price above 90, I will break even (since I will have bought stock at 100, bought through exercise at 80, and delivered it all through assignment at 90). If, at expiration, the stock price is below 80, the option position expires worthless and, since it was done for zero debit, my P&L is the just the stock P&L. If the stock is between 80 and 90, I wouldn't break even, but I would make something on the option trade.

Is this a bad trade? Not necessarily. At the right price with the right directional and volatility views, it might make sense. Do I give anything up? Of course, I do. I give up two of the things I frequently give up in selling options:

■ The opportunity to profit from a favorable remote event and
■ The flexibility to trade between now and expiration.

For example, in three or four weeks, PQR might be back at 100.00. Without the options, I could still hope for a good profit on the position. With the options, the best I can do is break even. Without the options, I could sell the stock at 100.00 and get out even. However, the option prices would probably be about 22 and 14, and to clean up the position, I would have to take a 6.00 loss on the spread. Instead, I would probably wait and hope that PQR's price would still be above 90 at expiration. Meanwhile, I'd have some of my risk capacity tied up in the position.

CHAPTER 18

Living with a Hedge

The complexity resulting from the multidimensional nonlinear nature of options does not end when a position is selected. While many hedgers prefer to let option positions remain untouched until they expire, in doing so they are giving up substantial opportunities to improve both profitability and risk management.

When it comes to managing an existing position, option positions have three characteristics that distinguish them from one-dimensional, linear instruments.

1. *Often, it's not easy to get out.* If you are trading spot foreign exchange, cash Treasury bonds, or stock index futures, you might be able to liquidate a position quickly, at a narrow bid/offer spread, and with minimal transaction costs. Traders of these instruments might rely on the ability to get out easily. In some cases, a core risk management principle is to "take losses fast." This might not work in options, especially if the position is complicated.

2. *An option position can change itself.* The classic example is the zero premium fence hedge described in Chapter 16 on page 202. Initially, it had about a 50 delta, with no significant gamma, theta, or vega. Over the position's life, if the underlying price were to stay about midway between the strikes, the delta of the aggregate position would increase while the other "Greeks" would remain insignificant. However, if the underlying price approached the short strike price, the delta would not change as much over time, but the gamma and vega would become negative and the theta would become positive. If the underlying approached the long strike price, again the delta would not change as much over time, but the gamma and vega would become positive and the theta would become negative.

3. *Each position reflects multiple views.* For an option position to be appropriate, it should normally be consistent with the hedger's forecast for:

- The direction of underlying price movement.
- Future actual volatility.
- Future implied volatility.
- Variations from the normal "bell curve" assumptions.

If you think about characteristics 2 and 3, you might conclude that many option hedges require ongoing management. With so many opportunities for a significant change either in the position characteristics or in one of the forecasts, we should constantly be aware of the possibility for a perfectly sensible position to become inappropriate. To deal with this possibility we should:

1. *Plan ahead.* Traders usually do not like to spend time on contingency planning (fantasizing about favorable results is more popular). It can seem like a waste of time, and it's more exciting to rely on reaction. But option analysis can be complicated, can take time, and can be influenced by the emotion of the moment. If this is to be a business, we need to think, in advance, about
   - *Risks.* As the variables change, what might be a position's changes in sensitivity? Might its characteristics be reversed?
   - *Size.* Can the position get bigger or smaller with respect to any parameter? Most often this happens as an underlying price approaches, or moves away from, a strike price. Sometimes, it happens as expiration approaches.
   - *Structure.* For example, sometimes a position's principal initial exposure will be to IV change, but, after a while, its vega will decrease, and it will become more sensitive to future actual volatility.
2. *Review frequently.* Many traders don't like to think about positions that aren't working well. Others don't like to "mess with" a winner. In the options business, it can be too easy to think of yourself as "locked in," and it can be a big mistake. Things change. A trader can't afford to be surprised or to miss opportunities.
3. *Think prospectively.* Don't be influenced by your P&L or by your original view(s). Can the position be justified *as it is?*

To illustrate some of the position management issues faced by hedgers, it will be assumed that you are a corporate foreign exchange hedger who has initiated the position in Example 1 on the following page. This is the same fence example of Chapter 16. Next, it will be assumed that 60 days have passed, no further trades have been made, and the spot and forward prices have declined to $1.5500. Your new situation is reflected in Example 2.

EXAMPLE 1

You work for a US$ based firm, expecting to receive a £10 million payment in 90 days.

> Spot £ at $1.6000
>
> 90-day forward £ at $1.6000

You hedged with

> Long £10 million 90-day/1.55 put at $0.0100 (Delta = 23)
>
> Short £10 million 90-day/1.65 call at $0.0100 (Delta = 25)

You selected this hedge because you expected the pound to appreciate over the next three months. You did not have a view with respect to future actual volatility or future implied volatility. You did want limited exposure on the downside. In this case, your maximum exposure was $500,000. You didn't mind selling the 1.65 call because you thought you would be quite happy, maybe even anxious, to sell your sterling asset for $1.65 per pound.

Has This Been a Satisfactory Hedge?

So far, the value of the asset has declined by $500,000. The options have a mark-to-market profit of $145,000. As in many hedging situations, there are several ways to view this result. Here are some things you might think about:

- You are $145,000 better off than if you hadn't hedged at all.
- You are $355,000 worse off than if you had sold the pound forward.
- Your hedge was initially 48 deltas short, with no significant gamma, theta, or vega. Now it is 52 deltas short. That information alone might lead you to expect about a $250,000 profit on the options. However,

---

EXAMPLE 2

> Long: £10 million asset at $1.5500
>
> Long: £10 million 30-day/1.55 put at $0.0150 (Delta = 49)
>
> Short: £10 million 30-day/1.65 call at $0.0005 (Delta = 3)

because the underlying price has moved to the long strike price, the position has become theta negative and vega positive. Your hedge has performed poorly compared to a simple 50 delta forward hedge, mostly because of the 60 days that have passed, but partly because of a small IV decline.

■ You weren't looking for protection for the first $0.0500 of a sterling price decline. You were self-insuring the first $500,000 of exposure. So far you are "wrong" by $0.0500, but you could get out now for only a $355,000 loss.

We often find ourselves taking this kind of retrospective look at the performance of our trades. While we might be able to learn a lot from that process, this kind of analysis can be mostly distracting if we're thinking about what to do next. We should focus on what we have now, what we *expect* for the future, and what *might happen* in the future.

What Is Different about This Position Now?

The position has changed in two significant ways:

1. Although the delta of the option position is still about 50, you might feel closer to being fully hedged. With only 30 days to go, your now-ATM put has a gamma that can be very helpful if the sterling price decline continues. In fact, the aggregate position can lose only another $145,000.
2. The position has changed from having no significant theta 60 days ago to being vulnerable to substantial time decay losses for the next 30 days.

What to Think about Now

The first step is to face reality. Although you might be tempted to think that the position is still alive and you haven't lost anything yet, the fact is that you really have lost money. You are $355,000 behind on your speculation (most firms would choose to use a different word here than speculation, but a euphemism doesn't change the nature of the position). Alternatively, you might focus on the fact that you were willing to risk $500,000. Then, you might think you have something like a "free call" here. That is, if the pound doesn't rally, your loss won't get worse than the $500,000. If it does rally, you can get some money back and maybe make a profit. In reality, however, you have the choice of getting out now. You have lost only $355,000, but you could lose $145,000 more. Your "free call" costs

$145,000, but you're not married to it. Even if you are emotionally involved, this position is not a permanent commitment.

The next step is to start over with respect to your views. You're not married to them either. Do you still have a reason to think the price of the pound will increase? It's okay to change your mind. You can't afford the self indulgence of continuing to take risk just to have a chance to avoid being "wrong." Also, do you now have a view on actual or implied volatility that might be significant in view of current option pricing?

Your Alternatives

Although there are many possible decisions available to you, it might help to focus on three of them:

1. *Keep the position as it is.* This might be a good idea, but only if
   a. You still have reason to think the price of the pound will rise, and
   b. You can forecast that the actual volatility of the pound will be greater than the current IV (about 8.5).

   Originally, with no gamma, theta, or vega, you could justify this position without a volatility forecast. Now, with a long position in a one-month ATM put, this position is likely to be attractive only if the price of the pound can be expected to be quite volatile. You might notice that, with a one-month option, the vega is probably too low to justify a bet on IV change.
2. *Close out the options and hedge with the 30-day forward.* It might be difficult to give up on the chance to get your money back, but, if there is no directional or volatility edge, there is no excuse for taking further risk.
3. *Close out the old fence and replace it with a new one—perhaps buying the 30-day 1.52 put and selling the 30-day 1.58 call.* Each option would have a price of about $0.0050 and a delta of slightly less than 25. If you still have the view that the pound price should go up, and you still have no significant volatility view, this might make sense.

Some Considerations

If you are choosing among these three alternatives, you might be influenced by many concerns, some sensible, some emotional, some arguable. Consider five of them:

1. *The fantasy of getting a good ultimate result.* To the extent that you are anxious to have a chance for this to turn into a winner, you would tend

to keep the position unchanged. To move to a forward hedge is to accept the $355,000 loss. If you roll to the 152/158 fence, you would have a chance to get back all but $55,000 of the loss. (With the new fence, if the pound finished above $1.5800, you would receive $1.58 for your asset upon assignment of the call. This would be $200,000 worse than getting the original $1.60 price, but that loss would be partially offset by the $145,000 gain on the initial option position.)

2. *Concern for the worst case.* If you are very concerned about the worst result possible, you might want to move to the forward hedge. That would end your loss at $355,000. To keep the current position would be to retain the original worst case of −$500,000. If you roll to the 152/158 fence, you might lose another $300,000 (in addition to the $355,000 you have already lost). A key consideration here is whether the original maximum exposure of $500,000 was (and still is) an important limit, or if you have more risk capacity. If this £10 million is a very large cash flow for the firm, you probably should be very concerned about the worst case. If it's a small cash flow, you probably have more flexibility.

3. *Fear of losses due to time decay.* While money lost because of time decay is no more or less real than money lost through any other dynamics, you might be very aware of it. Your awareness might be the result of a trade orientation (in this case, a bad reason) or it might come from the recognition that you don't have an actual volatility forecast that justifies taking that kind of risk (a good reason). If time decay is your dominant fear, keeping the current position is probably the least attractive choice and moving to the forward probably seems best. If you roll to the 152/158 fence, you don't have immediate time decay exposure, but you might have some later if the price of the pound moves toward $1.52.

4. *Desire to profit from a slight, 30-day bounce in the price of the pound.* Clearly, rolling to the 152/158 fence provides the best opportunity to cash in on a 1% or 2% bounce. Moving to the forward eliminates this possibility. Keeping the initial position would permit partial participation, but the bounce had better be bigger than $0.0145.

5. *The emotional pain of getting whipped.* It might be one of your fears that, after watching the price of sterling move against you for 60 days, you would make an adjustment, only to watch the pound whip back up, while you feel foolish for changing your position. This is the negative side of consideration 1, above. Clearly, you can avoid being subject to that pain by keeping the original position. You can partially avoid it by rolling to the 152/158 fence. If you move to the forward, and the price of the pound whips back up, you will be miserable.

What Should You Do?

When you think about all of these considerations, it should be clear that none of the alternatives can always be the best or the worst. You should start each analysis by being specific about your yardstick and your forecasts. You should think prospectively. You should specifically address each kind of risk. You should assume that there is no correct or perfect position. You should look at alternatives, remembering the transactional nature of options, asking yourself what you are getting and what you are giving up. Within the limits of sensible risk management, you should be statistically passive in describing the reasons for your decisions and in evaluating the results.

What If the Price of the Pound Went Up Instead of Down?

Example 3 below describes another scenario for the Example 1 position after 60 days.

At this point, the value of the sterling asset has increased by $600,000, but the option hedge has lost $256,000. Still, given the fact that the hedge's delta was initially 48 and now is 60, giving up about 43% of the appreciation might not seem too bad. Now that the underlying price is near the strike price of the short call, the hedge's P&L has suffered from an IV increase from about 8.5 to about 11.0, but has benefited more from the 60 days that have passed.

With the underlying price only $0.0100 above the call strike price, you might be tempted to rationalize that you haven't really lost anything by selling the call, since its sale price was $0.0100. If this were expiration day you would be correct, but it isn't. The call price is $0.0260 and the loss is real. You can choose to wait and hope the pound stays at its current level, but then you have lost something. You've lost the flexibility to sell your asset before expiration. Much as in the short strangle example of Chapter 17, this can be a frustrating situation. Part of your rationalization for selling the call was that you'd be happy to sell the asset at $1.65. Now, the result of your

---

EXAMPLE 3

Long: £10 million asset at $1.6600 (Spot = Forward)
Long: £10 million 30-day/1.55 put at $0.0004 (Delta = 2)
Short: £10 million 30-day/1.65 call at $0.0260 (Delta = 58)

short call position is that you have *given up the right* to sell it at that price before expiration.

Your potential frustration in waiting for expiration day should not necessarily make you dissatisfied with the hedge. Presumably, if you were going to speculate on the direction of the pound's price movement, you were going to have to hedge in some way. At least, your hedge left you with a $344,000 profit which is 57% of the move and 68.8% of what you thought you were playing for. In addition, it might have left you with a position you like for the short-term future.

If you keep the position as it is, you might not like the fact that you have only $156,000 more to make, while you face the possibility of giving back all of your $344,000 profit, and maybe more if the pound collapses. Notice, however, that you are comparing a reasonably probable positive event with your exposure to a remote event. Maybe you can manage the remote risk without seriously impacting your everyday exposure. For example, you might buy a 30-day 1.61 put for $0.0050, thereby ensuring that the position's profit does not turn into a loss. Is this a good idea? One of the purposes of the discussion of put purchases in Chapter 17 was to discourage you from being excessively concerned over whether a particular gain turns into a loss, and to encourage you to have some balance in your concerns about *all* of the risks in a position. In the present example, if you want to limit the remote risk, the 1.61 put doesn't seem like a better choice than the 1.60 put or the 1.62 put. The fact that buying a put at that particular strike ensures a small profit seems irrelevant. On the other hand, if this position is large for your firm, you certainly should do *something* about remote risk, and buying the 1.61 put might be a good choice.

Whether or not you buy an OTM put to manage the remote risk, you still need to address the everyday exposure. You should resist the temptation to "play with the house's money"; that is, to protect the position from turning into a loser while being too casual about gambling with the unrealized profits. As in Example 2, you should think prospectively. Your current position is much like a short 1.65 put position. If, at an 11.0 IV, your forecasts don't describe enough edge to justify the risk of such a position, maybe you should buy the 1.65 put or take off the options and do something else (such as sell the pound forward). Either of these choices would require a cash outlay for 30 days. Maybe one of the reasons you hedged with a zero premium fence is because it is organizationally difficult for you to pay a debit. If that's the case, you might try a call bear spread (buy 1.65 call, sell 1.55 call). You might give away a little in bid/offer spread, but you would temporarily generate cash and you would wind up with an essentially riskless forward conversion:

Long £10 million asset

Long £10 million 1.55 put

Short £10 million 1.55 call

If you are going to think prospectively about this position, you will have to take another look at your forecasts. Do you still expect the price of the pound to rise? Do you have a forecast for actual volatility that differs much from the 11.0 IV? You could also think about a forecast for implied volatility, but with only 30 days left until expiration, there isn't likely to be much vega action compared to the gamma and theta action.

As for Example 2, there are many possible choices, but here are the major possibilities:

- If you are still a sterling bull, and your forecast is for low actual volatility (compared to the 11.0 IV), you probably should keep your current position, possibly with some kind of remote risk management trade.
- If you are still a sterling bull, but have no helpful volatility view, you should consider rolling your fence up to the 1.63 put/1.69 call fence. The fact that this would assure you of giving back no more than $300,000 of your $344,000 profit is not as important as the fact that it gives you:
  —Delta exposure that is consistent with your directional view,
  —Reasonable remote risk, and
  —No immediate exposure to gamma, theta, or vega.
- If you no longer have a directional view, clean the position up and go on about your other business. Don't speculate without an edge.

What Kind of Business Is This?

If you are looking for a simple way to summarize the options business, you might be tempted to focus on its mathematical nature. For many of us, the mathematical complexity of options and the attractiveness of the Black-Scholes model played big roles in our decisions to be involved in options. However, survivors in the business soon learn that there is much more to it than models. There are the apparently less sophisticated disciplines of analyzing potential positions, of dealing with evolving position characteristics, and of risk management for both everyday risks and remote risks. There is the struggle of recognizing the forces of supply and demand and of working within a strategic structure to identify inefficiencies and to construct positions to take advantage of them. There is the ongoing challenge of making tradeoffs when the market doesn't give us what we want and when alternative decisions have both desirable and undesirable implications. Finally, there is the big world of human and organizational behavior, of temptations, of strengths and weaknesses, of supervision and coaching.

The business of options is a business of all of the above and more. As a maturing industry, we are much too far along for an organization to try to do a few things well and hope that the other issues won't matter. The options business is a multifaceted, ongoing challenge. It is a business like any business.